Woulda, Coulda, Shoulda

Handicapping Tips
for Anyone Who Ever
Bet on a Horse Race
or Wanted To

Dave Feldman
with
Frank Sugano

D0872895

Bonus Books, Inc., Chicago

©**1989 by Bonus Books, Inc.**
All rights reserved

Except for appropriate use in critical reviews or works of scholarship, the reproduction or use of this work in any form or by any electronic, mechanical or other means now known or hereafter invented, including photocopying and recording, and in any information storage and retrieval system is forbidden without the written permission of the publisher.

93 92 91 90 89   5 4 3 2 1

Library of Congress Catalog Card Number: 89-62256

International Standard Book Number: 0-929387-02-3

Bonus Books, Inc.
160 East Illinois Street
Chicago, Illinois 60611

Printed in the United States of America

Past performances and charts courtesy of Daily Racing Form.
Copyright (©) 1989 by News America Publications Inc. Reprinted with
permission of copyright owner.

To my wife Fern,
my good friend Leonard Schaller
and to millions of Broken Down Horseplayers

Contents

●
_____

One

Count Fleet
He Ain't

"I think I've got the horse for you, Dave."
"Is he sound?"
"Yeah."
"Is he cheap?"
"Yeah."
"Can he run?"
"No."

I looked at Joe Bollero, the guy who was giving me the tip. If he was laughing, it wasn't so that I could notice. We were at Washington Park, where I was covering the races for the *Chicago Herald-American*. Joe was a trainer friend of mine. He said he had the line on the horse because he trained him.

1

"Slow, huh?"

"He ain't Count Fleet."

"But you say he's sound?"

"Sure. Doesn't run fast enough to hurt himself. Maybe you could say he's smart. That's something."

I pretended I didn't hear that. I pretended I was deep in thought. I could feel my blood doing quick fractions. (Which was OK, because this was June 1944, and I hadn't had a quadruple bypass. I was 29. I could get excited painlessly. There weren't two overweight jockeys sitting on my pacemaker.) I was like some raggedy kid who hears he's going to get a new bicycle. All right, it wasn't exactly new and it wasn't by Schwinn out of Montgomery Ward, but it was a *bike*.

"How much is he?"

"Two hundred. But I think the guy will take 10 bucks a week."

"Jesus!"

I guess my face lit up because Joe cracked a smile.

"What's the horse's name?" I asked.

"Random Breeze."

Random Breeze. The name itself was worth $200. Ten bucks a week anyway.

"He's a hog, Dave, but he's a sound hog."

A hog is a dog, a bum, a plater, an eating machine, the brother-in-law who never works. I didn't care.

"Tell the owner I want to see him," I said.

The hog's owner was Bill Faires, a guy I knew

slightly. He had some beauty parlors in the Loop. That seemed to fit because he was a dainty and dapper fellow. He could walk along the back-stretch in white summer shoes and never get them dirty. Around him I always felt three sizes too large and a little sloppy. Was my tie straight? Was there chocolate ice cream on my chin? Faires was a hand-shaker. If he saw you 10 times in one day, he'd shake your hand 10 times. Got so that I was shaking everybody's goddam hand. I stopped that after a while. Everybody thought I wanted something.

We shook hands, Faires and I, when I caught up with him on the grandstand lawn. I asked him about Random Breeze and learned that the horse was for sale all right, but not for 10 bucks a week.

"Sorry, Dave, it's $200, and it'll have to be cash."

My heart stopped. At the quarter-pole, turning into the stretch, it just stopped.

"The horse ran yesterday, as you probably know," Faires said. "And he ran a wonderful race. We told the jockey not to move until the stretch and he finished quite strong."

I wanted to step on his white shoes. "Strong finish, my ass," I said to myself. After talking with Bollero, I had checked the chart of the race. Random Breeze finished 10th in a 12-horse field and probably would've come in dead last if two horses hadn't pulled up.

I didn't bother to straighten Faires out on his

champion. I just went into my pockets and fished out all the money I had. Fifty, 100, 150, 170, 190...

"I've got $191."

"Give it to me."

Random Breeze was mine.

Dumb, right? Yeah, but as they say, when you get an itch, you've got to scratch it. The thought of owning a horse had spread in my mind like a rash. I probably picked it up in New Orleans, where I had spent the winter covering the races at the Fair Grounds for the newspaper. On a lark, I bought a horse, the first I'd ever owned, a filly call Oomph Girl, who was named after Ann Sheridan, the actress. My partner and I got the horse cheap because we promised to pay the owner $1,000 when Oomph Girl won a race. Hah! The first three times we ran her she was beaten like a flyweight matched against Jack Dempsey.

My partner, Francis Gray, came from a wealthy family and everything for him was fun and games. We spent a lot of time in the book joint across the street from the Jung Hotel and he would bet hundreds. And many mornings we were on the backstretch at the Fair Grounds, where he would look in on his string of horses. It was Francis's idea to buy Oomph Girl and I said, sure, what the hell. I like his style. Trouble was, when you were pals with a guy like that you started thinking that everything for *you* should be fun and games. The difference was that Francis had monthly checks coming from home and I didn't. My father was a tailor at Hart Schaffner & Marx and he made peanuts. No, worse, he made shells. So after Oomph Girl lost her first three races under our ownership, I started to get nervous. Francis was the horse "expert" and he always entered the filly in $2,500 claiming races. I wanted to run her where I felt she belonged—in the cheapest races, $1,200 claimers.

Oomph Girl was a drain. My share of the expenses came to about six dollars to eight dollars a day—for the trainer, blacksmith, vet, etc. That was $42 to $56 a week. My weekly salary at the paper wasn't much more than that. I had plenty of schooling. It didn't take me long to dope it out. Just before her fourth start, I sold my half. I kicked myself all the way to Chicago.

Another racing season was opening locally at Washington Park, and I got back into the routine of covering the turf beat and handicapping the races for the newspaper and making a buck here, a buck there, doing odd jobs. And when Sportsman's Park opened its meeting, I'd be back in the announcer's booth calling the races.

I worked 14 to 16 hours a day. At the end of every week, I had six or seven different paychecks in my pocket. I was flush but I felt flat. What was missing was a charge, the kind I got when I was in New Orleans and had Oomph Girl. It was something special to wake up in the morning with your guts churning because your horse was going to run that day. The feeling was like nothing else. It was better than sweating out a photo finish with everybody telling you that your long-shot had it by a mile. I wanted it again; I wanted another horse. I hadn't been working my tail off with that idea in mind, but now I saw that it was something I could do because I had the money. And there were some questions that I wanted answers to. What if Francis and I had run Oomph Girl in $1,200 claiming races? Would she have finished in the money? Would she have won? Francis's mistake was thinking Oomph Girl was better than she was. The filly didn't stand a chance because she was outclassed. I wouldn't make that mistake.

After I paid Faires, I went to the barn to see Random Breeze. He was a big bay 4-year-old gelding. He walked toward me, stuck his head beyond the webbing and started sniffing at my coat pocket. I fed him some mints.

"You're mine now, Randy."

Joe Bollero had said he was well-bred. Still, he hadn't shown anything, which made him a bum. But that didn't matter. What did matter was that he was mine. Now I had to figure out what I was going to do with him. I had no trainer, no tack, I had nothing.

I asked around and finally went to another trainer friend, Angelo Cilio. He agreed to handle my horse. He had two other horses, and when I offered to pay a third of the expenses, Angelo said, "No, no, Dave. I like you. You're a friend. I take care of the horse."

Random Breeze had a home in barn 5 at Washington Park. Next door, taking up all of barn 6, were the horses belonging to Calumet Farm and its great trainer, Ben Jones. Who was to say that in a couple of years it wouldn't be Feldman Farm and its great trainer, Angelo Cilio?

Angelo disappeared two days later. I learned that he owed the feed man, the van man, the tack man, the pony boy, the hotwalker—every human at the racetrack. He couldn't pay, so he took off. There I was with Random Breeze and two other platers I had inherited, not to keep, but to watch out for, and I didn't know *anything* about taking care of horses. Being half-owner of Oomph Girl hadn't prepared me for this.

I got some guy who owed me a favor to take care of Angelo's "stable," but he wouldn't take my horse. The only help I could find was an exercise boy, Bob Killen, and a broken down guy who said he was a groom.

One day, when I was at the barn, this terrible odor hit me. Barns were not the greatest smelling places in the world, but this odor stunk worse than a fixed race. I wanted to gag. The smell became stronger as I got closer to Random Breeze's stall. I poked my head into the stall and pulled it out fast.

"Hey, what's this?" I asked the groom, who

7

was sitting on a little bench outside the stall. The smell didn't seem to bother him at all.

The groom was a nice enough fellow, but Seabiscuit probably could have outlasted him in a spelling bee. He turned to me and said, "He's crapping."

"I know that, for chrissake. What's *wrong* with him?"

The groom shrugged his shoulders, got up and walked away. Random Breeze was crapping his guts out and my groom couldn't figure out why I was going crazy. I could see flecks of straw under a oozy lava flow of crap and my groom didn't see anything out of the goddam ordinary. I didn't know much about horses, but I knew this wasn't normal. I mean, who can crap that much? An elephant, maybe, but not a horse.

This went on for weeks. I asked everybody— veterinarians, trainers, grooms, exercise boys, hotwalkers. Had they ever seen anything like this before? No, they hadn't. Was there some horse plague going around? No, the other horses were crapping like clockwork. It was only Random Breeze. Finally, I persuaded Ben Jones to look at my horse. He shook his head in wonderment, remarked how awful it smelled and said he didn't know what the hell was wrong. He recommended using a stomach sweetener, whatever that was. Others suggested Kaopectate. I tried them both and everything else on the tack room shelf. Nothing worked. My horse was going through clean straw like an adobe factory.

Meanwhile, it was business as usual for my groom. One day I was watching him as he carried a tub of feed to Random Breeze. He was a small guy and the tub looked as if it weighed 50 pounds. I spent a lot of time in the barn, but never gave much notice to feeding time.

"My god, that's a lot of feed," I said. "How much do you give him?"

"Four quarts."

By now I knew that the average horse ate about eight or nine quarts of feed a day—two quarts in the morning, two at noon, and four or five quarts in the evening. I looked in the tub again. This was the evening meal, so there should have been four or five quarts of mash. It looked like more, a lot more.

"You use a measure?" I asked. My groom said yeah and pointed to a can hanging on the wall. I got it, walked down the barn and asked another groom for his measure. I compared the two and they were the same.

"What does this measure hold?" I asked.

"Two quarts."

I went back to my groom and held up the measure. "How much does this measure hold?"

"A quart."

Holy mackerel! No wonder my horse was crapping all over the place. He was eating 18 to 20 quarts of feed a day!

I fired my groom.

Once I got Random Breeze regular again, Bob and I started to train him. Who else was there? No one had heard a word from Angelo and I still hadn't been able to find another trainer. I was on the backstretch every morning at six and Bob worked or galloped the horse. When we thought he was fit, we entered him in the cheapest claiming race at Washington Park. He ran like a horse that cost $191.

The next time he ran, I went up to the booth next to the announcer's box so I could get a better look at the race. I wasn't listening to the announcer's call because I was an announcer myself and could track the horses pretty good. I kept my binoculars fixed on the bay making a big move on the backstretch. I started yelling, "Go, Randy! Go! Go! Goddammit! Gogogogogogogogo." I leaned out past the edge of the windowless booth, so I could see the field on the far turn. I leaned out farther, farther, yelling, "Gogogogogogogo—*Jesus*!" I nearly fell out of the booth. Scraps of paper fluttered down to the grandstand below. It seemed to take forever for those white sheets to land. Where was I? What was I doing? Then I remembered. I caught the bay coming across the finish line, third. But it wasn't Randy. He was last.

I ran him another time and he didn't do anything.

My horse got to be a big joke at the track. One day a smartass jockey came by carrying one of these big clocks you hang in the kitchen. He said that since I didn't need a stopwatch to time my horse, I could borrow his Big Ben. I swore at him and said I'd never ride him on one of my mounts. He thanked me and walked out.

I didn't mind the ribbing, but I did mind the fact that I had another bottomless pit on my hands, another money destroyer, another Oomph Girl. One more race, I said, and if Random Breeze didn't finish in the money, I would sell him or give him away and call it quits. I would never buy another horse. Never. Owning was for the Whitneys, the Phippses, and the Vanderbilts—and guys like Francis Gray, who was a playboy, or Bill Faires, who had a successful business and could afford an expensive hobby. It wasn't for guys like me who had to work their tails off for every dime.

The meeting at Washington Park closed and everybody went to Hawthorne Race Course. Random Breeze was stalled across the street at Sportsman's Park, which took the overflow. One day I was headed toward the barn when my new groom came running up to me.

"Dave, our horse is gone!"

"What!"

"He's not in his stall and nobody knows where he is."

I ran into the barn and went to Randy's stall. No horse. I said to my groom, "Where were you?"

"I was in the tack room. When I came back, he was gone."

I shook my head. "What the hell is going on?"

"Looks like someone stole our horse."

"Come on, you're crazy. Who'd steal my horse? Who'd steal a hog? Maybe this horse here, maybe that one there, but not my horse."

"Maybe they stole the wrong horse."

I looked at him. I looked at him as if he were a tout who had sold me on a horse that was 20 lengths behind and losing more ground.

"You want to be helpful? Go find my horse! How can a horse disappear? Horses don't go for walks. They don't go out for a bite to eat. They don't go visiting their pals in other barns. Go find my horse!"

He went running out of the barn.

I went up and down the barn asking the other grooms and backstretchers if anyone had seen my horse. Nobody had seen anything. I couldn't believe it. They were probably all lying. I went back to the stall and checked the ground in front of it. What was I looking for? Tracks? I was losing my mind. I thought I was an Apache.

I called the security office and told the guy that my horse was missing. He was really on the ball. He said he would check it out and get back to me. Then he hung up. I called Charlie Bidwill, the managing director of Sportsman's and Hawthorne, and he said he would send out a couple of guys to help me look for Randy.

I went to the next barn and looked into every

stall. Nothing. I checked another barn. Nothing. I went through every barn down the line and then hit every barn across the way. It took more than two hours. Still nothing. Someone really had stolen my horse. But why would anybody want a cheap horse like Random Breeze? Someone was mad at me. That was the only explanation. Someone had a score to settle. The groom I canned? No, he was lazy and not too bright but he was honest. Maybe it was the jockey I had written about the other day. He had finished third on the 3 to 5 favorite. I wrote that he had ridden a dumb race because he let his horse get trapped on the rail where the going was deep. The next day this itty-bitty jock birdwalked up to me, yelling and cussing and flapping his arms. He had on his dazzling silks and his little-billed cap. He looked like one of those South American parrots, feathers all ruffled. I told him if he didn't go away I would step on him.

It was the jock all right. He probably hired some backstretch bums and they took my horse for a ride. No, that was crazy. The jock was dumb but he wasn't that dumb. I wasn't thinking straight. The worry was getting to me. If I didn't find him, I was out $191 and the hundreds more I spent to keep him. I headed back toward the barn, muttering, swearing and kicking rocks along the way.

"Dave, where have you been? I found our horse!" It was my groom.

"Where is he?"

"In his stall! I went around all over the place looking for him. When I got back, there he was."

Random Breeze was back behind the webbing munching on some hay. I went into the stall and checked him out. He seemed OK. Probably some practical joker had taken the horse. I was too tired to think about who might have done it. I patted my horse and said, "Our luck's got to change sometime. What else can happen to us?"

Later, someone tipped me that the horse thief was Bidwill. That's why the security guy hadn't gotten excited; he was in on the joke. That's why everybody had said they hadn't seen the horse; they were in on it, too. Charlie and I got along pretty good, but rich guys—and old Charlie was rich, believe me—sometimes figured guys like me were monkeys on a chain. They called the tune and we were supposed to dance around. Once, when Charlie was blind drunk, he emptied his pockets and put everything on a table. Then he took off his watch and put that on the table too, next to his wallet, keys and God knows what else. "Here, Dave, I want you to have everything. Take it. Take it all. You're my friend, Dave, my good friend. Take it all." He had his arm around me, blubbering away. His breath stunk.

I accused Bidwill of playing stupid games, that I didn't think it was funny of him to steal my horse. Charlie just laughed. The hell with it, he held all the cards. What could I do? Quit my job as announcer? Refuse to enter my horse at Sportsman's? That would have been a bigger laugh. I put the incident behind me and concentrated on getting Random Breeze ready again to race.

During one stretch in mid-September the weather turned rotten. Gloom closed in like a 20 to 1 shot running down your bet. Rain, rain, and more rain. Horses were slipping and sliding all over the track, which was sloppy one day, muddy the next. When the track was off, people joked that my daily selections belonged on the comic pages. Yeah, yeah, screw them. None of the other newspaper handicappers were doing so hot, either. A good handicapper averaged 25 to 29 percent winners. When the track came up slop or mud, a guy was lucky to pick two winners on a nine-race card. You could throw the *Daily Racing Form* out the window, because anything could happen.

I decided to enter Random Breeze again. What the hell. He had won one race in his life, at some small track in Ohio, and it had been in the mud. I entered him in a six and a half furlong claiming race and took a call on Steve Brooks, a close friend and one of the best jockeys in the country. Another trainer had first call on his services; I had second call. Brooks's other horse was on the also-eligible list. If that horse didn't get in, Brooks would be free to ride my horse.

The day came up mud. I poked my head into the racing secretary's office and asked, "Did Brooks's horse get in?"

"No, Dave, he rides your horse," someone said,

and I could hear everybody in the office laughing.

The word was out. Random Breeze was running in the first race and Steve Brooks was going to ride him. Trainers and jockey agents stopped me on my way to the barn and wished me luck. "I'm betting a hundred to win on your horse," a trainer said. He walked away in hysterics.

At the barn, I told Bob Killen, "Let's do everything we can because this is the last roll. Let's put him in an ice tub in case his legs are bothering him. And I've seen him fool with his tongue, so let's use a tongue strap. Let's not have any excuses."

When it was time for the first race, my groom and I took Random Breeze to the paddock. I met Monte Weil, a trainer who was running a horse in my race and another in the second.

"I can't lose the second race, Dave. You'd better bet on him."

Brooks came down and I told him, "I've done a lot of favors for you, given you good write-ups. Now I want you to do me a favor. This horse has been cheating. He's a sulker. The assistant starter is going to whack this horse at the break. I want you to hit him every jump. As soon as you know he's dead beat, forget it. But while you think he still has a shot, don't miss a jump with him. Let him know he's been at the races."

While Joe Bollero was saddling the horse for

me (I didn't know how to do it), I went to the windows and made a two dollar double, pairing my horse in the first race with Weil's horse in the second. I took another double with the favorite in my race and Brooks's mount in the second, a first starter. That was it.

I took a spot on the rail near the middle of the stretch. I was right across from the odds board. Random Breeze was 40 to 1. He was the second least popular choice among the bettors. A horse called Total was 99 to 1. Random Breeze had the No. 1 post, but I didn't count that as a plus or minus. Post position had never been a factor in his losses. Just speed.

The bell rang and the assistant starter hit my horse in the ass. Random Breeze popped out. He was a nose out in front. Then boom, he dropped back all the way to eighth. Then Brooks hit him and he hit him and he hit him. The horse started to move. After the first quarter he was third. At the half he was in the lead. I couldn't believe it. Through my binoculars I could see Brooks whipping away, his right hand coming down so hard that I jumped a little each time. Turning into the stretch, Random Breeze was ahead by *three* lengths and still driving. I started running toward the finish line.

The next day in the *Herald-American* Jim Enright wrote, "Random Breeze won in a big upset. Dave Feldman finished second."

FIRST RACE
6 8 6 8 6
Sept. 20-44—Haw

6 1-2 FURLONGS (Out of Chute). (Talked About, Sept. 17, 1940—1:17⅗—6—115.) Purse $1,500. 3-year-olds and upward. Claiming. Non-winners of two races since May 1. 3-year-olds, 116 lbs.; older, 121 lbs. Non-winners since May 1 allowed 4 lbs.; in 1944, 8 lbs. Claiming price, $1,200.

Net value to winner $1,000; second, $300; third, $150; fourth, $50. Handle, $65,457.

Index	Horses	Eq't	A	Wt	PP	St	¼	½	Str	Fin	Jockeys	Owners	Odds $1 Str't
68023	R'DOM BREEZE	wb	4	113	1	8	3^h	$1\frac{1}{2}$	1^3	1^5	S Brooks	Mr & Mrs D Feldman	47.20
67920^2	BLACK MARK	w	5	109	3	4	2^h	$3^{1\frac{1}{2}}$	2^2	$2^{1\frac{1}{2}}$	R Ca'pbell*	Mrs G H Emick	3.00
68023	ESREVINU	w	7	108	11	1	4^1	4^2	3^h	3^n	H Keagle*	H Kennedy	12.40
68134	WOBBLE PUMP	wb	4	116	10	9	11^6	$10\frac{1}{2}$	$6\frac{1}{2}$	4^n	B Nichols*	J Pugh	8.30
67920	FREE MISS	w	6	109	4	10	8^h	9^1	7^2	5^n	J W M'tin*	Ericson & Jenson	25.90
68252	FLOR'AN ACE	wb	3	108	5	3	$1^{1\frac{1}{2}}$	2^2	$4^{1\frac{1}{2}}$	6^2	S Freeman†	E E Pershall	23.40
67920	ERAZAL	wb	3	116	12	2	9^1	$7^{1\frac{1}{2}}$	9^2	7^h	W Bailey	B Fogelson	3.30
67817^3	MINEDDA	w	7	113	8	11	$10\frac{1}{2}$	8^3	$8\frac{1}{2}$	8^n	D Erb	H White	15.30
50752	LIBERATOR	wb	4	113	7	5	5^h	$5^{1\frac{1}{2}}$	5^h	9^2	G Burns	Mrs M Weil	40.70
67692	MAN O' MINE	wb	3	112	2	6	$6\frac{1}{2}$	$6\frac{1}{2}$	10^3	$10^{1\frac{1}{2}}$	A Skor'ski	Mack Brothers Jr	4.50
67920	HALSEY	wb	3	105	6	7	7^1	11^6	11^3	11^2	T Bates	Mrs E B Carpenter	11.40
66677	TOTAL	w	4	110	9	12	12	12	12	12	W Mor'sey	Mrs I Wendt	112.60

Time, :24, :48⅗, 1:15⅕, 1:22⅗. Track muddy.

Mutuel Prices

	$2 Mutuels Paid			Odds to $1		
RANDOM BREEZE	96.40	35.20	16.20	47.20	16.60	7.10
BLACK MARK		4.80	3.60		1.40	.80
ESREVINU			7.20			2.60

Winner—B. g. by Chance Shot—Zephyretta, by Lemberg, trained by A. Cilio; bred by Mr. Joseph E. Widener. Winner entered to be claimed for $1,200.

WENT TO POST—2:16. OFF AT 2:16½ CENTRAL WAR TIME.

Start good from stall gate. Won ridden out; second and third driving. RANDOM BREEZE took command as FLORIZAN ACE bore out and opened up a good lead under pressure and, ridden out, had little left. BLACK MARK, a strong factor from the start, tired after reaching the last eighth, but held the others safe. ESREVINU, never far back, also tired in the drive. WOBBLE PUMP closed well between horses FREE MISS could not get up. FLORIZAN ACE took command quickly, but bore out badly on the turn and otherwise could have been a much stronger factor at the end. ERAZAL was outrun. MAN O' MINE showed little.

Scratched—67817 Joe Burman, 113; 67581 Joe Schenck, 116; 68245 Enaj, 105; 68496 Free Style, 116; 68252^2 Duolc, 109; 63982 Treviscot, 108.

Overweight—Free Miss, 4 pounds.

Random Breeze had won by five lengths and paid $96.40. Brooks went on to win the second race too, with his first starter, and the double paid $988. I didn't have a separate win bet on my horse and I didn't have him in a double with the winner of the second race. But my share of the purse came to $1,000.

September 20, 1944. I got to the winner's circle and waited for Brooks and Random Breeze. Brooks doubled back at the clubhouse turn and jogged toward the circle. I grabbed the bridle and patted my horse on the neck. Then I shook

Brooks's hand and thanked him for a terrific ride. He smiled and said, "I had a lot of horse under me today." He could have said, "The rest of the field was worse than this dog," but he didn't.

"OK, everybody turn this way," the photographer said. I turned and, still holding onto the bridle, faced the camera. A crowd of railbirds and racetrackers rimmed the circle. It was like being on stage. But I felt confident. I knew my lines.

"Hey, Feldman," someone shouted. "You'll never win another race with that bum."

"Go to hell," I said.

•
_____

Two

And We're Off

I was the perfect oddball human interest story.
I was like the millionaire who gives a bum a quarter and finds his long-lost father. I was like the
farmer who grows a 1,000-pound pumpkin, or
the old lady who talks to mushrooms.

There wasn't anyone else in the country who
was doing what I was doing. I handicapped the
races and covered the turf beat for a major newspaper; I was the track announcer at Sportsman's
Park; I owned a racehorse, and now I was a winning trainer. I could enter my horse in a race,
handicap the event, call him home to the wire,
and interview the winning owner and trainer—

me. Not that I would ever interview myself. I couldn't, I wouldn't go that far. So Jimmy Enright did it. He wrote about me when Random Breeze won.

The headline read: "$96 Winner—No Bets; Feldman Horse Scores."

> Random Breeze, the horse with the so-called 'slows,' came to life altogether too fast for his owner yesterday.
>
> Random Breeze is owned by Dave Feldman, *Herald-American* handicapper. Whenever there's talk of slow horses, Random Breeze is front and center—a position he seldom enjoyed in competition.
>
> That was, until yesterday.
>
> It's all different today. Random Breeze is king and his owner is blushing. He failed to wager on the big, bay beast of his one-horse stable...

But the oddball story was old news the next day, even if the pumpkin turned into a carriage, even if the lady called in to say the mushrooms were talking back. So Enright wasn't around the next time Random Breeze ran. Only the everyday bettors and the racetrackers took notice when Randy won again. People at the track figured the first victory was a fluke. They gave most of the credit to the jockey, Steve Brooks, and little to me. But that changed after Randy won a second time with no big-name jockey aboard. I was starting to get some respect. At least, no one was laughing at me. I won those races because my horse was sound to begin with and I kept him race fit. I also knew what kind of horse he was, that he wasn't a budding stakes winner. I knew that a good trainer didn't run a horse for the exercise. He ran him in the right company.

With my winnings I claimed a filly called Silver Toy and then another horse, Swift Action. In the meantime, Random Breeze won his third straight race, looking better and better. He always was a handsome, solid-looking horse. Now I knew he was smart, too. Got so that when the jockey just showed him the whip, he would get into higher gear.

Then, right before his next outing, Randy injured his right hind ankle during a workout. I had him treated, but the ankle kept blowing up every morning. I knew that his days on the track were numbered. I couldn't afford to keep a horse that wasn't sound, so I sold him for $1,000 to a guy who raced in Ohio, where they had cheaper races. I had a few pangs, all right. Randy and I had been through a lot together. But I didn't have a farm. I didn't even have a backyard. What could I do? Bring him back to my apartment and give him the extra bedroom? I just patted him on the neck and let him go.

Winning with Random Breeze was the turning point of my life. I would have quit the racing end of the business, owning and training, if Randy hadn't won that day at Hawthorne. His victory proved to me that I could challenge the game and win. When I started out, I didn't know a fig from a fetlock, but after six months, I was a trainer who had won 50 percent of his races—three victories in six starts. Every day I was learning more and more about how to judge horses, how to keep them fit, and how to place them in the right races.

I won a number of races each with Silver Toy and Swift Action. The victories with Swift Action, though, came over a longer stretch of time—a couple of years maybe. I claimed him back three times—at $2,500 a pop. Still, I figured it was better to lose horses through the claiming route than run them out of their class and never win a cent. Years later, Harry Howard, Brooks's jockey agent, cracked to someone: "That Feldman, he never thinks too much of a horse. He'd run one for a ham sandwich." Harry was a midget. He never stood nose to nose with me, otherwise he probably would have said roast beef. Harry thought I played it too safe. My thinking was that the horses I ran had to carry only the jockey; they weren't weighed down by big dreams and other excess baggage. I was a realist. Platers like Randy, Silver Toy and Swift Action didn't stir the dreamer in you, unless you were batty to begin with.

Being a professional handicapper gave me an

edge. It was my job to pick winners and I couldn't do it if I wasn't objective. I could look at Swift Action, say, in the same cold way I looked at any other horse. The fact that he was mine never entered into it. If he didn't figure in a race, I didn't run him. Your average trainer couldn't do that. He was like the horseplayer who bets every race thinking the next two dollar wager will get him out of the hole. He also had an owner breathing down his neck, demanding to know what the hell was wrong and threatening to take away the horse. A trainer's head was up in the clouds or up somebody's ass. What a life. Me? I didn't have to deal with jerk trainers or jerk owners. I had it made.

So, naturally, I started training horses for other people. I was flattered. Shocked, maybe. Here was a guy telling you, "I got a horse I bought for $10,000. See what you can do with him." He had faith in me. What was I supposed to do? Say, "Are you sure you don't want Ben Jones?" and turn him down? Besides, training for a rich owner gave me the chance to prove myself with good stock. If I trained only the horses I could buy, I would always be running in claiming events. I wanted to race at a higher level, against good competition.

Of course, there was another reason why I took on other people's horses. Money. I did a lot of things for a buck. Except for the time I booked thoroughbred races at the walkathons at the

Coliseum (I figured that people watching a bunch of goofballs walking around a track needed some sort of action), everything I did was on the up and up.

—In 1929, when I was 14, I became the mascot for the Chicago Blackhawks. The first three seasons they played in the Chicago Stadium, I sat on the bench next to Johnny Gottselig, Mush March and the rest of the players. I had a ringside seat when fights broke out on the ice. I'd lean over and yell, "Kill him! Kill him!" It was a great sport. The Blackhawks paid me two dollars per game and gave me all the dented pucks and chipped sticks a kid could ever want. I probably could have made some money selling the equipment, but I gave it away.

—I was the relief announcer for the six-day bicycle races at the Coliseum, filling in for the main guy when he wanted time off or when the basic crappiness of the sport got to him. For some reason the fans went crazy watching these riders zip around the track on their skinny bikes. I was the announcer, so I had to pretend I was having a heart attack in the booth, so excited, so goddam *thrilled* was I by the spectacle. It was a stinking sport, probably fixed, too.

—In the late 1930s, I wrote publicity for midget auto racing, working for Norman Alley. Alley, a newsreel cameraman, was on the gunboat Panay when it was bombed by the Japanese off Nanking, China, in 1937. He was cranking the camera while the boat was under attack and sinking. The newsreel made him famous. When I met him he was just starting to promote indoor auto races at the armory on 51st and Cottage Grove. On the first night of the races, Alley and I stood by the door eating peanuts and counting the number of people who went through the gate. About 2,500 turned out. They loved it. Roaring motors, accidents, injuries (none fatal), the smell of gas fumes strong enough to asphyxiate you. What a great night! Two weeks later 7,500 people showed up. We had to turn people away.

—I announced harness races, filling in for Stan Bergstein and other regulars. That was almost as bad as announcing bicycle races. I hated the buggies. It seemed as if every horse had three names. Star Spangled Hanover. Star Hanover Banner. Hanover Spangled Banner. By the time I finished calling their positions the first time, the race was half over.

But publicity and part-time announcing paid peanuts compared with training. That was where the money was. In 1945-46, a trainer netted about $3 per day for every horse in his stable. If I trained four horses, I could make $84 a week. *Plus* 10 percent of any purse money. What was that? Maybe another $100? Who made $184 a week? Doctors, lawyers, hoormasters and horse trainers.

When you had money, it was like having the

only speed in the race. And the more I had, the more distance I could put between me and wherever I came from. Things aren't so good that they can't be better. That's from the Bible. Exodus, Leviticus, Numbers, Parlays, Johnstown—somewhere. My father read the passage in Hebrew. Things can't be so bad that they can't get worse. He was a good Jew.

———————————

How old was I? Guessing? Six, seven, maybe eight. No more than eight. Every day at school the teacher would have a bunch of us go up to the blackboard and do arithmetic problems. It was like a test. We would stand up there and face the blackboard with stubs of chalk in our hands. The teacher would give each of us a problem to do. "Johnny, add 36 and 81," and while Johnny was writing the numbers down and figuring out the answer, she would go on to the next kid. I was usually the last kid in line because I was usually the last kid to get to the blackboard. I had the spot right next to the clock, the flag and the picture of the president of the United States. Harding it was, or maybe Calvin Coolidge. Anyway, by the time the teacher got down to me, I was asleep on my feet.

On school days my mother had to wake me, dress me, stuff food in my mouth, take me outside, point me in the right direction like a windup toy, and push. It wasn't that I was lazy. I was just dead tired. I worked every day until midnight and woke up at 7 a.m. to go to school. My father Hyman, as I said before, was a tailor for Hart Schaffner & Marx. He was a terrific tailor, but when suits weren't selling, he would get laid off and have to work at Wrigley's Gum or some other factory. My mother Anna was mostly a housewife. She was sick a lot when my older brother Charlie and I were growing up.

Both my parents were from Minsk, Russia, and came to Chicago around the same time, 1895. One of my father's relatives introduced Hyman to Anna. "So what a coincidence. You're from Minsk and I'm from Minsk. So what a coincidence." They got married, probably figuring it was fate.

I was born in 1915, four years after Charlie. When I was six, I got my first full-time job, selling newspapers near my house from five in the afternoon until midnight. (I've been fighting sleep ever since. I can sleep at a red light. I can doze behind binoculars during a distance race. I can be out on my feet in a slow betting line on trifecta day.) I was a natural newsboy. It probably helped a lot that I was a cute little kid. At least that's what my customers said I was. Anyway, after a year or so working the dead corners, I was rewarded and given the opportunity to sell my papers in front of the Broadway Strand theater on Roosevelt Road near Ashland Avenue.

The Strand was the nicest theater on the West Side. It always did good business because it had first-run movies and a stage show. Before I got the Strand spot, I was lucky to make 50 cents a night. (Newspapers cost three cents, and newsboys made a penny for every one sold.) Now I was going home with more than a buck and a half, sometimes two bucks. I got a break because the Strand had all these amber lights in the lobby and under the marquee. My customers sometimes couldn't tell the difference between a penny and a dime. Neither could I, until I got out from under the lights and checked the coins. By that time, of course, it was too late to correct the mistake, too late to return the money. Some nights I came home with a bunch of pennies and two or three dimes. I dumped it all on the kitchen table. In the morning it would be gone, put away somewhere for family expenses.

The Broadway Strand was in an area controlled by the 42 Gang. The leader was Joey Colaro, who called himself Babe Ruth. He kind of liked me. He let me store my papers in his car, which he usually parked near the Strand, and at midnight when I was finished he would drive me home. There were also some kids in the neighborhood who called themselves the Little 42 Gang. They were just punks, about 14 or 15 years old, and three or four times a week they would come by the Strand and steal one of the cars parked in front of the theater. They would open the hood, get the motor started somehow and drive away. I'd see it all but never say a word. I minded my own business. When the show would let out, I'd hawk my papers, knowing that when the crowd cleared there would be one guy left standing in front of the theater with his wife or girlfriend.

"Hey, kid, my car's gone. Did you see anything?"

"Nothing, mister. Not a thing."

One night the Little 42 Gang came to the Strand and took out the yellow bulbs in the coming-attractions window. Then one of the guys came up to me and socked me in the jaw, knocking me down.

"You didn't see nothing, right?"

I was seven, maybe eight. I was scared all right, but I was mad too. The manager came out later and asked me if I had seen anything. The manager kind of liked me. When Babe Ruth's car wasn't around, the manager would let me store my papers in the lobby so they wouldn't get stolen or rained on. I told the manager that it was the Little 42 Gang and the next time they came around I'd let him know.

That day came. A couple of gang members dropped by the Strand to see a movie. I went inside, got the manager and pointed them out just as they disappeared into the darkened theater. The manager waited until the movie was over and as everybody was heading out, he grabbed the gang kids and hauled them off to the side. Once the lobby was cleared, he started hitting, kicking and banging them around. Then he threw them out the door. They took off, but I knew what was coming. Around midnight I saw them across the street waiting for me. When they started crossing Roosevelt Road, I lit out. I was skinny and fast and I lost them easily. I said good-bye forever to the Broadway Strand.

Around that time, we moved to the South Side on Marquette Road near Spaulding. We lived right across the street from the golf course in Marquette Park. I needed a job and found one there. In the evening, after the last golfers had left, my friends and I would sneak onto the course and head for the water holes. There, we'd take off our shoes and walk around in the water and try to feel golf balls with our feet. When we felt one, we'd reach down and pick it up. On good days we could find 20 or 30 golf balls. A lot of them were like new, just a little discolored. Those we kept and painted. We sold the "Re-painted Golf Balls" for 50 cents each.

Summers I swam for golf balls at night and caddied during the day. Marquette Park, Olympia Fields, Black Hills, Jackson Park, I caddied all over. Caddying paid pretty well, especially the way I did it. Everybody liked me. I would go down the fairway and wait over a hill. If a ball went into the water or into the bushes, I would retrieve it and throw it back onto the fairway. After the round was over, the golfer would be pretty happy and give me a good tip. Between caddying in the afternoon and swimming for golf balls at night, I had a good business going.

Like any kid, though, I played around. I had a bike which I bought myself. I played baseball. And I went to the racetrack. I was around 12 when I saw my first horse race. A friend of mine, Jack Connors, lived next door and his uncle, Bert Ralston, took us to Arlington Park the first year it opened, in the summer of 1927. We piled into his car and the trip from the South Side all the way north to Arlington Heights took about two hours. It was a big deal for me. My father didn't have a car and because we had no money to throw away, we never went anywhere, not even to a movie. A trip to Arlington Heights was like going on a vacation. It was a different world—clean air and wide open spaces.

Ralston had money. He had a blind pig, one of those joints that sold booze, on Archer and Ashland. It was illegal, of course, this being the time of Prohibition, but no one seemed to care. At the track, Ralston made bets for Jack and me and gave us the winnings when our horses finished in the money. It was a good introduction to horse racing. Ralston showed us the *Racing Form* and tried to explain the charts and past performances. None of the stuff he was telling us made any sense. But just to make him happy, I would nod my head and look serious. Jack didn't have to because he was family.

Ralston took us to the track once or twice a

month. His picks didn't win very often, so I usually returned home with my lungs filled with clean air but no more money in my pockets. I had to work that much harder to make up for the time I wasted going to the track.

Strange way for a kid to think? Maybe, but I had been paying my own way since I was six. My parents never had much to say about what I did, because I didn't see them that much. I was out of the house most of the day, coming home only to sleep. Sometimes my independence drove my mother crazy. "What are you? Some kind of king?" she would say to me. In Yiddish, usually. And I would say something back, always in English. (I understood Yiddish but I couldn't speak it. The words sat on my tongue, like a jockey on his mount, waiting to rush out, but my gate never opened.) I was a wiseguy, a smart aleck, a know-it-all, but I never gave my folks real trouble. Except for the fact that I wasn't a good Jew.

My father was Orthodox, very religious. Every morning he put on his shawl, his tallis, and read his prayer book before putting on his hat and going to work. On Saturday, sabboth, he couldn't turn on the lights; some outsider had to be called in, from some Gentile bullpen, to flick the switch. He couldn't handle money on Saturday, either. If my father and my mother wanted to go anywhere, they walked. Riding a streetcar on sabboth also was forbidden. But you needed money to hop on a streetcar, right? If you couldn't touch money, what point was there in having the rule against riding a streetcar? I didn't mention it to my father. I didn't want his whole world to come crashing down on him.

My mother kept a kosher house, but I ate out most of the time and probably broke more eating rules in one day than my father did in his whole life. My parents and Charlie went to the synagogue on holidays, but I usually managed to get out of it. Once, when I was around 10, my father dragged me to the synagogue. After he dropped me off, I went out the back door.

Everybody needed religion, though. I was a Boy Scout. I got a good deal on a second-hand uniform and went pretty regularly to meetings. I learned about "being prepared," making knots and what to do in case I came across a bear. When I couldn't go to the meetings anymore, I quit. I didn't feel too bad. I made a little when I sold my uniform.

I went back full-time to caddying and swimming for golf balls. One day some cops grabbed me. They said I was breaking the law by selling on Park District property and hauled me off to the police station. They told me to call my parents and have them come down to the station. I got to thinking. My parents got off the boat a long time ago, but they still acted a little seasick. What did they know about talking to big, tough Irish cops? I called my friend Jack Connors. Four hours later, his father came to the station. He talked to the cops and everybody had a good laugh. I was sprung. I quit swimming for golf balls.

My brother Charlie by that time had gotten a job at the *Examiner*, working as a junior copy editor in the sports department. He got me a part-time job working on straw ballots. In the weeks before elections, I stood on street corners with other kids and we asked people to mark up ballots. There were six or seven of us, and I was the only one who actually got people to fill in the ballots. The other kids marked up their ballots themselves and then went to the movies. I never fooled around like that. If someone was going to give me $2.00 to work, I was going to give him at least $2.00 worth of labor, maybe $2.25 or $3.00.

After the elections, I got on part-time as an office boy in the sports department. A short time later I was full-time, working until midnight. Naturally, I started falling asleep at school again. That worried my eighth-grade teacher, Miss Fitzgerald, who kind of liked me. She started nosing around and asking questions. She found out I was working at the *Examiner*. One day I got a tip that the school was going to send a truant officer to the paper to raise hell with my boss for employing a child and working him until all hours of the night. I told my boss. He took my name off the payroll and started paying me by voucher. That made it almost impossible for the school to check up on me.

I probably slept through most of eighth grade, but I graduated when I was 13 and went on to Lindblom High School. Around that time my real education began. No, not at Lindblom. It was at the bookmaker's, where I would run bets for the guys in the sports department. Ruby Raff was a bookie who operated in the back of a cigar store in the Weston Hotel, on the corner of Madison and Market (Wacker today). Raff's place was across the street from the Opera House and kitty-corner from the Hearst Building, where I worked.

At first that was all I did—place bets and return in a flash to the office. But that was like sending me to a strip joint to deliver G-strings. It was difficult for a kid not to get interested. I started placing my own bets, too. Like most bookies, Ruby took small bets, as little as 50 cents. That's what I would bet. I would check the horses and the odds that were written on these large sheets taped to the wall. (The sheets came from a printing company owned by Sportsman's Park's Charlie Bidwill.) I didn't know how to read a *Form*, but I didn't bet blind. I understood odds and I began to remember the names of horses and jockeys that did well. I would bet a couple of dollars a day and try to chisel a small profit.

Every so often Ruby would get a tip that the cops were coming and he would close up shop fast. The sheets would come down, and the cash would be stuffed in bags. He would start yelling and we would all follow one of his employees into the toilet. It had a secret door that led downstairs to a tunnel that led to another secret door. We ended up in a toilet with one urinal, in back of a restaurant. There might be 10, 15 of us, and we'd troop out of the toilet, march around the tables while customers choked on their food in surprise, and walk out the front door. The next day Ruby would be back in business and I'd be running bets for the guys. And making a few of my own.

I started going to the track again. This time I went with John Carmichael and some other guys from the sports department. They kind of adopted me because I was Charlie's brother and, like Charlie, I was a hard worker. At the track, they ran bets for me because I was underage. I didn't make many, though. Unlike bookies, the guys at the mutuel window wouldn't take a bet for less than two dollars. Two or three losers and I'd be wiped out for the week.

I got to be pretty good. Other kids my age read comic books, I read the *Form*. There weren't any pictures, except the ones I made up in my mind. Being a regular racegoer helped me when it came to reading the past performances. At the track I had seen horses get boxed in or forced to go wide. I had seen horses go to the lead too early or wait too long. I had seen how a poor post position can hurt and how a fast rail can help. A horse wasn't only as good as his last race. A horse was as good as his most recent outings, going back five, six, seven races.

When it came to picking winners, I was a couple of lengths ahead of the other guys in the sports department. Once my mother (as a joke, I think) said, "You make more money playing the horses. Maybe you should quit your job." I was no genius. I was a kid, and like all kids, I figured I knew everything. Most horseplayers outsmart themselves; they try to weigh too many factors— past performance, strip, jockey, trainer, breeding and so on. They get confused and finally pick a horse on a hunch, saying, "He's gotta win *this* time." I didn't know enough to outsmart myself. I just went on the evidence.

One day during the winter when there were no local tracks operating, the circulation manager came up to the sports department and said the paper could pick up some readers on Sundays if there was a line for the races at Agua Caliente in Mexico. This was a big deal. When the circulation manager came up with a suggestion, department heads took that as an order. It was said that "only hoors and horseplayers read the *Examiner*." I didn't know what the hoors read, but the horseplayers got their three cents' worth every day. The *Examiner* was a broadsheet and we had almost a page of racing news in our three- or four-page sports section. We ran racing stories on Page 1 of sports, and entries and results for five tracks on an inside page. And for a while we printed the past performances, until the *Form* threatened to sue us. Although we had more racing news than any other paper in town, we had only one guy on the staff who knew enough about horse racing at Caliente to do a morning line. That was me. I played Caliente races at Ruby Raff's and knew which horses, stables and jockeys were doing well. To me, Caliente was like Sportsman's or Arlington, a local track.

I became a professional handicapper at the age of 14.

Later, I began making one-two-three picks for the outside tracks under the name Track Ace. I never got credit for the selections; that is, my name didn't appear in the paper. (Back then, most stories and features ran without a credit or a by-line. The idea was you had to earn the right to have your name appear on a story. These days reporters think it's part of the First Amendment.) I got extra money for being Track Ace, so I didn't care about getting any credit. Besides, it would have caused problems. Lindblom High would have sent a truant officer or some other school cop to the paper to raise hell. I was happy being a newspaperman. I was happy being Track Ace. I was happy running bets to Ruby Raff's. I was happy because I had something going for me and the last thing I wanted was for my school to spoil things.

How many kids at Lindblom could say they saw Knute Rockne? The Notre Dame football coach came to the *Examiner* officer one day in 1931 to meet with Warren Brown, the sports editor. A few hours later, the office was really buzzing when the news came over the wire: Rockne was killed in a plane crash in Kansas.

Another time, Damon Runyon, the sportswriter, dropped by the office. Runyon was syndicated out of New York and his column ran in the *Examiner*. After talking some business, he asked Brown where he could make some bets. "Dave can do it," Brown said. I looked up from my desk just as Runyon turned to me.

"You know a book, kid?"

I said there was one across the street.

"I don't want to go out. Get him on the phone," he said, taking the seat next to me.

Runyon pulled out a *Form* and turned to the entries for the New York track. I got Ruby on the phone and told him that Mr. Damon Runyon—would I lie, Ruby?—wanted to make some bets. I heard Ruby tell one of his guys that Runyon was at the *Examiner* office and to keep the line open.

Runyon checked his watch against the wall clock and said to me, "Give me $20 to win" on so and so in the first at Aqueduct. I placed the bet and held the line for a few minutes until the call of the race started coming through. Then I turned the phone over to Runyon.

"Ran out," he said, handing back the phone.

Runyon had nothing much else to say to me and I was too shy to get any conversation rolling. Besides, he was busy. He played 45 races, every race at five tracks. I must have been on the phone for six hours. He ended up winning about $25. He gave me $15.

I was 16 or so when Track Ace became a one-column line and not too long after that it was set two columns and called Feldman's Form. I also started selling my selections to other news-papers, like the *Providence Evening Journal*, the *New York American* and the *Detroit Times*, and to a radio station in Chicago, WIND. Russ Hodges used my picks on his morning radio show. When Hodges began doing baseball broad-casts, he had to quit because he couldn't fit the races into his schedule. I got his job.

Radio was perfect because I loved to talk. Once I got going I was a set of springy plastic teeth—nonstop chatter, chatter, chatter. Listening to me, my father probably thought there were locusts in the Philco. The program was only 15 minutes, but I crammed in lot of racing news. I talked about the national and local scene, then went over the results of the previous day's races, giv-ing a comment or two on a horse's form or a jock-ey's ride. I closed the program with my selections for the afternoon card. Actually, they were picks by "Dave King." (What was I? Some kind of king? Yeah, Ma. David King, radio star.) I used a bogus name because I figured the *Exam-iner* would get mad if it found out I was compet-ing against myself. I changed around a horse or two, but I always had my top choices in the pa-per.

So there I was, 17 or 18 years old and cashing a

half-dozen paychecks every week. I was making $70 or $80 a week, at a time when the Depression was busting balls. Bad times were good times for gambling because everybody was desperate to make a score. The racetracks were more popular than ever and the mob got rich off book joints and numbers games.

While I was working all my jobs, my brother Charlie was covering basketball and baseball, and editing stories on the copy desk. He was more of a workaholic than I was. I worked long hours because I enjoyed it and wanted to make money. Charlie didn't care about money. If one of the guys on the desk needed a day off, Charlie would work his shift without asking for anything in return. I didn't think he was a sucker. Nobody else did, either. They all liked him, respected him. It was my brother who went to Warren Brown and suggested the paper run each player's batting average in the box scores. Great idea, Brown said, but who's going to figure them out every day? Charlie said he would. So, during the baseball season, Charlie worked two extra hours a day without pay. Well, he got some money. The paper gave him a one-time bonus of $10. That didn't upset Charlie, because working was one of the two things he lived for. The other was eating. As far as I knew, he didn't go out with girls. He wasn't a queer or anything like that. He just worked and ate. After work he would come home and clean out the refrigerator before squeezing in a few hours of sleep. That was his life.

Somehow, before or after or in between the

time I was handicapping, talking on the radio, going to book joints, freelancing as a publicist and God knows what else, somehow I squeezed in a couple of hours every day to go to school. I graduated on time, in June of 1932. My class ranking? Probably off the board. But I could name every top stakes horse in the country and what each had won up to that time. And I knew all the practical math I would ever need: percentages. I was college material.

Both Northwestern and DePaul at that time had campuses downtown and they took part-time students. I would go to Northwestern for one or two terms, switch to DePaul, then switch back to Northwestern. It all depended on which school offered classes that fit my work schedule. I wanted to become a sportswriter and I figured that college wouldn't hurt. Charlie graduated from Lewis Institute, a college in the city, and Charlie was doing well at the paper.

But after going to school part-time for four or five years, I was still six months from getting a degree. I felt like a sprinter in a route race. My legs were getting tired. I couldn't go on any longer, so I slowed to a gallop and then to a trot before finally dropping out.

Besides, I already was a sportswriter. I was writing about sporting events as a publicist. One year I covered, mostly by telephone, all the games played by Buck Weaver's Cooneys, a semi-pro baseball team.

"And then what happened, Buck?"

So-and-so got a hit and then so-and-so drove him in and then they got two runs in their half.

"And then what happened, Buck?"

After I got all the details, I'd write a five- or six-paragraph story and ship it to the City News Bureau. The CNB would then send it over the wire where it would be picked up by the other papers—the *American*, *Daily News*, *Daily Times* and *Tribune*. It was sportswriting, sort of.

Weaver was a well-known figure. "Infamous" probably was the word used back then. He was one of the eight White Sox players banned from major league baseball in the 1919 Black Sox scandal. The players were accused of taking money from gamblers and throwing games. Weaver, though, never took a cent, but he still got bounced because he *knew* about the fix and didn't say anything.

Maybe Weaver's reputation wasn't deserved. But Duke Cooney's was. Duke was Al Capone's treasurer. He also was a hoormaster, managing the syndicate's vice operations. When he died in 1942, the obituary in the *Daily News* began:

> Dennis "The Duke" Cooney, who was something out of Freud by way of the woodwork under the sink, died just before midnight in Mercy Hospital. He was 63 years old...

Cooney had tried to get some respectability by doing good deeds and getting into legitimate

45

businesses, like buying a semipro baseball team and opening up a big night club. I spent many nights at the Royal Frolics, on South Wabash, watching the 16-girl chorus line and waiting and waiting for Cooney to give me my week's pay. The waiters kept me supplied with food and drinks, but I wasn't going to be bought off. When I was the mascot for the Blackhawks, the team wanted to give me two game tickets instead of two dollars. I held out for the cash and the dented pucks. Cooney tried it with food and drink. Never once, though, was I offered a couple of passes to one of his homes for soiled doves. But I wouldn't have taken them anyway. I wanted the cash. I needed every bit of it.

There was a stretch when my father, mother and brother all were in the hospital at the same time. My father had a nervous breakdown, my mother had heart trouble and other problems, and my brother was in for tuberculosis. In those days the policy was no work, no pay. And if you had to be hospitalized, you paid the bills, not some insurance company.

Everybody got out of the hospital, and my father and brother returned to work. Later, Charlie had to be hospitalized again. This went on for several years, in and out, in and out, until 1939, when he died. He was only 28.

From my way of thinking, Charlie didn't have much of a life, but I don't think he felt that way. He loved his work and he loved to eat. If he loved anything else it was baseball. During the season, on his day off, he would go by himself to Comiskey Park or Wrigley Field, sit in the stands eating hot dog after hot dog and watch his teams play. He didn't care how long the game was. The longer they played the better. Ten innings, 12, 15, 18. He liked the idea that a baseball game could be played forever. Me? Give me a horse race anytime. Six furlongs in 1:10; a mile in 1:36. Nine races a day. Bang, bang, bang. Charlie and I were alike in some ways. We both worked hard and took care of the family. But he was quiet and easygoing; I was a dynamo, going in three directions at once. He was good-looking, like my mother; I looked like my father. Different though we were, we got along, Charlie and me. He was a good man.

It was a rough time. My folks seemed to get sick more often and now I was their sole support. I continued to hustle 14- to 16-hour days, picking up a buck here, a buck there, before showing up for work at the paper.

One of the jobs I had grew out of my radio work on WGN, where I described the feature race every Saturday. In 1940 Jack Keeshin, who was president of Sportsman's, asked me to fill in for the regular track announcer, Frank Ashley, who got sick. Two weeks later Ashley came back and started announcing again. When he saw me, he chuckled and said, "I understand you weren't too good." When Keeshin said he wanted to dump Ashley and hire me, I said OK. I didn't like the idea of taking somebody's job, but I was willing to make an exception in Ashley's case. I became Sportsman's regular track announcer in 1941 and held the job for 32 years.

In 1942 I was called up by the draft board to take a physical. I failed because I had had a hernia operation sometime back. Later I was called up again. Same thing—4-F. When I went to take a third physical, I said, "I wish you guys would make up your mind. I'm announcing the races at Sportsman's. They can't keep delaying the first race." I was rejected again. When I took my *fourth* physical, I was told I was fighting material. The war was going that badly. Then Uncle Sam found out my parents were in the hospital and there would be nobody to take care of them if I went into the Army. I was 4-F again.

I spent the war years announcing at Sportsman's and working at the *Herald-American*, which was begun in 1939 when the *Herald-Examiner* merged with the *American*. Late in 1942 I went down to New Orleans for the first time to cover the winter meeting at the Fair Grounds. Back then, the racing season in Chicago was only six months and many of the stables went south for the winter to New Orleans or Miami.

This was big-time for me and I loved it. I hung around with Joe Bollero and Angelo Cilio, two trainers from Chicago, and stayed at the Jung

Hotel, where we drank mint juleps in the bar, played gin, and talked about racing. Bollero and Cilio turned in pretty early because of their schedules, so I would spend the rest of the evening across the street at the book joint.

The book joint gave house odds and if you knew anything about handicapping you could score big with overlays. You might get 8 to 1 odds on a horse that you figured should go off at 3 to 1. In Chicago, I was chased out of some book joints because I was always beating the odds. Problem was, when I made a bet, the bettors who knew me would make the same bet. The guy who ran the joint on Canal and Adams told me, "I like you, but do me a favor. Don't bet here anymore." I didn't argue.

There weren't many overlays at the book joint I went to in New Orleans. Frenchy Schwartz of the *Form* made the house line and he was pretty good. When there were no horses for a price, I bet like a piker. That wasn't the case with Francis Gray, a guy I had just met. He loved to gamble. It didn't have to be on a horse. He once bet a guy $100 that he could run faster backward than the guy could run forward. Gray won.

Gray had a string of horses, about 10 or so, and many mornings, at first light, I would be with him on the backstretch to watch his horses work. Gray's horses were like some women who look terrific with the right lighting. The nose doesn't seem so large and you can't see her mustache.

Gray's claimers looked like champions, all muscle, speed and heart, running against the empty grandstand in the friendly gloom.

The first time I visited a backstretch was with Leadpipe. I was an office boy at the *Examiner* and Leadpipe sold the racing editions of the paper at the track. He knew everybody at Sportsman's. As he made his rounds, he introduced me to trainers, jockeys, grooms, hotwalkers, exercise riders and the old guys with the old dogs. I walked through the barns and a horse here and there would stick his head out. "It's near feeding time," an old guy with an old dog said. "They think you're bringing dinner. They say horses are dumb. But, tell me, how many animals you know can read that clock on the wall?" I had heard of kids running away to join the circus, but I wondered whether anyone had run away to join a backstretch.

Years later, on February 12, 1943, I did join the backstretch. That's when Francis Gray and I bought Oomph Girl. Gray had mentioned once that he thought we should buy a horse together. I said sure. If I could ever find a horse at the right price, I would buy him. By right price, I meant cheap. So when Gray heard about a filly for sale, he and I went to dicker. Gray did all the talking. The guy was asking $2,500. Gray said no. They talked and argued and haggled until finally a deal was made. Gray got the filly, Oomph Girl, for $300 and a promise to pay $1,000 after she won her first race. I gave Gray $150 and went into the horse business. Without Gray it would have been impossible. I didn't have a stall, a trainer or any tack. Gray had everything. It was the perfect setup for me. I was happy and excited. I would have kissed Gray, but he wouldn't have understood. Besides, I was going to get married the next day.

Fern Bayles had come down to New Orleans after I proposed on the phone. I met Fern on a blind date in 1938 and had been going with her since. We got married and had our reception at the Jung Hotel. Only the day before I had gotten involved with another female, but Fern didn't make a fuss. We spent our honeymoon visiting Oomph Girl at the Fair Grounds.

It didn't last, our honeymoon with Oomph Girl that is. The horse couldn't win because, as I mentioned before, she was always in too tough. Fern, who knew something about racing, said maybe Gray and I should drop her down. "Francis doesn't want to," I said. "He's the expert. He's calling the shots."

The expense was getting to be too much. "Six bucks a day, Fern. Six bucks every goddam day! That's my share. That's what I have to pay to keep that horse in oats and keep her fit to lose. I can't afford it. This has got to stop."

When Oomph Girl was beaten badly in her third straight race, I put out the word on the backstretch that my half of the horse was for sale. I couldn't figure out why but pretty soon I had a buyer. I got $1,000! I said goodbye to Gray, packed up and headed back to Chicago with Fern. I was through with the horse business, the ass end of it anyway. But little did I know.

In June 1944, I bought Random Breeze and three months later I was a winning owner.

The morning after Randy had paid $96.40, I was sitting in the office working on my selections for the following day. The phone rang. I reached for the receiver, but even before I picked it up I knew who was calling me. Sometimes I had these premonitions. I would be thinking of somebody and boom!—there he would be. A few seconds ago I had been thinking of Angelo Cilio.

"Dave? This is Angelo."

"Angelo, how've you been? Where in the hell are you?"

At a friend's place, he said.

"Everybody's looking for you—the stewards, the tack, the feed man, the van man. You'd better come back and square things."

He said he would in a few days. Then he asked, "Did you bet on the horse?"

"*Did I bet*? Money's coming in from *everywhere*. I had people betting in China so it wouldn't show on the board. You're asking me if I bet on him?"

Angelo said he wondered whether I had, that was all.

"Didn't you read Jimmy Enright's story?"

No.

"I bet nothing, Angelo. *Nothing.* Makes me sick."

That news probably cheered him up.

Cilio came back to the track, paid everybody off, and got back his two horses. But within six months I had a bigger stable than he did. I had Silver Toy and Swift Action and another horse I claimed in partnership with Joe Maumas, the first guy I trained for.

Maumas owned a casino in Biloxi, Mississippi. We got along well because he was more than fair and I was able to win some races. We did well. After a year or so, I sold out to Maumas because he wanted to race in New Orleans during the winter and I favored Miami. We parted friends.

That wasn't always the case.

●

Three

If I Could
Train the
Owners

You need money to make money. Somebody
said that. Maybe it was me. Anyway, I always
knew that was true. The purses I won were just
enough to keep me operating in the black. That
was fine for a guy who wanted a hobby, but I
never was much for collecting stamps or saving
string or making furniture. I wanted a stable of
horses—good horses—and the only way I was going to get it was to work for someone who could
buy decent stock. So, I hung out the sign that
read Dave Feldman, Trainer.

55

In walked some of the nicest people in the world, the kind that made me happy I was in the horse business. They had faith in me, trusted my judgment and didn't meddle in things they didn't know anything about. And then there were the jerks, the egomaniacs, the two-bit millionaires. They were like the platers running at bush-league Balmoral Park—unpredictable. They made me wish I were like a lot of trainers who saw every owner as a sucker waiting to be fleeced.

That's the sad truth. Training is a hustle. At least, in the majority of cases it is. Many trainers make big money by devoting 25 percent of their talent and energy working the horses and spending 75 percent of their time working the owner. A hustling trainer knows how to nurse an owner, play with him, feed his ego and blow smoke. An owner is like the "teaser" in the breeding shed. He's the cheap stallion whose job it is to get the mare all worked up. Just when he thinks he's going to score, he's led away, screaming and kicking, and the million-dollar stud comes in to take over. A trainer is like the guy standing outside the shed spraying the teaser with cold water. "Bad break, sir. Your horse will win next time. No doubt about it."

If a trainer can't train, he hustles; it's the only way he can survive. I knew one guy who trained for a zillionaire couple that owned a liquor company. The wife had all the money, so the trainer kept close to her. She had a face that looked like both ends of a horse but that didn't bother him. He treated her like a ringer. Wash the paint off and she was Marilyn Monroe. Schmoozing and smooching. "Every kiss," he told me once, "is worth $10,000."

Even a lot of good trainers have to be promoters because a hustle usually is the only thing an owner understands. The average owner, you see, isn't too bright. Oh, he's smart in his own business or profession, but once he gets to the track he always checks his brains at the clubhouse gate. Owners think horse racing is like some exclusive club. They're willing to pay a big membership fee to join, but they want a lot more than purse money. They want camaraderie, good times. They want to feel as if they're on the "inside," where the action is, the excitement, the glamor. You may have crap on your shoes from walking in the barn, a welt on your leg from getting kicked by a horse, sharp pains in your chest from yelling at a groom you don't dare fire because the next guy will probably be worse, and then along comes the guy you work for, this jerk, this twit, who wants to talk about the sport of kings and practice a secret handshake.

Sometimes I got to thinking, maybe God was testing me, maybe He was saying, "If Feldman (He never called me Dave) can work for this schmuck without slashing his wrists, I'll give him the champion he wants." I didn't kill myself, or the schmuck, but God never came through. With Him, everything's a Pick Six. I must have 100 Triple Crown winners in my Pick Six pool. It's been rolling over every day for 40 years.

I trained for this one guy, a lawyer, and he called me one night to ask how his horse figured in the race the next day.

"I don't think he'll be in the money," I said. "Maybe fourth or fifth. There's no other race for him so I'm running him. His only chance is that anything can happen in a horse race."

"The guy in the *Tribune's* got him second," the owner said. He was referring to the morning line in tomorrow's edition.

"The guy in the *Tribune's* got him second? Well, that changes things, doesn't it?" I said, sounding a little sarcastic. "Chrissake, I've been *sleeping* with the horse. The guy at the *Tribune's* never been to the barn. He's never seen him. Who would know more, the guy at the *Tribune* or me?"

The horse ran out and not too much later so did the owner. I had no finesse, no style, no fast talk. I never led my owners into the breeding shed. I sent them out to the pasture with the other horses, telling each one, "Your chances of scoring today are 4 to 1." If winning a horse race was like getting laid, my owners got a lot of nooky. But they like the *thought* of getting laid as much as actually doing it.

I could never hustle an owner. For one thing, I didn't have the time. I was at the barn in the morning, I was calling the races in the afternoon, and I was at the paper at night. For another thing, I was pretty honest. By nature maybe, because nature gave me a big mouth. I usually said what I was thinking, only to realize later that I was sucking on my wing tips.

Oh, I had some larceny in me, but it was mostly petty stuff. It wasn't anything I planned or plotted. It spilled out when I got excited. I remember one day at Sportsman's. I was running a horse, Light Moon. He figured to win easily if he ran *off* the lead. If he ran *on* the lead, it shouldn't be by more than a length or two. That was what I told my jockey Evan Anyon before the race.

The horses broke and pretty soon Light Moon was on the lead and—goddamit!—running away from the field. "IT'S LIGHT MOON IN FRONT BY EIGHT! LIGHT MOON IN FRONT BY EIGHT!" I was screaming. It must have sounded funny because I called the position of the other horses in a normal voice.

"IT'S LIGHT MOON BY 10!" Didn't the goddam jock know where he was? "IT'S LIGHT MOON—BY 10 LENGTHS!"

Sure enough, my horse stopped in the stretch and got beaten.

"What the hell were you doing?" I asked Anyon after the race. He said he didn't know he was that far in front. "First of all, you should have looked back," I said. "And second, didn't you hear me yelling?"

Dishonest? OK, but it was like taking pencils

home from the office. Maybe if I had more larceny in me I wouldn't have gone through so many
owners. For some guys, the surest way to end a
love affair is to marry the girl. For me, the quick-
est way to kill a relationship was to train for the
person.

That was what happened with me and Dave
Paper, who owned a company in St. Paul, Minne-
sota, and was the first millionaire I trained for. I
met him in Florida and we got to be good friends.
He loved racing and wanted to become an owner.
He kept pestering me to pick out a horse for him
to buy. I kept saying no.

"If I do that, we'll split up," I said. "You'll get
dissatisfied and we'll get in an argument. That'll
be the end of our friendship. It isn't worth it."

"No. No. If you get me the horses, we'll still be
friends and partners, even if you spit in my face."

He kept asking and I kept refusing. I tried to
call him one day. He wouldn't talk to me. I called
again a few days later and he still wouldn't talk.
OK, OK. I heard that some trainer was going to
sell his horses, so I called Paper's office in St.
Paul and told the secretary to tell Paper that I'd
buy him a horse.

Paper got on the phone. "You mean that?"

Yeah, I said.

"Go ahead and buy him."

Paper set the terms of our partnership. I would
claim the horses and build him up a stable, he'd
pay all expenses and I'd get 50 percent of all the

money that came in. He also said if it got to the point where the stable became worth more than he paid for it, I would become half-owner. What a dream deal that was! And it was *his* idea. I didn't make one demand.

So I ran the horse I bought for him. Boom! He won. I ran him again. Boom! He won again. I claimed five or six more horses, one of them called Sunny Dale for $12,500, and we were going! We were winning races and making money.

Then I hit a bad streak. Some of the horses got hurt and those that ran, lost. Uh-oh, here it comes again, I thought. I could see that Paper was getting upset.

Paper said, "I think I'm going to get somebody else to take care of the horses. You're too busy with your other work."

I was never too busy when the horses were winning. Now I was too busy. "OK, if that's the way you want it," I said.

In the meantime, some of the horses that had been sore, recovered, and I won a couple of races, one of them at Sportsman's with Sunny Dale.

"We're winning again, huh?" he said.

"Yeah. It was just a matter of time."

Then, one day Paper told me to come to the Ambassador West where he was staying in Chicago. I got there and we beat around the bush for a while. Then I said, "Go to hell." Paper turned the horses over to Dwight Denham. Sunny Dale went on to win the Columbiana Handicap at Gulfstream Park in 1953. Paper later was offered $100,000 for her. According to the deal we had, I should have been half-owner of Sunny Dale and the others, but I didn't press it.

I probably would have felt worse if Paper had gotten another horse I had had my eyes on. It was 1952 and I went to Keeneland to cover the yearling sales for the *Herald-American* and to buy a horse for Paper. He had given me $10,000. After checking the breeding of the horses for sale, I picked out a filly for Paper. I asked Allie Reuben of Hasty House Farm what he thought the filly would sell for. He said about $15,000. I figured the same, so I didn't wait for her to go on the block. I bought another horse instead the next day and returned to Chicago.

The following year I was walking along the backstretch at Washington Park and Reuben called me over. "I want to show you a nice filly," he said. The horse was Queen Hopeful and she had just won the Arlington-Washington Lassie Stakes. Reuben and I got to talking about her breeding and it suddenly hit me. I said to Reuben, "Isn't this the horse I asked you about at the sale?" "Yeah," he said, "she went for $6,000."

Harry Trotsek wound up with the filly to train. Queen Hopeful finished 1953 as the leading money-winning 2-year-old. As a broodmare, she was worth about $500,000. If I had stuck around for the bidding, I probably could have gotten her.

And Paper would have been that much richer.

I never knew why Paper let me go. It wasn't my training. I had won races, built up a strong stable and made money. Yet, he forced me out. Screw him. I wasn't going to sit around and stew about it. There were other millionaires.

Like Ethel Haffa.

She wasn't in the horse business when I first met her in 1955. She was just your average horseplayer. She came to the track with three furs, changing into a different one as the temperature dropped. When she bet, she spent $1,000 on each race, $100 going on the horse with the longest odds and the rest divided among two or three other picks. One day, one of her $100 long-shots came in, paying $140 to $1. All the papers wrote about her $14,000 jackpot.

Ethel loved publicity. So did her zillionaire husband, Titus, who owned Dormeyer Manufacturing. Publicity was good for Ethel's ego and Titus's business. I had dinner with the Haffas one night and said I had a great idea for a publicity stunt. I told them that secret bids were being taken for Nashua, who had finished second in the Kentucky Derby and won the Preakness and Belmont. The colt was put up for sale after the owner, William Woodward, was killed in a shooting accident. I suggested to Titus and Ethel that they submit a bid for $800,000 and send a deposit of $80,000 to the New York bank that was handling the sale.

"I'll write an exclusive story for my paper," I

said, "and everybody will pick it up. Other papers, the wire services, TV, radio—everybody!"

Ethel thought the idea was great. Titus, though, wasn't so sure.

"What if we win the bid and get the horse?" he said. "Then what?"

"First of all," I said, "if I know my horses, Nashua will go for more than $1 million. And even if you do get him for $800,000, you don't have anything to worry about. He may be worth $5 million when he goes into stud. Send in the $80,000 and you won't be sorry."

Titus said OK.

The next day I had a scoop in the *Herald-American*. I wrote that Ethel had put in a bid for Nashua and that her offer was in the neighborhood of $1 million. (OK, the news was manufactured, but that didn't bother me. Nashua *was* for sale and the Haffas *were* willing to pay $800,000 for him. No problem. Besides, a lot of the so-called "news" in the papers and on radio and TV came out of pointless press conferences and publicity stunts.)

When the news broke, everybody in town was calling Ethel for interviews. She told the *Sun-Times*:

"I filed my secret bid, but I have told no person, not even my husband, the amount of the bid. I am not at all certain how much it will take, perhaps as much as $1,100,000, to get this great horse, but I am anxious to obtain him. . . ."

In the same article, the *Sun-Times* said there

were reports that Ethel's bid was $850,000. Ethel denied it, probably sniffing at the suggestion that only a ditz would expect to get a champion for that amount. "I did not, as reported, bid $850,000," she said.

That's right, Ethel. It was $800,000.

After Nashua was sold, the *Tribune* came out with this story:

> Mrs. Titus Haffa...was one of the five who bid more than $1,000,000 for the race horse, Nashua.
>
> The Chicago sportswoman, who previously had refused to reveal the amount she had offered...told a *Tribune* reporter yesterday that her bid was $1,153,000. That was $98,200 less than the successful bid of $1,251,200 made by a syndicate headed by Leslie Combs II of Spendthrift farm, Lexington, Ky.
>
> Mrs. Haffa, who owns no horses, also disclosed that she plans to attend the next yearling sales and start a thoroughbred racing stable.

Maybe after all the interviews and stories and reports, Ethel got confused. Maybe she really believed she had bid more than $1 million for Nashua. And maybe she was so swept up in the excitement that she really was planning to go to the yearling sales. Maybe. Anyway, she milked the story for all it was worth.

The publicity died down and, so did Ethel's enthusiasm for owning a horse. It wasn't until two years later that she said, right out of the goddam blue, "I think I'll buy a horse."

I liked Ethel, but I liked Titus even better. He was a great guy. I knew that some hustler would get to Ethel and work her over but good. Titus ran the business and Ethel ran him.

"You want to buy a horse?" I said to her. "I've got one, Pasha Saied. He's running tomorrow."

Ethel bought him. He ran and won, paying $14.40. I was out a couple thousand dollars because she got the purse, but it was a good beginning to our owner-trainer relationship. Too bad it didn't last.

Early on we ran cheap to fair horses. As she got more involved in the horsey set, she wanted better thoroughbreds. One day she handed me a blank check and said, "Go to New York and buy some good horses."

When I returned from the trip, I gave her back the check. "I couldn't find any," I said.

"There weren't any good horses?"

"Yeah, but they're all overpriced. Word got out I was looking and everybody jacked up their prices."

She was hot. "I don't care how much they cost!"

"Well, I do."

"Dave," she said, ripping the check, "you're a *jerk*."

After that I wasn't too friendly with Ethel. But

I still liked Titus, liked him enough to go to dinner with him and Ethel from time to time. After dinner we would usually go to their place on Lake Shore Drive and play gin rummy. Ethel cheated. Titus would whisper to me, "Let Ethel win." Fat chance. We never played for money, just blood. Ethel and I did, anyway.

Sometime after the "jerk" incident, Titus said to me, "Dave, I hate to tell you this. Ethel bought two horses from Europe for $100,000 and you're not going to train them. She's got this other guy lined up."

I had seen this "other guy" talking to her at the track. Every time I came around, he would take off.

"Good," I said. "Because I once told Ethel, 'If you ever buy any horses from anybody else, he's the trainer, not me. He's going to die with the horses, not me.'"

The biggest hustle in racing is the horse sale. If a horseman found the right pigeon owner, he could make a "commission" of $10,000 or $20,000. He would get the owner to agree to buy a horse for $50,000 and work out a deal with the horse dealer, or whoever owned the horse, to sell him for $40,000. Now Ethel was paying $100,000 for two horses that probably weren't worth $10,000. After Titus told me about Ethel's plans, I heard that somebody had tried to sell those two horses for $50,000 to Allie Reuben. Allie turned him down.

Ethel got her high-priced horses. And sure enough, the trainer had them six months and never started them. They both had serious leg problems.

She showed up at Hialeah one day and started talking to me as if I were the garbageman, "You're going to take these horses."

"No, I'm not. You bought them with that guy, and he's going to suffer with them."

We broke up.

I shouldn't have been surprised by her reaction when I asked her, at the start of the 1959 racing season, to buy this horse I had my eye on. He was a 3-year-old and the trainer, Elliot Burch, said I could have him for $175,000. I wrote Ethel a letter telling her about Sword Dancer and followed it up later with a phone call.

"This horse could win the Derby," I said, thinking I sounded like a hustler. But I wasn't hustling. The horse was going to be that good. I just knew it.

Ethel screamed into the phone: "How dare you ask me for that kind of money." Then she hung up.

I had tried Ethel first because I thought Titus, who liked me, might have some influence. When she turned me down, I went to see the owner I was training for, Jack R. Johnston, who was also vice president of Sportsman's Park and the Miami Beach Kennel Club. He had an office at the Miami club during the winter. I went there and begged him to buy the horse. I was down on my knees pleading.

"Offer them $150,000," he said.

"Somebody already did and they wouldn't take it."

"One-fifty, that's as high as I'm going to go."

It was hopeless. Johnston was a guy who never wanted to pay full price for anything. I knew that, but I wasn't thinking when I walked into his office. I should have told him the horse cost $200,000. Then he would have said $175,000 and I would have had Sword Dancer.

In the 1959 Triple Crown races, Sword Dancer finished second in the Derby, second in the Preakness and first in the Belmont. He was named the horse of the year. I woulda, coulda, shoulda.

It was a lousy year, 1959. Sometime after the Triple Crown races, Johnston and I were going to go to South Carolina to look at horses. A horse agent there named Fat Charles told us about a 2-year-old that was on the block for $35,000. His dam was sired by Count Fleet, who won the Triple Crown in 1943 (the same year Francis Gray and I were running Oomph Girl in $2,500 claiming races). I liked the bloodline—he was by Your Host—and Johnston liked the fact that this young colt was owned by Mrs. Richard Du Pont. He would have given almost anything to tell everybody in Chicago he bought a horse from a Du Pont.

Johnston and I set up an appointment to fly with Fat Charles to South Carolina. We didn't go because Johnston got drunk. I set it up again. We missed that one, too. Johnston got drunk again. We had to cancel a third time when I got drunk. After three misses, we scrapped the plan.

The next year I saw that one of the entrants in the Arlington Classic Stakes was a Du Pont horse. I didn't remember the name of the horse Johnston and I thought of buying but I did remember his bloodline. This was the same horse. Kelso.

The strip was sloppy and Kelso, going off at 4 to 1, finished eighth. He didn't lose again that year, winning six straight to take horse-of-the-year honors. He also was horse of the year in 1961, 1962, 1963 and 1964. His career winnings totaled nearly $2 million.

Fat Charles, who had tipped me on Kelso, also figured in another woulda-coulda-shoulda episode. It was at Hialeah and I was running Hill Rose, a mare I had claimed from Sunny Jim Fitzsimmons for $10,000. After she ran out, Fat Charles told me he had a buyer for my horse and offered me $13,000. I said no. When she ran out the second time, I looked up Fat Charles and sold Hill Rose. Some years later, I went to a sale and one horse caught my eye. It turned out to be one of Hill Rose's foals. That same horse, True North, went on to win the Widener and Seminole handicaps at Hialeah in 1971. He was one of the many terrific foals out of Hill Rose. That was made clear one day at Gulfstream Park. I was with Fat Charles, when this guy came up and said to Charles, "Boy, you made a millionaire out of me selling me that mare." I got sick. Probably would have just given up and died if I didn't think I had a shot at the double that day.

Then there was Hard Rock Man. I was racing in New York about 30 years ago and was about to claim the horse for $7,500. The claim was all written. Then outside the racing secretary's office, Buddy Jacobson, the horse's trainer, came up to me and said, "Say, this kid who's working for me used to work for you. Says you're a helluva guy." I tore up the claim. I hardly knew the guy, but I couldn't take the horse away from him. What a softhearted squirrel! What mush for brains!

So Hard Rock Man ran and won, of course. Then Jacobson took the horse to Delaware, where a trainer named Clyde Nix claimed him. When Nix brought him to Arlington, I said to myself, "I'll get him now." As far as I knew, Nix didn't have some kid on the payroll who had worked for me once and thought I was a great guy. Nix was fair game, so I put in my claim. What happened? Another trainer, Bobby Cramer, put in a claim too and outshook me for the horse. Hard Rock Man went on to win stakes races and sired some fair to good foals. Guessing? The whole deal was worth a half-million. I didn't get a slice. All because some kid had said some nice things about me. Woulda, coulda, shoulda is the worst kind of hindsight. It's a view of a horse's ass as he walks away. I was due for a break.

It came with Glass House. I first saw him in 1961 at Hialeah. I was in the paddock area checking him out as a possible claim. I liked his breeding and he was a 4-year-old that hadn't raced much. There was an inquiry into the race that had just finished, so all the horses had to stand outside the paddock gate for about 10 minutes. I was inches away from Glass House and could see that his left fore ankle was slightly enlarged. But, I could also see it was an old injury and that the bone probably had set. I decided to put in a claim for $10,000. He was a good-looking horse. I figured if he couldn't win for $10,000, he should win for $7,500.

Glass House ran out that day. When I got him in my barn, I checked him out, feeling his ankles. They were OK, tight and cool. A couple of days later I gave him a worm ball to kill any parasites and a physic to clean out his system. I ran him back too quickly, though. The worm ball and physic weakened him and jockey Bobby Ussery just about eased him in the stretch. He was beaten by some 15 lengths by $12,500 claimers. "You'd better get rid of this horse," Ussery said.

I waited a while before running Glass House again. When I did, it was for $7,500 at Gulfstream. He finished second. After the race, a trainer told me he saw a guy drop a claim for my horse. I looked down and saw my groom leading Glass House back to the barn, so that meant I hadn't lost him. A steward told me later the trainer had used a Hialeah claim form, so the claim was void.

The strong finish for second place was just a sign of great things to come. Glass House won race after race, including the New Year's Handicap at Tropical Park with Ussery riding. He won in Florida, New York and Chicago. Always on the dirt. A trainer asked me once why I didn't run him on the grass. "When a horse wins a bunch of races on the dirt, why put him on the grass?" I said. "Why try to fix something that isn't broken?"

But it was threatening to break. Glass House came back from one race with a puffy knee. That was a bad sign. Fluid was building up. The knee wasn't going to get any better, but I could prevent it from getting worse. I started putting him in the whirlpool. He'd soak in hot water for a while and then I'd dump in ice. Glass House was in the whirlpool for an hour every day, and on days he raced he got a double treatment, before and after he ran. Got so he started asking for reading material. I could have asked a vet to tap and drain his knee and then inject cortisone. But too much of that and there's bone damage. The whirlpool was best, followed by a poultice applied to the knee. It was time-consuming. Trainers with 40 to 50 horses couldn't do it. I only kept as many horses as I knew I could handle—six or eight mostly, no more than a dozen.

Glass House kept winning, but I knew it would be wise to sell him while he was on top. I put an ad in the Form saying my horse would be on the block at the horses-in-training sale at Hialeah. Lou Wolfson must have seen the ad. He offered $25,000 for Glass House. I told him I wanted $35,000. He said no. Wolfson, another zillionaire, wanted a bargain.

A week before the sale, I checked the list of races that would be run, if they filled. Two allowances, one for six furlongs and the other for seven, were scheduled two days before the sale. I figured if Glass House won again, I could get close to $50,000. If he lost, I would be lucky to get $30,000 or $35,000. The key was to get Glass House in the easier of the two races. I was afraid of a horse owned by Dixiana Stable.

Kenny Noe, the racing secretary, said I should run Glass House in the seven-furlong race. He said the Dixiana horse probably was going in the six-furlong event. I told him I'd think about it.

Later, I saw Howard Battle, the assistant racing secretary, and asked whether both the races would fill. He said he thought so.

"Which race is Dixiana going in?" I asked.

"Don't know yet."

I decided to take a chance. I entered Glass House in the seven-furlong race. Later in the day, when the entries came out, Glass House and the Dixiana horse were in the same race!

"Hey," I told Battle, "you've got us together."

"The other race didn't fill," he said.

I guess I was turning green.

"Something wrong?" Battle asked. "You can always scratch him, you know."

I could, but that would be like telling the buyers at the sale that something was wrong with Glass House. I had to run him. If he lost, I probably would have to take him off the block and keep him. That wasn't what I wanted to do.

Everything came down to a race I didn't think Glass House could win. Thank god I smoked cigarettes—five packs a day. The only guy I knew who smoked more than I did was another trainer, Boo Gentry. I never saw him without a butt in his mouth. He didn't chew Clorets to freshen his mouth, he drank Weed-Be-Gone. Cigarettes were a comfort to me. They gave me other things to worry about. Smoking made me cough so much I thought I was dying. I could run a loser and kick the bucket at the same time. A real deadheat. Leave it to Feldman.

I rode Steve Brooks and, goddam, Glass House won! I called the *Form* and added two more inches to my ad: "GLASS HOUSE WINS AGAIN." Wolfson called and offered $30,000, plus another $10,000 if he won in New York.

I told him, "I'll get $40,000 or more for him and won't have to worry whether he'll win again."

"I don't want to quibble," he said.

"I'm not quibbling. You are."

Goodbye.

At the sale the next day Glass House went for $45,000! Top bidder was a guy named Roxie Gian, whom I knew from way back. He was from Buffalo and he built shopping centers, mostly on the East Coast. He had called me before the sale, asking whether he should try to buy Glass House. I told him the truth: The horse needed care, but he could still win a lot of races. When Gian got Glass House, he turned him over to his regular trainer, Frank Merrill.

I didn't have a star in my stable anymore, but I inherited some decent stock in 1963 when I went to work for Jack Hogan, the president of United Insurance Company. He was a hard guy to figure out. He kept me off guard by saying this and doing that. Nice guy but something of a screwball. When he flew, he traveled with his jeweler. Whenever he met a stewardess he liked, he would tell his jeweler to give her a ring or a diamond watch. No strings, no hanky-panky. He just liked playing Santa Claus at 25,000 feet.

One day I told him there was a race at Sportsman's that was right for either his horse or one that I owned, Hatchet Bay. I said if he wanted me to run his horse, I wouldn't run mine.

"I think my horse has a better chance," I said, "but I'll do what you want."

No problem, he said. I could run mine.

Well, Hatchet Bay, a horse I claimed for

$15,000, won the race. And Hogan was hot. He didn't like his trainers having their own horses, he said.

"But I asked you if I could run him and you said yes," I said.

"Come up and see me tomorrow."

My back! I called a friend of mine, Alex Dreier, the television newscaster and Hogan's brother-in-law.

"I think Jack's going to turn me loose," I said. I explained what had happened. Dreier said he would drop in on the meeting.

The next day I went up to see Hogan and he lit into me again. Dreier walked in, all smiles and greetings. "How're you guys doing?"

I told him. Then Hogan told him.

Dreier turned to me and said, "Dave, will you sell Jack your horse?"

"Sure."

"How much do you want?" Hogan asked.

I paid $15,000 so I said $15,000.

Hogan bought him.

I ran Hatchet Bay a few days later and he won. The purse was $6,000, which now went to Hogan. So this multimillionaire got my horse for only $9,000. I should have had Hatchet Bay and $6,000. Instead, I had $15,000—and no horse!

But I kept my job. I took Hatchet Bay and the rest of Hogan's stable to California for the Santa Anita meeting. Hatchet Bay ran and looked good finishing in the money. A few days later, I saw a race for 2-year-olds and put out a feeler for the winner. No dice. I wondered whether the horse that ran second, a speedball called Hempen, was available. He had impressed me. I had seen only one horse break out of the gate faster than this young colt and that was Spy Song. Hempen, I was told, was for sale. The price was $75,000 and the horse I ran—Hatchet Bay. Hogan came out the next morning to look at Hempen. He made the deal, writing out a check on the spot.

When we got Hempen, he had a cough. All 2-year-olds cough, so I wasn't too worried. If he had a cough and wasn't eating, that meant trouble, but Hempen never missed an oat. He coughed for six weeks. After that we shipped him to New York with the other horses. He started training and the rest of the horses started winning.

One month into the meeting I had nine victories and was tied for the lead in the trainer standings. I also shipped to Laurel, where I won two more races. I called Hogan one day and told him to come down to Laurel because I thought we had a shot at winning some purses. He said he didn't want his horses all over the country and told me to ship them back to Chicago.

I came home and Hogan took the horses away from me. I had taken his 12-horse stable and won 38 races for him in 10 months. It wasn't good enough. Hogan gave the horses to Steve Ippolito.

I should have guessed Hogan was loading crap

into the fan. Hogan had rehired Ippolito for the second or third time and given him a nice horse called Oink. Before Hogan and I left for Santa Anita, Oink developed a big ankle and Hogan thought he was through racing. I persuaded him to let me have a shot. I knew this veterinary surgeon in the East, Dr. Jenny, who has operated on a plater for me. This was the same guy who had saved Tim Tam by operating on his sesamoid. Tim Tam won the Kentucky Derby in 1958.

I called Jenny and he said to mail him X-rays. He would study them to see if he could operate on Oink. After a few days, Jenny called and said he couldn't operate but an injection might help. "Put your vet on the phone tomorrow and I'll tell him what to use," Jenny said.

Oink was injected and pretty soon he was bouncing around and ready to race again. I thought Hogan might want to reward me by giving me Oink to train, but he returned him to Ippolito. Oink won some nice races after that.

And everybody, except me, cashed in big on Hempen. He was sold as a quarterhorse stud for about $200,000. Then he was sold again to be bred to thoroughbreds. Hempen's son, Annihilate 'Em, won the Travers in 1973 and some of his other foals did pretty well, too.

Even though Hogan let me go, we remained friends. He never screwed me out of any money. He was always fair in that respect. In fact, after we split, he would give me $400 or $500 every time one of my old horses won. But because of his rule against my owning horses or training good stock for another owner, I had to start almost from scratch again. After 20 years of training I had three mules in my stable.

I asked around looking for horses to train, thinking that it wouldn't take that long to find an owner or two. I went here and there but nobody would give me a horse. The problem was very few people knew I was a trainer. I always kept my stable small, never training for more than two owners at a time. The other thing was I never put my name down on the program as trainer. It had been that way since 1944. I always figured the papers I worked for wouldn't care for that. I was also worried that some jerk would slip my horse a mickey or something stronger and I'd have a horse with a positive test. I didn't need that. I had enough problems. All those years I had someone else down as trainer. Since 1958, I had been using the name of my assistant, John Sullivan.

So when I needed horses and started asking owners, they would give me a funny look and say, "When did you train?" I'd tell them I trained so-and-so and so-and-so, and they'd say, "Your name wasn't on the program."

If I wanted to stay in the game, I'd have to do something drastic. I'd have to do some hustling. I decided to take out an ad in the *Form*. Some trainers did that but it always was a small one-column, two-inch blind ad. Only breeders selling foals from their studs went full-page. I figured I had something to sell, so why not do it in a big way? I bought a full page.

Four

Dr. Dave

In mid-1964 the ad ran in the Midwest edition of the *Form*. It looked impressive. Our names were at the top: "DAVE FELDMAN (General Manager and Adviser) and JOHN SULLIVAN (Trainer From Ireland) Six Years in United States." Then big bold letters jumped out saying:

ANNOUNCING

**Opening of a Public Stable Immediately
Not by Accident—Not by a Longshot**

Two Men Who Have Operated One of the MOST, If Not THE MOST, Consistent Racing Stables in America

Blossom Stable (owned by Dave Feldman) operated a very successful stable since 1943. Horses have been claimed and have improved with CONSISTENCY. Believe it or not, more horses have finished 1-2-3-4 in Feldman's silks than have been out of the money in 20 years. It is also a known fact that in the last five years, with John Sullivan as trainer and operating with other horses owned by various sportsmen, this combination has had AT LEAST 75 percent of their horses in the money...

The ad listed the number of our victories and earnings for 1961 (71, $220,515), 1962 (32, $149,357), 1963 (45, $197,754) and half of 1964 (14, $76,000).

All this has been accomplished because of personalized service...

Now, for the FIRST TIME, they are building a public stable. They'll be happy to START or build your current stable up. Horses can be purchased or claimed for those now in the business. Foreign-bred horses can be purchased immediately for reasonable prices for those seeking grass specialists.

> Sullivan & Feldman are not soliciting a one-horse stable worth $3,500 unless the prospective customer definitely wishes to build a strong outfit.

Then there was a long list of horses beginning with Glass House:

> Stake horse. Claimed for $10,000 and within 24 months won $98,000 and 24 races. He was out of the money only twice in 45 starts. Glass House was sold at auction for $45,000. He was the world's most consistent performer.

Among the others on the list were Deux-Moulins ("Plater champion. . . . He equaled the American record on the turf for two miles."), Sunny Dale, Potomac, Futuresque, Light Moon, Spanish Fort and Country Squire.

The bottom of the ad read:

THIS WILL BE MAJOR RACING THE YEAR AROUND

I got some inquiries but no offers except one—from a guy named Frank Sullivan, who owned a big paint company in Ohio. He sent me 20 horses. I shipped 15 of them right back. My fee was $15 per day per horse for training and feed.

By returning 15 horses, I was throwing $225 a day out the window, but I knew John and I couldn't handle 20 hogs in addition to the three we already had.

A trainer with too many horses had to let others do too much of the work. When that happened, he really wasn't training anymore; he was managing. I believed in giving each of my horses personal care, like getting down on my knees to feel his ankles or running the tube up his ass to give him an enema. I couldn't do that with 23 horses. The enemas alone would kill me. Also, I couldn't keep that many horses straight in my head. (I was still working for a newspaper and announcing the races at Sportsman's.) I would screw up somewhere. Put the wrong jockey on the wrong horse and put the wrong horse in the wrong race. With John's help, I could handle 12 horses, but no more.

The five horses I kept were the ones I thought could finish a race without getting lapped. Dopey, Dippy, Sleepy, Sneezy and Wheezy. They weren't much, and I couldn't do a lot with them. One of them, maybe it was Dopey, won a race, beating a miserable field and paying $38. I was shocked. I was ready to give him a urine test. It just went to prove that anything could happen in a horse race. What was even crazier, some jerk claimed him.

Frank Sullivan, though, was peeved. "What did you do?" he said. "Have somebody claim him?"

Jesus! He thought I wanted the bum for my-self. After a while Sullivan took back the other horses. I didn't mind.

Then about a year or so later, he called and said he wanted to send me a 2-year-old maiden. I said OK, ship him. The horse was called Te Vega. I prepped, schooled and trained him. I took the greenness out of him. Given time, he'd be a racehorse.

After I had Te Vega about three months, Sullivan called and told me to run him in a stakes race at Gulfstream. I said he wasn't ready to meet that kind of competition.

"He'll run out," I said. "Run him in a race for maidens."

Sullivan said no. He liked the idea of running him in a stakes. Prestige.

After Te Vega ran out, Sullivan wanted to run him in the Bashford Manor at Churchill Downs. I said the horse wasn't good enough yet. Sullivan said he liked the idea of running a horse in a stakes race at Churchill.

Te Vega ran way out in the Bashford, and Sullivan told me to ship him back. A year later, in 1968, the horse won the Ohio Derby, which was only a $25,000 race back then. When he stopped winning, Sullivan sent him back to me.

Te Vega was now four and he had hoof trouble. I told Sullivan I wanted to "heel-nerve" the horse. When the nerve above a bad foot is taken out, a horse usually will run better because he isn't bothered by pain.

"No!" he said. "You do that and his foot will fall off."

Sullivan didn't understand. He thought it was risky. After I explained what a heel-nerve was, Sullivan said OK. "But if his foot falls off, I'm going to come after you."

Dr. Tom Gorman pulled the nerve at Hialeah. Then I brought Te Vega back slowly. Three months later, I entered him in a feature race at Gulfstream Park. He ran a big second to War Censor, one of the best grass horses in the country. The heel-nerve seemed to do the trick. I figured Sullivan would let me keep him. I was wrong.

We split again. I sent him a bill for $2,500. He gave me a check for $850 and wrote on the bill, "Paid in full." What was I going to do? Get a lawyer and sue Sullivan? It would take too long and besides, the lawyer would get most of the money. The hell with it. Some months later, I read in the *Form* that Sullivan had died. I had forgotten about him until I saw the obituary. Then I remembered I still had his check. I rushed to the bank and cashed it. Years later I met his son in Florida. A real nice guy. My father was a tailor and I can't sew a button. So much for breeding.

It was during the stretch I trained for Frank Sullivan, the first time, that I happened to see Glass House's past performance in the *Form*. Roxie Gian had bought Glass House the previous year and Frank Merrill still hadn't won a race with him. After Sullivan took his horses away from me the first time, I decided to give Gian a call. Maybe I could persuade him to let me have Glass House to train.

"What do you think you're going to do with him?" Gian said, meaning: Did I think I was a better trainer than Merrill?

"He doesn't know the horse, but I do."

Gian said something about losing $5,000 when he bet on Glass House in New York. "I'll send him to Woodbine and if he doesn't do any good, I'll send him to you," he said.

I called Tom Gorman in New York and asked that he give Glass House a quick look-see. Gorman went to the barn, but stayed out of the stall because he knew I didn't have Gian's consent. Later, he saw Glass House walk around. He looked OK, Gorman said. But, he warned, unless a horse was very lame, it was hard to tell just by looking at him whether anything was wrong.

I took a shot. I phoned Gian. I told him not to send Glass House to Woodbine.

"Send him to me. I'll pay for everything—the van, vet, feed, everything—if you let me have the horse for 21 days. If I don't win in that time, I'll return him."

Gian agreed. It was going to cost me about $2,000 to get the horse back. If he didn't win, it was money down the drain.

But I had tremendous confidence in myself. Like all good trainers, I was part medicine man. I had as many home remedies stored in my head as a vet had treatments written in his horse book. I didn't go in for frog balls and newt eyes and witch doctor potions. I just relied on experience.

Some months earlier in California, when I was training Hogan's horses at Santa Anita, I helped a vet of mine, Dr. Jock Jacoy, save a horse that was owned in part by actor Audie Murphy. I had called Jacoy to see whether we could have dinner together. He told me he couldn't make it.

"I have a high-priced broodmare here and she's got the colic. I think she's going to die," Jacoy said. "If you want to come up, that's OK, but I can't leave this horse."

The mare was at a ranch near the track and I drove up. When I arrived, I saw Jacoy in the yard chasing the mare with a whip. He cracked it from time to time, but he wasn't hitting her. He just wanted to keep her moving because a horse with colic sometimes may give up and die if it gets a chance to lie down. The wind had picked up and was blowing dirt and sand all over the place. I leaned into the wind and headed toward the yard.

"That's not going to help, Doc," I yelled. I told him I had had luck with colicky horses by giving them enemas.

"OK," he said, "let's try it. I've tried everything. I injected her with everything I could think of."

We filled a five-gallon bucket with soap, mineral oil and water, fixed up a pump with a long tube and stuck one end of the tube up the mare's ass. Jacoy and I took turns. While he pumped, I held the tube. Then we switched. I didn't mind pumping.

When it was my turn again to hold the tube, I felt as if I was standing next to an active volcano. The wind whistled and whipped, but I thought I could hear rumbling coming from deep within the earth's crust. In this case, the horse's ass. Five gallons of molten shit. Omigod!

"Doc!"

"What is it, Dave?"

"Your turn."

"We just switched."

"Doc!"

"Yeah?"

"Doc!"

"What?"

"She's *coming*, Doc. She's *coming*. She's your horse, Doc. Let's switch!"

Too late.

I read somewhere about a big eruption that occurred in Java 100 or 150 years ago. The mountain blew up and lava flowed down the sides burying hundreds of villages, each no larger than a backstretch, and killing thousands of people. Some of the lava shot up and set fires miles and miles away, killing more people. Then there was tons of ash that got picked up by the wind and carried around the world. You couldn't see the sun. You thought the world was coming to an end. It was horrible.

My clothes were ruined. I had put on a surgical

apron but that was like covering a tit with a pas-
tie. The mare kept exploding and I was standing
there holding the goddam tube as if I were the
Dutch boy trying to put a finger in the dike. The
poor horse must have thought she was coming
apart. Crap and soapy water were flying everywhere. Some of it probably got swept up by the
wind and carried across the Great Plains.

It slowed, first to a trickle, then drip, drip, drip,
until finally it stopped. Although the mare
seemed a tad better, she was still in pain.

"I give up," Jacoy said. "I'm going to let her lie
down. I don't think she'll live."

"Wait, Doc. I've got one more idea," I said.
"Do you have any brandy? I had an old groom,
Tom Lloyd, who said the best thing for colic was
brandy. Let's give it a try."

Jacoy went into the house and came back with
a quart bottle that was almost full. I took a drink.
The sun was going down and I was wet and cold.

We took a syringe, filled it with brandy and
gave it to the mare. We kept doing it until the
brandy was gone. The horse lay down. We covered her with a blanket and let her sleep.

"She's going to die," Jacoy said.

"Maybe not," I said, although she didn't look
good.

Early the next morning I called Jacoy and
asked how the horse was.

"You saved her, Dave! You saved her! She's

running around like she can go six furlongs in 1:10. She's 100 percent."

Call me Medicine Bear.

But I wasn't sure whether I could get Glass House back to running 100 percent. One thing I did know—if I couldn't do it, no one else could.

Glass House arrived and I saw that he was a bit sore. I went to work. He was back in the whirlpool every day. As the deadline drew near, I started working him a bit. Two and a half weeks after getting Glass House, I called Gian and told him the horse would be running the day after next, although the racing secretary doubted whether the race would fill. Gian said he would fly in. The next day I began having second thoughts. The horse just wasn't ready. I called Gian and said I changed my mind and wanted to enter the horse in the next available race.

"I need a few more days," I said.

"Send the goddam horse back! You said he was going to run tomorrow. He's sore, isn't he?"

I begged. I pleaded. It was like talking to a creditor. Hang on. Glass House's victory was in the mail. Finally Gian said OK.

I wasn't through begging and pleading. This time it was with the racing secretary. I told him there was a race in three days for Glass House and if he didn't do everything he could to make sure it filled, I would lose my horse.

The race "went." I phoned Gian and told him

Glass House would be racing three weeks to the day he was shipped in. "I'll be there," he said. "See you in the paddock."

Glass House won, paying $14.60. I looked around for Roxie but couldn't find him. I called his home in Buffalo and he answered.

"What did he do? Lose?" Gian asked.

"Yeah, he lost," I said.

"I knew it," he said. "What do you think you are? A genius? I had him for a year and couldn't win. You thought you could win with him in three weeks."

"Did you bet on the horse?"

"No. Do you think I'm crazy?"

"Roxie, are you near a chair?" I said. Gian had a bad heart.

"What is it?"

"Get a chair and sit down."

OK, he said, he was sitting down.

"Glass House won," I told him.

"What are you doing? Lying to me?"

"I figured if I said he lost, you'd tell me you bet $5,000, so you could squawk. If I told you he won and you played him, you might not want to tell me because you would figure that I figured you should stake me because of the chance I took. Got it?"

"What in the hell are you talking about? Did he win or lose?"

"Won by two lengths. Paid $14.60. Are you sure you didn't bet?"

Gian let me keep Glass House, but when I wanted to run him again, Roxie insisted I ride Herberto Hinojosa. He said Hinojosa's agent, a guy named Polish John, had told Roxie to give Glass House to me. "We owe Hinojosa the mount," Gian said. "He'll win on the horse."

Trouble was Hinojosa had injured his left wrist and wasn't dead fit. He couldn't whip Glass House when the horse lugged in nearing the wire. Glass House was beaten by a neck.

"Don't ever tell me who to ride," I told Gian. "You cost me a race."

"OK. I promise."

Gian and I got along after that, so I said OK when he asked me to ship Glass House to Fort Erie, across from Buffalo in Canada. He wanted Glass House to run against this top sprinter based at the track. Roxie wanted to show off his horse before his friends. I went to Fort Erie in the morning and flew back to Chicago in time to announce the card at Sportsman's. I left John Sullivan in charge, but Merrill was listed as trainer on the program. Merrill trained at Fort Erie, and I didn't want the horseplayers razzing Merrill in case Glass House won. Which he did.

Gian was happy—and a little skeptical.

"What are you doing to this horse?" he asked me. "You hopping him?"

I laughed. He couldn't figure out why I could win with Glass House and his regular trainer couldn't.

The next stop was Detroit, where Gian had tons of friends. Winning a stakes at Detroit would be like winning the Derby, he said. Glass House ran and won, setting a new track record for six furlongs—1:08—on August 1, 1964. (It still stands.)

I got Glass House back to Hawthorne where he was beaten by a neck in a stakes. I decided to ship him to New York for his next race. After the horse ran out, Gian demanded that I send him to a farm, which was Roxie's way of telling me he was giving Glass House back to Merrill.

I had won another $40,000 with Glass House my second time around and gotten Gian out of a hole. But Gian, it turned out, was another Dave Paper, another Jack Hogan. At least in Gian's case, I had only one horse to lose.

Sometime later, Merrill ran Glass House in a $10,000 claiming race in Florida. I went to the track that day with a $10,000 check all made out. I felt lousy. I had pneumonia and had gotten out of bed just to see Glass House run. But I didn't put in the claim. It wouldn't be like last time; Glass House wasn't a three-week project anymore. I felt I didn't have the energy. Maybe the pneumonia had something to do with it. Glass House won and was claimed. That was the last I saw of him. Months later, someone told me Glass House was running against $2,500 claimers at a track near Boston. I decided to buy him and find some nice home for him. I made some calls but came up empty. No one knew who his owner was or whether Glass House was still racing. I should have claimed him back in Florida. Now, he was going to spend the rest of his days racing at bush-league tracks until he couldn't walk anymore. He deserved better.

It wasn't until 1968 that I got another horse that compared to Glass House in class. I was at Hialeah training for Izzy Hecht, who was president of the Flagler Kennel Club in Miami. He had his eye on a horse running in a $10,000 claiming race. He wanted to know what I thought. I told him no because the people who had him used the same barn I did. If I claimed the horse, the people who owned him would think I was a rat-bastard. It was like a broker using inside information to make a killing. It wasn't kosher.

"Well, I'd like to have him," Hecht said. "You look the race over and call me back."

I studied the past performances, made some calls and then got hold of Hecht.

"The horse you want is OK," I said, "but I think there's another one in the race that's better. Frigid Aire II. Bred in Ireland. He might be the sleeper."

The other day Frigid Aire II was beaten by 20 lengths, but the race was on the dirt. He was a grass horse. I told Hecht that I had done some checking and everyone was high on the horse.

"This is the horse I want." I said.

"OK. Go claim him."

The horse Hecht wanted won the race and

Frigid Aire II, despite getting knocked all over the track, finished second. He should have won the race. I felt a lot better when I heard that Pete Battle, who trained for a big outfit, was mad when he learned his horse got claimed.

Going to the post, Frigid Aire pranced like a dancer, light on his feet, head high, confident, in control of every muscle. He looked like the Black Stallion, an outlaw that might rear up on his hind legs, whinny a signal and lead the other horses in a stampede around the track, through the paddock and out the gate.

But no, he was pure racehorse. He ran like a ringer in his first start for Hecht and me. He won a *$40,000* claiming event at Hialeah. I nominated him for the Hialeah Turf Handicap, a $100,000 race. About three days before the race, Frigid Aire began to cough. It got better, it got worse, back and forth, this way and that. We worried, we sweated, we prayed. The morning of the race we were all standing around—Hecht, Tom Gorman and myself—looking at one another and waiting for a sign from God to tell us what to do. Then Frigid Aire coughed again.

"That's it," I said. "I'm scratching. If I run him, I'll ruin him."

About a month later, I ran him in a $30,000 handicap at Sportsman's—on the dirt. For some reason, grass horses that can't run on dirt elsewhere like the strip at Sportsman's. Frigid Aire came from last, circled the field and won. I ran him back again, in another $30,000 handicap, and he won the same way. This time he beat Gentleman James, who had just won the $150,000 Gulfstream Park Handicap. Next time out Frigid Aire finished second after getting pushed to the outside fence going into the stretch.

The next morning I got to the track at 6:30 and spotted my assistant trainer, Raul Martinez, coming out of the barn. Something was wrong. I followed him to Frigid Aire's stall.

"I just got here and saw this," he said. "Somebody tried to kill your horse."

I looked into the stall and saw Frigid Aire with his head down and eyes half closed, standing as still as a statue. Flies were buzzing around wounds all over the lower half of his body. The straw was blood-splattered. On the walls, where Frigid Aire had rubbed against them while trying to get away, there were bloody smears. During the night, someone had taken a pitchfork and stabbed him—maybe 10 times. There were deep wounds on his stifle, the area just above his hind leg, on his shoulder and on his legs.

I called the vet. When I returned to the stall, I began washing the wounds with hot water and soap. Frigid Aire didn't move a muscle, didn't make a sound. No twitch, no whinny, nothing. Sometimes the pain is so deep, so terrible, the only thing a horse or a human can do is remain rock still. Most good racehorses are well-mannered and trusting. Frigid Aire wouldn't have been frightened by a man coming into his stall in the middle of the night. He might have even nuzzled up to him, hoping for a mint or some sugar. Only when that first thrust pierced him would he have suspected something was wrong. Then the nightmare began, the screeching, screaming and kicking, the pain shooting through the body, the throbbings of burning wounds. The man who attacked my horse was insane. Why else would he do that to a defenseless animal?

A day or so after the attack, someone called and said he knew who stabbed my horse. He named a trainer, a guy who used to work for me. I passed the information to Dan Groth, who was in charge of security at Sportsman's, and told him what the caller said. Groth said he would look into it. The anonymous caller phoned several times until I finally told him to call me at the security office so Groth could talk to him. He did. Groth listened to what he had to say. Then he told me he would look into it. If Groth ever came up with anything, he never told me. I wanted to confront the guy who I suspected stabbed my horse, but I didn't have any proof. If I had cancer and was going to live only a few months, I would have gone to his barn and beat him with a horse whip until he confessed.

Frigid Aire was sidelined for five months. I got him back in training, then shipped him to Belmont for the Man o' War Stakes. He washed out badly in the paddock but still managed to run a decent race, beaten by only five lengths. But in the races after that, he started to fall apart. If a horse is hurting in one leg, he shifts his weight to the other. That puts more strain on the tendons. If he was raced anymore, he would break down for sure. Hecht eventually sold him to a breeder in Ireland for about $35,000.

Hecht believed in bargains. He got one with Frigid Aire II. He thought he had another one in an Irish bred that he bought for $5,000. I ran the horse and he lost. He had bad hocks; the elbow joints on his hind legs would swell up. I fired the hocks and let him rest. Then I ran him at Hawthorne and he won two claiming races. I shipped him to New York and he won for $8,000. Then I took him back to Florida and he won for $10,000.

"We'll run him next for $12,500?" I told Hecht.

"How about the Hialeah Turf Handicap?" he said. It was on his mind, like a girl who smiled at you in the elevator. What if, what if, what if. Hecht was like Gian. He wanted to win a big race at home in front of all his friends.

But Frigid Aire belonged in the race; this bum didn't. He had as much chance of winning the Hialeah Turf Handicap as I had of capturing the Pillsbury Bake-Off. I told Hecht I'd nominate the horse if he insisted, but he didn't belong in the race. "I want to run him for $12,500," I said.

Hecht was about five-foot-nine, stockily built, and had a big round head fringed with hair. He had cold fierce eyes. His look was a finger being jabbed in your chest. "What if we lose him?" he said.

Thinking to hell with him, I said, "Well, if we lose him, you've got the $12,500 claiming price, and the purse will be about $4,000, and you'll probably bet $500 to win and $500 to place on him and win about $2,000. That's about $20,000 for a bum you gave me from Ireland. That's not bad."

"Yeah, but he might win the Handicap."

"If he wins at $12,500 and we don't lose him, I'll run him in the Handicap."

The horse won, and Hecht started yelling "Dave, Dave," while pounding me on the back. I wanted to see his eyes pop out, so I told him that the horse broke the track record. He hadn't, of course, but Hecht wouldn't have known that.

"*He broke the track record?* We'll run him in the Handicap!"

We were on our way to the winner's circle when a guy from the racing secretary's office told us, "Sorry, boys, you lost your horse."

Hecht went bug-eyed again, only this time he was screaming at me. "Didn't I tell you they would claim him? He broke the track record! We could've won the Handicap!"

"He didn't break the record," I said. "I was only kidding."

That stopped him for three seconds. Then he yelled, "I don't care! I could've won the Handicap!"

A short time later we broke up. I went to his office to settle up. Some months back he had bought a horse from me for $8,500. He paid me $5,000 at the time and said I would get the rest later. I still had the registration papers, so I figured there was no way I wouldn't get my money.

"You owe me $3,500," I said, holding up the papers.

He held out his hand, but I wouldn't give the papers to him. "What's the matter?" he said. "Don't you trust me?"

OK, OK, I thought, and gave him the papers. Then he said he didn't owe me any money. I had taken his word when we made the deal for my horse. No witnesses, nothing signed. It was my word against his. He didn't get to be a millionaire by not playing all the angles. I left, but not before telling him what I thought of him. And I told him that within a year that horse he had all lined up for the Handicap would be running in $2,500 claiming races.

About a year later, I saw him at Tropical Park. I pulled out an old past performance I had clipped from the *Form*. I had been saving it just for that moment. Our old horse was running for $1,500 at some bush track. Hecht took it and walked away. Never said a word, never said a goddam word.

Through the years, whether I was training for an owner or not, I tried to keep my own string of horses. They were mostly horses I claimed. One of the few I ever bought for myself was Sport King. I got him in the summer of 1969, about the time Hecht and I were at each other's throat. Trainer David Whiteley was at Arlington and I asked whether he had any horses for sale. He mentioned a horse, Sport King, that I could get for $30,000. Whiteley was a good guy. His recommendation was enough for me. The only hangup was that they were shipping Sport King out in a few days and the guy the Whiteleys trained for would only take cash, no check, for the horse.

"I'm good for it," I said.

"I know, but I'm training for him," David said. "If he says 'get cash,' I'm going to get cash."

I had some money stashed away but not $30,000. While I was trying to figure what to do, Whiteley invited me to see Sport King work. The horse, a dark bay gelding, went five-eighths in :59 and 2. He flew! I *had* to get him. I called a friend, Jack Maisell, but he said his money was tied up. Then I called another guy, Jake Gottlieb, who was part-owner of the Dunes in Las Vegas. I had done him a favor in New York. He had wanted $5,000 to bet on a horse I tipped him on. But he couldn't cash a check because he hadn't established credit at the track. I had credit so I got $5,000 and gave it to Gottlieb. The horse won at 3 to 1 and he paid me back. The whole thing took about 30 minutes.

I called Gottlieb in Las Vegas. "Jake, I want to buy this horse at Arlington. I need $30,000 in a hurry. Can you help me out?"

Gottlieb said he thought he had that much in his account at Arlington. "Call me back."

I called back. Gottlieb had the money. "I told them to transfer it to your account," he said.

I got Sport King. With $15,000 I managed to scrape up and Maisell's $15,000, I paid back Gottlieb in a couple of weeks.

Sport King was a beautiful horse—sound, not a pimple on him. He was one of the few horses I ever saw that ran better when another horse hooked him. He loved to run on the lead and fought like hell to keep it. He had only one bad habit. Whiteley never told me that Sport King was a bad actor at the gate. He didn't want to get into the slot. He had to be muscled and pulled.

One of the first races I entered him in was a one mile handicap at Sportsman's named after a guy I had trained for, Jack R. Johnston. I figured Sport King could beat the field, but I wasn't sure whether he could handle the dark. The post time for the feature was around 5:30 p.m. That meant the race would be run under the lights. Any horse with a gate phobia might go crazy at night when things get spookier, when the lights create shadows that seem to jump out from everywhere.

Five days before the race Sport King turned in

a fast workout, going six furlongs in 1:11⅗. He was sharp. He was going to kill 'em. My only worries were that damn gate and racing under the lights. One evening, between the races, I took Sport King onto the strip and schooled him at the gate under the lights. The assistant starter put a sack over his head before sending him into the hole. Once he was in the slip, the sack came off. The gate opened and—boom!—he broke like a champ.

The sack worked like a charm for the handicap, too. I could see it from high up in the announcer's booth. I was calling the race. With Gerry Gallitano up, Sport King raced to the lead, hugged the rail around two turns and stormed into the stretch with two other horses.

"It's Sport King a head in front. Pit Stop is slipping through on the rail and that's Son Jack on the outside. The three are heads apart. It's Pit Stop by a head. Son Jack second. Sport King is third between horses. The three are still heads apart. It's Sport King, Son Jack and Pit Stop in midstretch. Son Jack regains the lead. Sport King comes on again. Pit Stop is making another move. They're still heads apart coming to the wire. The three are digging. Sport King is making another move. At the wire—it's SPORT KING—the winner by a head."

"I thought you were going to fall through the booth," my groom, Wendell Griffin, said after the race.

"What were you doing?"

He pointed to the dusty spots on his pants and said, "I was on my knees—praying."

Later, I happened to run into Ted Atkinson, the state steward and former jockey. "Hey, that was a smart thing you did," he said, referring to my schooling Sport King at the gate and getting him used to running at night.

"Thanks," I said. I couldn't think of anything else to say. I was almost speechless. It was the first nice thing Atkinson ever said to me.

Sport King's purses totaled more than $150,000. He won a bunch of allowances in Illinois, New York and Maryland, and another big race in December 1970, the Monumental Handicap at Laurel, Maryland.

I saw Frank Whiteley during the time when Sport King was winning consistently and he said, "You're doing a better job with the horse than I did."

For races that were a mile, Sport King was the best horse I ever trained. Glass House was my best sprinter. On grass, Frigid Aire was at the top of the second division when he was stabbed that night. He was still developing and just might have moved up to the top ranks.

Deux-Moulins, a horse I claimed from Frank Wright for $3,500 in 1954, was the best plater router I ever saw in my life. He wasn't much to look at but he got the job done. One year he won five of the six races in the Arlington-Washington distance series. He didn't lose the other race. The other trainers wouldn't enter their horses if

Deux-Moulins was in the race, so I had to scratch him. Deux-Moulins could beat good stakes horses if the race was far enough. In the summer of 1955, he set or tied three records in three consecutive races. He broke Arlington's mark for $2^{1}/_{16}$ on the turf, set the track record for $1^{3}/_{4}$ miles on the dirt, and on July 28 tied the American record for $2^{1}/_{16}$ on the grass: 3:30$^{4}/_{5}$.

The best off-track horse I ever had was Spanaqua. He ate mud, *real* mud. Up until the 1970s, racing strips were composed mainly of dirt and clay, not sand. Sandy strips can turn fast when it rains because some of the cushion gets washed away. Dirt and clay strips, during a rain, turned soft and mushy. That was perfect for horses with bad feet and bad ankles, like Spanaqua. The soft mud took the sting out of pounding.

Like Deux-Moulins and Glass House, Spanaqua was a record-setter too. At Hawthorne, during one rainy stretch, I ran him twice in three days, knowing once the strip turned dry and fast he'd be just another horse. After finishing second on a Thursday, he was entered to run again on Saturday.

Just before the Saturday program got under way, a steward told me the horse that beat Spanaqua the other day had been disqualified because of a positive test. I would get first-place money. As for Saturday's race, Spanaqua couldn't run unless he picked up a three-pound penalty now that he was a winner. I jumped at it. The field was tougher but the race was longer, 1³/₁₆ miles instead of 1¹/₈ miles. Spanaqua could run all day in the mud. He would wear everybody out.

That's what he did. He won two purses in one day. It was a record, maybe for Guinness.

The only standout filly I ever had in my stable was Sunny Dale. I should have had more—Queen Hopeful back in 1952 and, about 20 years later, My Juliet. My Juliet, a 3-year-old filly, had just run a good race at Hawthorne and was for sale for $40,000. No one I was training for at the time would put up that kind of money, so I went to see Jack Hogan, who had paid $75,000 for Hempen on my recommendation. I told Hogan he had a chance to own the champion he never had. This filly, I said, was going to be great. Hogan said later maybe, but not now. He said his accountant advised him not to buy anything until after the first of the year. Well, My Juliet was sprinter of the year in 1976, went on to win more than $400,000 and as a broodmare produced foals that sold for big money. Sometime later, Hogan tried to explain to me why he had taken a pass on My Juliet. "I thought you said she was Illinois bred," he said.

Every trainer needed a star and My Juliet would have been mine if Hogan had come through. I hadn't had a consistent, quality horse since Sport King and he won his last race for me in 1971. But things were about to change in 1976.

"Bet him, Dave," the jockey agent said. "He worked six furlongs in 11-3."

The horse was a strong-looking 4-year-old called Old Frankfort and he was running in a $20,000 claiming race at Arlington.

Old Frankfort ran out. When I saw the agent again, I told him that as a tout, he had a future as a stall cleaner. The agent gave me the palms up. "I don't know what happened, but he did work that fast. Honest."

When Old Frankfort ran back—for $10,000!—I claimed him for the guy I worked for, Charlie Windle. I couldn't pass it up. Old Frankfort was a good-looking, sound horse and he'd be eligible for an easy maiden race.

Windle pretty much let me claim any horse I wanted because he figured I knew what I was doing. He had once given me O So Big, a horse with a bowed tendon. "See what you can do with him," he said. I won six straight. Then in his seventh race he broke down.

The thing about Windle was he wanted his horses to run once a week, no excuses. "That's the way I make money," he said. A week after I claimed Old Frankfort, Windle asked why his horse wasn't running. I couldn't tell him the truth, that I had forgotten to enter him. I was goddam president of the goddam Horsemen's Benevolent and Protective Association. Something had come up and everything else slipped my mind.

"He was coughing," I said.

When the next race came up, I didn't enter Frankie because during a workout, his right hind foot clipped the heel of his right front foot.

"He grabbed a quarter," I told Windle, using the term for Frankie's injury.

Meanwhile, the guy who lost Frankie told me he would have sold him for $2,500. Bad knee, he said. What in the hell was he trying to tell me? I went to the barn and checked the knee. Nothing. I figured the guy wanted me to drop him down so he could claim him back at a cheaper price.

Windle was still waiting for Old Frankfort to run. When I finally entered him, the race didn't fill.

"That's it," Windle said. "I'm going to sell him."

"You just did," I said.

"To who?"

"Me."

I gave Windle $10,000.

I started him out against $15,000 claimers but by the end of 1976 he was running in, but not winning, stakes races at Hawthorne. He was third in the Sun Beau Handicap and Charles Bidwill Memorial. About a week later I ran him in the Gold Cup. I told the jockey, Larry Snyder, to stay off the rail because it was deep. So what did he do? Going into the stretch, in third about two lengths back, Snyder went to the rail and stayed there. Old Frankfort finished sixth, beaten by about seven lengths. Frankie might not have won, but he should have got some purse money. He finished the year with five victories in 21 starts and earned more than $60,000.

I didn't race him much in 1977, only five times, because he had leg trouble. But he came back strong the next year. In March, I ran him in the 1 1/16-mile Canadian Turf Handicap at Hialeah. I really screwed up by giving Eddie Arroyo the mount. I wanted Mickey Solomone or Jerry Bailey because Frankie was a big, powerful horse and he needed a rider who was strong enough to control him. But neither Solomone nor Bailey was available. Two weeks earlier Arroyo had ridden Old Frankfort in a $45,000 claiming race. Frankie broke fast and Arroyo was able to rate him on the lead. Frankie was ahead in midstretch. Then boom! He got beat by a neck. I had no problems with the ride; Frankie just wasn't fast enough that day. But I still doubted whether Arroyo was strong enough. I named him, though, because I needed a rider and he was the best one available.

The horses broke and I could tell right off that Arroyo didn't have any control of Frankie. The horse was too damn strong. He had taken hold of the bit and started to roll. Arroyo fought him; Frankie fought back. That was the only battle Frankie won that day. Arroyo couldn't rate him and Frankie ran his best too early. After three-quarters, Frankie was third, 2 1/2 lengths behind the leader. Then he fell apart, finishing fifth, beaten by almost 10 lengths.

I lit into Arroyo after the race and he didn't say one goddam word in defense of his ride. In fact, he admitted Frankie's poor finish was his fault. A few weeks later, Arroyo retired. He had never mentioned it to me. If I had known his plans, I wouldn't have given him the mount. I would have ridden somebody else, an apprentice even, but not some guy who felt he was getting too old and was ready to hang it up.

Three weeks later, in a $40,000 claiming race, Old Frankfort won by two lengths with Solomone up. Then, going off at 4 to 5, he won an allowance with Bailey. At Calder Race Course, Frankie made it three straight by winning the Palmetto Handicap with Tommy Barrow. He paid $16!

In five months, Frankie had won four times in nine starts, finished second twice and third once. His winnings totaled nearly $50,000. I never had a horse that had won that much that quickly. Frankie was special. I decided that Old Frankfort's next race would be at Arlington Park on July 4—the Grade II Stars and Stripes Handicap.

About two weeks before the race, Frankie's ankle started to bug him. It looked as if he was getting an osselet, a bony growth. Every day I was on my hands and knees tubbing him, first in hot epsom salt water and then in ice. Hot and cold. I wanted to keep the heat out of his ankle. If a horse has hot joints, you've got problems.

The day before the race, I had the vet come in to check the ankle. He took his goddam time.

"What about it, doc? Can I run him tomorrow?"

"I'm checking, Dave. I'm checking."

I never had children but that didn't mean I didn't know what it felt like to be a parent. My kids were like a lot of other 2- and 3-year-olds. They ran around naked all the time and couldn't be potty-trained. Only difference was my kids had four legs. My worries and responsibilities were the same. I called in the doctor when they were sick. I made sure they got their shots. My kids ate food that would make them grow big and strong. I made sure they took their vitamins. I didn't brush their teeth, but they saw a horse dentist regularly. Most important, I didn't let them play with kids that were bigger, stronger and faster than they were.

"C'mon, doc, you're not getting paid by the hour."

I should have been a vet. A vet didn't charge for examining a horse, but he figured to get the work if any fixing had to be done. Some vets were like auto mechanics.

"You got bad rotor lining, pal, and your thermostat needs a new semicondensor. Also, I don't like the look of your steering hinges. You don't plan to take any long trips, do you?"

"No, just six furlongs."

"Well, don't go over 30 miles an hour."

"Not over 30? The others will be running close to 40! My horse will come in at 1:25!"

"What can I say?"

"OK. Fix him up."

The longer the vet took, the more worried I became. I got to thinking about the last time I had a horse entered in a big, big race. Ten years ago, in 1968, I had scratched Frigid Aire II on the day of the Hialeah Turf Handicap because he coughed. Was it going to happen again? Goddam it all!

The vet stood up.

"Looks OK to me. Run him."

I had a good vet.

Race day. The handicap was on the grass, which was wet from an overnight rain. The course was soft but that was OK. Frankie could run over anything. That wasn't the case with another horse, though, and his trainer, Peter Howe, scratched him. This was the horse that Ron Turcotte was supposed to ride. He had flown in from New York for the race. Now he was free. I had another jock lined up but I wanted Turcotte, the guy who rode Secretariat, the Triple Crown winner in 1973. He also had ridden a lot of winners for me, including two on Sport King.

I went to look up Howe. I was a little worried about what he might say. Some trainers were hard cases. They got ticked when you asked to borrow their jockey. After all, their stable shelled out for the jockey's first-class plane fare. Why give a free ride to some local guy who was too cheap to import a top jock? Bud Delp went crazy once when he learned that Bill Shoemaker, an old friend of mine, had agreed to ride my horse. Delp had flown Shoe in from California for a big stakes race at Arlington. The feature was the eighth and my horse was entered in the ninth, so I didn't see any problem. Delp screamed at me, "Shoe isn't riding for you!" OK, OK. Shoe looked at me and kind of rolled his eyes upward. "Sorry, Dave," he seemed to say. "What can I do?"

I found Howe and he said sure, it was OK with him if I rode Turcotte, but I would have to ask Ron. I caught up with Turcotte in the jockey's room and told him the horse he was going to ride was scratched. Would he ride my Old Frankfort? Yes, I said, I cleared it with Howe. Yes, my horse had a shot. "OK," he said. "I'll ride him."

In the paddock, I told Turcotte: "I'd rather see him come from behind, but he likes to fly out of the gate. If he breaks on top and you can't hold him and nobody goes with him, take the lead."

Frankie walked out of the gate. In a 10-horse field, *he walked out of the goddam gate.* I panicked, but Turcotte didn't. He had control of Frankie, didn't let him take the bit. Turcotte took his time. He sat still. Then along the backstretch, he asked Frankie to run a bit. Going into the far turn, they were in third, about three lengths back. Around the turn and heading into the stretch, Frankie was in the lead by a half-length! Turcotte had rated him perfectly, saving the best for last. Frankie won by one and one-half lengths.

I had to sweat out an inquiry because jockey Jerry Bailey, whose horse finished *fifth*, claimed foul against Old Frankfort. Bailey was a friend of mine, for chrissake! What did he expect to get? Fourth-place money? I could see it if his horse finished second and he stood a chance of getting first place on a disqualification. But fourth place! The claim was disallowed. The crybaby lost and Frankie stepped into the winner's circle. The $50,000 Stars and Stripes Handicap was the biggest victory of my career. First-place money of $34,000 raised Old Frankfort's lifetime winnings to $148,000.

Turcotte flew back to New York and five days after the Stars and Stripes he was involved in a spill at Aqueduct. The fall left him paralyzed from the waist down. I hated to see any jockey get hurt like that, but Turcotte's accident hit me hard. He was one of the "good guys" of horse racing. You needed guys like him. He helped make up for the screwballs, crooks and hustlers you met every day at the track. Turcotte was clean and honest. He never shortchanged a trainer on a mount, always gave it his best, whether he was on Secretariat or a claimer. He rode smart and he was smart with his money too. During the winter I would see him and his family at the little cafe near Hialeah. He was making good money but there they would all be—Ron, his wife and the kids—eating hamburgers.

After the Stars and Stripes, Old Frankfort didn't race for seven months. He had come back sore after a workout. I shipped him to Gulfstream and he ran in an allowance race in February 1979. He finished last. It was time to think about selling him to a breeder or breeding him myself.

I did the wrong thing. I took out an ad in the breeding magazines, giving notice that Old Frankfort—winner of "10 races, one a Grade II stakes, and a total of $148,234"—was ready to service any mare for only $1,000. I sat back and waited for the telephone calls. And I waited.

I couldn't get the sunuvabitch laid.

I thought back to Arroyo's miserable ride on Old Frankfort. Now it was costing me plenty. In the 1¹⁄₁₆-mile Canadian Turf Handicap at Gulfstream, Practitioner's winning time over a firm grass course was 1:41 ³⁄₅. Three weeks later, in the $40,000 claiming race at Gulfstream, Old Frankfort and Solomone covered the same distance over a firm course in 1:40 ⁴⁄₅, three-fifths of a second off the track record. If Frankie had run 1:40 ⁴⁄₅ in the Handicap, he would have beaten Practitioner by four lengths.

Although time is a tricky thing (someone once said it's only important in prison), it meant something in Frankie's case because of the other races he ran against the same horses. In the Canadian Turf Handicap, Practitioner beat Haverty by a head and That's A Nice finished third. Old Frankfort beat Haverty by nine lengths two months later when he won the Palmetto Handicap at Calder. As for That's A Nice, Frankie beat him by five lengths in the Stars and Stripes.

Frankie would have gotten some nooky if it wasn't for Arroyo's bum ride. A winner of *two* Grade II races would have meant something to breeders looking for a stud.

Oh, I got Frankie some mares, but they weren't the kind you'd want to bring home and introduce to your parents. They were claimers from my stable. Frankie couldn't have cared less. It bothered me, though. He wasn't going to get a chance to prove himself as a stud. And, of course, I wasn't going to make any money as a breeder.

Woulda, coulda, shoulda.

●
───────────────────────────

Five

Good Jock,
Bad Jock

Some years back, Herbie Litzenberger and I were at a restaurant having dinner and I had a chance to ask a jockey something I had always wondered about.

"When I'm driving my car I can think pretty fast. If I see traffic jamming up, I'll maneuver to avoid it. How is it for a jockey when he gets into close quarters? He must have a tough time thinking, huh, because I see so many getting shut off? Is that right? Is it hard to think—Herbie, where you going?"

He got up and left me all alone at the table. Worse, he stuck me with the bill.

Touchy. Like a lot of jocks I knew.

It was an innocent question. I guess he thought I was trying to make a fool out of him. Usually it was the other way around. Jockeys were the ones always playing games. If they weren't so little, I would have knocked a few of them on their ass.

Some jockeys made me feel like Moe—or was it Curly? Maybe it was Larry. Anyway, I felt like the Stooge who couldn't hit back, so he kept slapping himself in the face.

I felt like a Stooge that day when Eddie Arroyo rode Old Frankfort in the Canadian Turf Handicap. And I had that same feeling that day more than 20 years ago when I saw Bobby Ussery come walking toward my barn with a smile on his face and spit on his tongue.

I knew what he wanted. He wanted to get off my horse, Glass House. I had named Ussery to ride him in a stakes race at Hialeah, but now he wanted out because he had a shot to ride Intentionally, a horse that figured to beat me.

"Bobby, what's the matter?"

"Well..."

"Well what?"

"Would you get mad if I rode that other horse?"

"Would I get mad? I'd *hate* you, Bobby."

I would too. I had given him a lot of winning mounts in the past. Now he was spelling loyalty f-a-v-o-r-i-t-e.

"I was going to ask you to do it, to let me off your horse," he said.

Willie Shoemaker (left) and Eddie Arcaro shake hands before a 1955 match race between Swaps and Nashua at Chicago's old Washington Park. Nashua (Arcaro up) won.

Above. After 20 years of riding race horses, Ted Atkinson finds his 3,500th win, at Hialeah in 1957, as thrilling as his first.

Right. Eddie Arcaro fought calories during his entire Hall-of-Fame career. Here he loads up his plate pretty good after announcing his retirement in 1962.

Left. Robert Baird . . . after a tough race in 1968. Obviously, he wasn't leading the pack.

(Courtesy Field Enterprises, Inc.)

(Courtesy Field Enterprises, Inc.)

Above. Steve Cauthen, "The Kid", as I dubbed him, was the nation's leading jockey in 1977, his first full year on the circuit. He eventually took his less aggressive riding style to Europe.

Left. Walter Blum, shown here in 1967 when he made his debut as a Kentucky Derby jockey, was in my view a very good rider.

Left. A true superstar, Angel Cordero rides hard
and rough, and is unfailingly cheerful. *Right.*
Pat Day won 1,257 races each year from 1983–85
—the only jockey to reach that mark since 1895.
He is still setting records on horses such as
Easy Goer, the 1989 Belmont Stakes winner.

Jean Cruguet is in the winner's circle with Seattle
Slew after winning the Kentucky Derby in 1977
in 2:02:01.

(Courtesy Hawthorne Race Courses, Inc.)

Above. Earlie Fires (center, behind cake) surrounded by friends and fellow jocks, celebrates his 4,000th career win. He did it at Hawthorne Race Track on July 1, 1986 when he had four winners. *Right.* Next to Steve Brooks, Fires was the best whip rider I've ever seen. Here he weighs out after setting an Arlington Park record for most wins in a season (121).

Right. I was the one who gave Doug Dodson his start—a fine jockey but he cheated at gin rummy. Here's how he looked in 1948, at the beginning of his career.

Right. As a rider, Bill Hartack could do little wrong. Here is how he looked in 1964, smiling behind three of the four Kentucky Derby trophies he won.

Right. Harold Keene set a Sportsman's Park record in 1950 by booting in six winners in eight mounts. In the early 1950s he was a contract rider for the legendary Chicago owner-trainer, William Hal Bishop.

I think Julie Krone rides as well as most of the top male jockeys. In 1986 she held the record for one-year earnings by a woman jockey. She's still at it. *Below, left.* Chris McCarron holds the trophy after winning the Preakness Stakes in 1987. He captured the first two legs of the Triple Crown that year aboard Alysheba. *Below, right.* Conn McCreary won two Kentucky Derbys. I always considered him a great come-from-behind jockey. He was an outstanding jockey during the 1950s and 1960s.

Above. Another Kentucky Derby winner, controversial Don Meade had a trick for making his horse break fast out the gate. He was one of the best jockeys in the 1930s and 1940s.

Above, right. Craig Perret rode a lot of winners for me. Here he is in 1970 weighing in at Hawthorne Park after winning the second race.

Right. Randy Romero was a sensation at Arlington Park when he started out in the early 1980s. He still is—although we've had our differences of opinion several times.

Left. The great Willie Shoemaker after winning
his seventh Gold Cup at Hollywood Park in 1978.
What can I say? A great rider and a great friend.
The 1989 season is his last as a jockey.

Center. A jockey who can ride the hair off his horse,
Ismael Valenzuela started out riding burros. Here's
how he looked in 1968.

Right. Jorge Velasquez was a fine rider; he
missed a few wins in 1981 when he fell off one of
my horses and broke his collarbone, but he ended
up with his share of big winners that year.

All photos courtesy Chicago Sun-Times *unless otherwise noted.*

"Come on. The stakes isn't that big, and if you were going to ride Intentionally all the time I wouldn't mind it because you're my friend. But (Manual) Ycaza's his regular rider. For you it's a one-shot deal."

"Well, I'd like to do it. I'd like to win that stakes."

"Don't do it to me," I said.

"If I win, I'll split my 10 percent with you."

"I don't want you to switch, but I'll leave it up to you."

"I'll do it."

"Then I'll take that half."

Ussery won the race.

Glass House broke last in a 14-horse field. That wouldn't have happened with Ussery aboard because Bobby was a good gate boy. And my horse wouldn't have finished fourth. He might have finished second, which would have been worth $5,000. Or if he had gotten third, that would have been worth $3,000. The winner got $16,000, so Ussery collected $1,600.

After the race Ussery didn't come to see me, but I knew where he hung out, so I went there.

"Bobby, I think you owe me $800. Is that right?"

"Yeah."

"Write me out a check."

I got my money and wouldn't talk to him for two years.

That happened often—good jockeys switching to favorites—if you were a trainer with a small stable. Jockeys would think twice before crossing a big-time trainer because they might never get another mount from him. Small-time operators like me ended up going nyuk-nyuk-nyuk-nyuk-nyuk, slap, slap, slap.

Joe Culmone, a jock from Italy, was another guy whose neck I wanted to wring. This was way back in the 1950s, at Hialeah. My horse and Culmone's mount were coming down the stretch, head and head. My horse had a habit of hanging once he got on the lead, but Culmone, of course, didn't know that. About 100 yards from the finish line, Culmone took his elbow and hit my horse in the head. My horse lunged at Culmone, getting his nose out far enough to edge the other horse at the wire.

"I go claim foul," Culmone told me.

"For what?"

"He boddered me."

"Hey, I won a big bet. You're my friend. Why the hell are you claiming foul on me?"

"Goddam horse he gonna pass me. I hit 'em with my elbow and the sonabitch he turn around and wanna *bite* me."

Culmone also mentioned he had bet $600 on his horse. That was the real reason he was claiming foul and that was why he had pulled that dumb move. He got really mad when I told him my horse always hung when he made the lead, so that Culmone would have won if he hadn't hit him.

Culmone claimed foul but the judges threw it out, so I didn't have to slap myself too hard.

But for every crazy guy like Culmone, there was an Eddie Arcaro or a Bill Shoemaker or an Angel Cordero Jr. or a Steve Brooks. If there weren't, I'd have slimmed down long ago and taken up riding.

EDDIE ARCARO

He was one of the few jockeys I ever saw who probably had the strength to carry a horse to the wire. He was a natural athlete. We went out drinking one night, first at Gibby's on Dearborn and Clark and then to the Palmer House, where we stayed until 4 a.m. A few hours later at Arlington Park, my head was swimming as I watched Arcaro win a stakes and two other races.

Arcaro rode only one horse for me, Big Upset, a filly that could fly. I had just claimed her when John Heckmann, the jockey who rode the horse in the race, told me that something was wrong with her. Heckmann and I were friendly, so I had to believe him. Then on the morning of the day I was going to run her, Heckmann came to me and said he had had trouble sleeping because he had a guilty conscience. The filly's trainer had told Heckmann to lie to me. Heckmann said I had made a good claim and should scratch the horse because his boss was going to claim her back.

Heckmann probably believed that the filly was OK. But my mind works in crazy ways sometimes. I went to the barn, got on my stomach and checked the filly's legs. I felt around one ankle and came away convinced that she was going to develop osselets. When a horse gets osselets, the ankle becomes enlarged. It can mean a layoff of three or four months and there's no guarantee that the horse will return to her best form. I wasn't Calumet Farm; I couldn't afford to gamble. I decided to run her.

"They're going to claim her back," I told Arcaro, "but I'm going to take a chance that I'm doing the right thing."

"I hear this gal can really run," he said. "We'll see."

"Win by as much as you can," I said. "I want to know what I'm losing."

The filly won by several lengths. When Arcaro came to the winner's circle, I told him I lost the horse. "Well," he said, "you got $2,500 more for the horse and a $2,500 winning purse. You made $5,000 in five days. You can't squawk about that. But you did lose a fine filly."

I almost choked. Had I done the right thing?

I had. The filly did get osselets.

TED ATKINSON

I rode Ted Atkinson on one horse. It was at Tropical Park. I was pretty high on the horse and wanted to make a decent bet. The windows were about to close so I shouted to this one clerk who knew me, "Punch me six tickets!" I thought he was behind the $50 window. I was wrong. He gave me six $100 tickets! I went to watch the race, mumbling, grumbling and praying. At the first call Atkinson fell off my horse. I don't recall whether he was injured.

Atkinson stayed on mounts more times than he fell off and later was named to the Hall of Fame. After he retired, he became a steward in Chicago. That's when he started falling off horses again, so to speak. He never seemed to know what was going on. There was the time when fixers were rigging trifecta races and the track police tipped Atkinson. He never saw anything, never even *suspected* anything. He was the only one at the track who didn't know the fix was on. Atkinson wasn't crooked, just incompetent.

BOBBY BAIRD

He won on Swift Action, one of the two horses I claimed after winning with Random Breeze in 1944. A good front-running jockey, Baird rode like a monkey on a stick. He looked as if he were about to fall off as he urged his horse on, scratching his neck, screaming and pushing. He got out whatever a horse had to give. Baird's son, E.T., looks better on a mount than Bobby, but he'll never ride as many winners.

WALTER BLUM

Good rider but his trouble was he always wanted to run on the lead. He rode a horse for me called Spanish Fort at Washington Park. Spanish Fort was part of an entry I was running; the other was Country Squire.

Before the race, Blum asked why I was running the other horse. "You know I can win it with my horse," he said.

"I'll tell you why I'm running an entry, Walter. I'm going to tell you *not* to go to the lead, but you will. You and (the other speed in the race, Space Skates) will run head and head. Spanish Fort will tire and Country Squire will win."

"I won't go to the lead. I promise," Blum said. "Scratch that other horse, will you?"

We argued some more but I finally gave in. I scratched Country Squire.

Sure enough, Blum took Spanish Fort to the lead, fought the other speed horse, and hung in the stretch. Some longshot sneaked in to win. My horse finished second.

Years later, I asked Blum whether he remembered the day he lost on Spanish Fort. He said he didn't. He said I must be wrong. Jockeys only remember the winners they rode. I remember the losers too.

STEVE BROOKS

My life would have taken a different turn if Brooks hadn't ridden Random Breeze on September 20, 1944. I don't think any other jock could have gotten a sulker like Randy to put out. Brooks was the best whip rider I've ever seen.

Brooks was a star in the 1940s and 1950s, doing most of his riding for Ben Jones and Calumet Farm. He won the Kentucky Derby with Ponder in 1949. Beginning with Random Breeze, Brooks won more than 30 races on horses I owned or trained. One day at Hialeah, he rode three horses for me, winning two races and finishing in the money in the third. Extending his pinky, he said to me, "I would have given this finger to have won that other race for you." I believed him.

STEVE CAUTHEN

It was in the mid-1970s and Paul Blair, an agent, came up to me at Arlington and said I should keep my eye on his jockey, that he might turn into a good rider. The kid rode a winner here and there, but I didn't pay much attention. Then one day he rode two winners and I decided to watch him the next day through binoculars. I was impressed. The kid, Steve Cauthen, rode as if he had been riding 10 years, not just two, three months.

I gave him a mount, on Rusty K'on, and he put up a tremendous ride. The rail was deep and he had the No. 1 post position. Before the race I told him to get off the rail. That's easy to say but hard to do. If you rush your horse to the lead in an effort to get outside a bit, you'll burn up your mount. If you pull back to let another horse take the lead, you run the risk of allowing too many horses to pass and you're stuck way in the back.

Cauthen rode my horse perfectly. He broke and was on the rail running head and head. Then, seeing that he could swing around, he took back out of the spot and let the horse that was running with him take the lead on the rail. And Steve just went out and around. He won the race easily.

I nicknamed Cauthen "The Kid" in my columns. I guess I wrote about him quite a bit because one of the sports copy editors at the *Daily News* asked, "Who is this guy? Another Arcaro?" I said, "Might be. He just might be." Like Arcaro, Cauthen had natural ability, but he wasn't anything like Eddie when it came to riding style. Arcaro was rough and tumble, aggressive, a little mean. Cauthen was patient, heady, doing everything with his hands. Someone said he had the body of a boy and the mind of a man who's 40.

Cauthen rode in New York in 1977, but was scheduled to come back to Arlington to ride Sauce Boat in the Futurity. The night before the race I phoned him in New York and asked whether he'd ride my plater, Danny Crow, in a claiming race.

"The track is going to be a sea of mud," I said. "My beat-up horse needs a lot of warming up. You can gallop him up and down the backstretch and check out the strip. It may help you win the Futurity."

"OK," he said. "I'll ride the piece of shit for you."

Cauthen finished in a dead heat for first with Danny Crow. And he won the Futurity.

Cauthen was the nation's leading jockey in 1977, his first full year on the circuit, and won the Triple Crown with Affirmed the next year. Then he went to Europe, where he said his riding style fit in better. He didn't have to pound and push horses. "In Europe, I can do it all with my hands. Guide your horse, rate him, use your head and win. You don't have to overpower a horse."

ANGEL CORDERO JR.

He's the kind of jockey you've got to love. He rides hard and rough, always getting the best out of your horses. He rode only one horse for me, finishing second in a race at Gulfstream.

The other thing I like about Cordero is that he's so damn cheerful. You always go away feeling good after talking with him.

JEAN CRUGUET

A Frenchman, he won the Triple Crown with Seattle Slew in 1977.

He loves to train your horse as much as ride him. After finishing out of the money on my horse one day, he said, "Drop him."

"Don't train," I said. "You moved too soon. You got him tired."

He didn't say anything, but I could tell he didn't appreciate my comment. His neck rose out of his collar.

JOE CULMONE

In 1950 Culmone was at Tropical Park and battling for the national jockey title with Bill Shoemaker, who was riding in California. With four or five days left in the year, it was announced that on December 31, Shoe was going to go to Agua Caliente, where they had 15 races on the program. When Culmone heard about it, he said, "I lose, I lose. I canna win no more."

"No, you're going to win," I said. "I called Havana. I know the racing secretary there and he wants you to come on Sunday and race. They've got 12 races. They'll give you 12 favorites. You'll ride five, six, seven winners. You'll beat Shoemaker."

"What time boat leave?"

"Boat? We're going by plane!"

"I never been on plane. I not go."

The next day: "I not go."

The next day: "I not go."

Finally, on Friday, he said, "I go. Only for you."

"You sunuvabitch. You go for yourself. I'm going to make you the leading rider in the country."

So the Cubans chartered a plane and flew a bunch of us over. When we got to Havana it was pouring. When we got to the track it was flooded. The racing secretary ran up to me and said, "I got him all the favorites, but none of them likes the slop. I can't change the jockeys now. It's too late."

Culmone and Shoe went into the last day of racing tied with 385 victories. Shoe was at Caliente, where it was probably nice and sunny and dry, and Culmone was in Havana, where there was so much water on the track that you had to worry about the currents.

The horses went postward for the first race and I couldn't find Culmone. Where was Culmone? I saw a loose horse and somebody said the horse stumbled in the slop and Culmone fell off. He went down in the muck and I thought he had drowned. Finally he picked himself up, went plop, plop, plop to the gate and remounted. He must have picked up about 15 pounds of mud. He lost the race.

Culmone ended up with three winners that day. On the plane home we heard that Shoemaker also rode three winners, so they finished in a tie with 388 victories.

PAT DAY

He's a great rider, one of the best in the business. He has small hands like Shoemaker. Horses respond because he's easy on the bit. He can hand-ride most horses and beat jockeys who are whipping their animals to death. Sometimes, though, he just isn't mean enough. He'll blow a race because some horses have to be whipped. Day doesn't have the temperament to whack them.

Day was a hell-raiser when he was younger. But then he found religion. Now he mentions the Lord more times than I talk about my losers.

DOUG DODSON

I helped him get mounts in New Orleans, where he first became known. Later, I touted him on my radio program from Hialeah. Warren Wright heard my comments and told Ben Jones to make Dodson the first-string rider for Calumet Farm. He won the Preakness on Faultless in 1947.

Dodson was a fine jockey, but as a person he had one bad habit. He cheated at gin rummy. We played every day while he was in New Orleans and I never beat him. Later, when he was riding for Jones, somebody asked him how he got to be a star. "Dave Feldman did it," he said. That was nice of him, but he never did return a dime from the rummy games.

EARLIE FIRES

Next to Brooks, Fires is the best whip rider I've ever seen.

Fires has no great love for me. He says I'm always knocking Chicago racing. "You're always writing about New York or California," he said. What crock. What am I supposed to do, be a homer? Say that I love $5,000 claiming races? I boost when I think a race or program is worth boosting. If it's crap, I call it crap.

Fires's big beef goes back to 1981, when I wrote a column about complaints from readers. One letter said the only reason Fires won so many races was because there were no Shoemakers or Arcaros anymore. After that came out, Fires and the rest of the jockeys wouldn't ride for me. I was running a horse the next day and Rick Evans was supposed to ride him. He took himself off the horse. Terrific. The year before, when he was an apprentice, I put him on Liberal and he won the Bidwill Memorial Handicap. Now he was refusing to ride for me!

Chicago jockeys have big feet and small heads. I should have sued the bastards.

AVELINO GOMEZ

He was a great jockey in the 1950s and 1960s. In 1966 he led the nation's jockeys with 319 victories. I saw him ride first in Cuba, before Castro took over, and then at Gulfstream. I helped talk him into coming to Chicago. When he arrived, I introduced him to other trainers and we all started giving him mounts. In fact, he won with five of the first six horses he rode for me. I talked

Ivan Parke into riding Gomez when Parke came to Chicago with Lou Wolfson's stable. Gomez rode 9 winners in 10 mounts for Parke.

One day I rode him on Light Moon and the horse got beat. The next time out, I rode Kenny Church because Gomez was hurt. Light Moon won. When Church won again on Light Moon, Gomez screamed at me, asking why he hadn't been given the mount.

"You can't be mad at me after what I've done for you," I said. "I put you on all those winners and introduced you to all those people. Now you're mad at me because I had one damn winner. I don't believe it."

He listened. Yeah, he said, I was right. No, he wasn't mad at me.

The next time I put him on a mount, he went right up a horse's hinder. The steward, Aiden Roarke, came down and asked me what the hell kind of orders had I given my jockey.

"You don't think I gave Gomez those orders, do you?" I said.

Run up a horse's ass—that's a good way for a jockey to get beat and not be accused of pulling his mount.

Maybe I was wrong. I rode Gomez on another horse and told him, "Don't go to the lead." He went to the lead and the horse stopped to a walk.

"Yeah," he said. "I made a mistake."

No, I made the mistake. I didn't ride him again.

BILL HARTACK

He rode Deux-Moulins for me one day at Arlington and got beat, but I told his agent that I'd ride him back. In the meantime, I had a call on him to ride another horse, Latches. The day before the race, I spoke to Hartack and told him about my horse's quirks. Later, I saw the entries pasted on the wall. Hartack was riding another horse. I told his agent, Chick Lang, "Didn't I have the call on Hartack?"

Well, Hartack rode against me and beat Latches by a nose, only because he knew the bad habits of my horse. After the race, I spotted Lang and he was laughing. He was probably getting a kick out of the fact that Hartack beat me with the orders I gave him.

When I ran Deux-Moulins back, I had a call on Hartack, but I rode Shoemaker. Hartack and Lang both had a fit because Hartack and Shoe were battling for the jockey lead at Arlington.

Hartack said to me, "You told me I'd ride that horse back."

"What you did to me, I did to you," I said.

"I didn't do it," Hartack said. "Chick did it."

"Well, goddam, I did it to him then."

"No, you did it to me."

"Wait," I said. "Who am I dealing with? Whoever did it to me the first time, that's who I did it to the second time."

Hartack stopped talking to me.

As a rider, Hartack could almost do no wrong. He always seemed to make the winning move at the right time. He seemed to know where the horses were going and when they'd split to let him through. Like Arcaro and Shoe, he seldom got shut off.

Years later, Hartack became a steward in Chicago and I had high hopes. Although he's hardheaded and obnoxious, he's a man of principle. But after a while on the job, Hartack has shown he isn't any different. No better, no worse.

HAROLD KEENE

I bumped into Keene after the races one day at Sportsman's. I had just finished my selections for the paper and he was looking them over.

"Hey, I think I'm going to beat your pick in the ninth race," he said. "Put me on top, will you? I'll win it."

"I don't know. I like that horse I picked, but I am afraid of your horse."

"I'm telling you. I'll win it."

"God, I hate to change. But I'll put you on top. You'd better win."

Next day the horses I picked were all coming in. I had eight winners through eight races. I was the track announcer. I called Keene in the jockey's room.

"Hey, you'd better win the ninth. I've picked

eight winners. I've been trying to pick the card my whole life."

"Don't worry. I'll win it."

Keene finished second. The horse I originally had on top won.

A handicapper's dream is to pick the card. I've never done it. Nice guy, that Keene, but goddam him.

JULIE KRONE

I can't say I think highly of women jockeys, but Krone is a terrific rider. She is one of the two female jocks I've seen who helps a horse win. The other was Robyn Smith (who retired when she married Fred Astaire), but she wasn't as good as Julie. Many female riders (and male ones too) can't keep a horse from lugging in or bearing out when he's being whipped in a drive. Krone has the strength and technique to keep a horse pointed in the right direction coming down the stretch, straight on course under a full steam of power. She rides as well as most of the top male jockeys.

CHRIS McCARRON

Great rider. He won a race for me during Arlington's International Festival of Racing in 1987. At that same meeting, he also agreed to ride my Have A Heart. I figured my horse would win easily, but for some reason he just didn't fire. After the race I kept asking McCarron what happened, and he kept saying, "Nothing." I told him the horse didn't have to win. I just wanted to know why he bombed out. I drove McCarron crazy telling him that *something* was wrong.

The next day, after McCarron had returned to California, I ran into a horseplayer who told me that Have A Heart had washed out at the gate. "He was soaking wet," he said. That sounded reasonable. A lot of horses were washing out because of the 90 degree weather. I ran Have A Heart back with Juvenal Diaz and my horse won. I sent McCarron a picture showing him in the winner's circle when he won with my first horse. I also added a note explaining why Have A Heart ran so poorly, and that he won when I ran him back. He wrote back saying that yes, my horse must have washed out that day and he was happy that the horse came back and won. "Congratulations." It was nice of him.

CONN McCREARY

He won two Kentucky Derbys, with Pensive in 1944 and Count Turf in 1951. I wrote one day that McCreary was considered a great jockey because of his come-from-behind victories. I pointed out that Conn always came from behind because he broke slowly and that any quality horse that hasn't been pushed early will come flying through the stretch. McCreary got mad. "They give me mounts that don't have much early speed," he said. I told him I was sorry he didn't like my article, but that was the way I felt. I said I still thought he was a nice rider.

RONNIE McPHEE

He woulda, coulda, shoulda been a great jockey. He was done in by booze, blondes and barracudas. He was a natural with horses. He even won ribbons in shows where horses jumped over fences and hedges. Poor Ronnie never could make it over other hurdles.

I bought his contract for $400 in 1946. He won a lot of races for me, but he put me through hell. I spent many nights going from hotel to hotel in Cicero looking for him. I'd usually find him drunk sitting with some big blonde. I'd drag him back and threaten him, saying once I got through with him he'd be mucking stalls in the bushes. He'd cry and say he was sorry, and I'd be relieved because I had money tied up in the guy and wouldn't know how to make good on my threat, anyway. The next day, he'd ride three winners.

But eventually he wore me out. I was ready to tear up his contract by the time we got to Florida for the winter season. Lucky for me, McPhee's riding caught the eye of a few trainers. Sunny Jim Fitzsimmons said he wanted to buy McPhee's contract for $6,500. And another trainer offered $7,500. I left it up to McPhee. He said he'd go with Fitzsimmons—only on the condition that I gave him $1,500. I cursed him but gave in. That was how sick I was of him.

McPhee did well with Fitzsimmons for a while, but then one day he showed up for work at six in the morning wearing a tuxedo and dragging along a blonde. That was pretty much the end of McPhee's riding career. Fitzsimmons wouldn't ride him anymore. Ronnie finally went to Fitzsimmons's boss, William Woodward, and asked for his contract. Woodward probably threw it back at him.

DON MEADE

He was a great rider in the 1930s and 1940s. He won the 1933 Derby on Brokers Tip and if you talk to any old racetracker he'll tell you that Meade and Herb Fisher, who rode Head Play, practically slugged it out coming down the stretch. A few years back in Florida, I asked Meade about that race and he said, "Survival of the fittest." What, Brokers Tip and Head Play? "No," he said, "between Fisher and me."

I never rode Meade but I saw him ride many times. The thing I remember best about him was that if he was riding a horse with any speed at all, he would always break out in front. He was the best gate boy I ever saw. He would bust out like tits on a showstopper. Meade said he got the edge because all the other jockeys had their horse's nose right up to the front of the gate, right where it snapped open. "I always took my horse back about a neck," he said. "Then when the gate opened, he wouldn't hesitate. Arcaro asked me once how I got out so fast. I told him and he started doing it too."

CRAIG PERRET

He used to ride around Chicago and he rode a lot of winners for me. If I asked him now to ride one of my mounts, he would turn me down. "I don't ride in claiming races," he would say. Oh my back! I never heard a jockey say that. Even Arcaro and Shoemaker rode claimers. But I guess Perret wants to be known as a guy who rides only in the "classic" races. I don't blame him that much. Claimers are more likely to break down. If you don't need the mounts, why ride them?

RANDY ROMERO

He rode my Gala Serenade in a $10,000 claiming race at Gulfstream in 1988. The horse was 10 to 1 and I bet a left lung on him—that's about $600.

Gala Serenade stumbled at the start, was rushed up into close quarters, had to be steadied, lost a lot of ground on the stretch turn, and finished third.

"He'll win next time. Don't worry," Romero told me after the race.

I was standing there with my tongue hanging out because I was breathing with only one lung, and I had a jockey making excuses. "He'll win next time, Dave. He'll win next time," Romero kept saying.

"He should have won today," I said. "He'll be 8 to 5 next time. He was 10 to 1 today and I bet big on him. What good is 'next time'?"

"Don't blame me," Romero said.

"I'm not blaming you," I said. "Just don't tell me about 'next time.' "

I never get mad at a good jockey, but I made a switch the "next time" Gala Serenade ran. He won—at about 8 to 5.

A year later, I was at Gulfstream again. Romero came to me near the paddock and asked whether anything was wrong. "You used to say hello before," he said. "Lately, you haven't been talking to me. What happened?"

"I haven't been talking to you because I thought you were still peeved at me for not riding you back on Gala Serenade last year."

"No, man, we're friends," he said. "Forget that stuff."

One thing led to another and I put him on Gala Serenade again.

Race day came and Romero was aboard. As Gala Serenade was about to go into the gate, Romero yells out. Some discussion followed and then it was announced that my horse had been scratched.

"He was sorer than a boil, Dave," Romero said after I had tracked him down.

I couldn't believe it. Gala Serenade looked OK to me. I called up my vet, Dr. George Burch, and had him check out the horse. "This horse is as sound as any horse on the grounds," Burch said. "The jockey must have been pulling your leg."

I had a jockey, Robert Lester, work Gala Serenade and he came back and said, "No problem."

The next day I went to the jockey's room.

"Randy, how old is your father?"

"Fifty-four. Why?"

"Well, I've been training horses almost as long as your father's been alive. I don't need anyone like you to tell me what kind of shape my horse is in. My horse is sound. Check it out with the vet."

"Aaah, stop bugging me about that goddam horse."

"You should give back the jockey mount," I said, referring to the $40 he was paid.

"Aaah, stop bothering me."

I swore at him and walked out.

Romero's no crook. He probably believed that my horse was sore. But he should have given me some credit for knowing my horse. He should have said, "Yeah, maybe I was wrong. Sorry Dave." And he should have returned the $40.

BILL SHOEMAKER

Shoe rode a number of winners for me. The best one was the time he rode my champion platter, Deux-Moulins, in 1955. I had to beg Shoe's agent, Harry Silbert, to let Shoe ride my horse. Silbert said no at first because the race was 2¹/₁₆ miles long and he thought Shoe would get tired.

"All he has to do is sit there and ask the horse to run when he turns into the stretch," I said.

"OK, OK, I'll do it for you," Silbert said.

In the paddock, I gave Shoe my orders. I told him Deux-Moulins would take off once he hit the stretch, that all Shoe had to do was wait. Shoe nodded and headed toward the track. Suddenly I remembered that this race was *two* times around. Deux-Moulins was going to turn into the stretch twice. Shoe was going to be in trouble when my horse took hold of the bit entering the stretch that first time. Shoe was heading for a long, tough ride. The horses broke and Shoe, crouched high, rated the horse nicely all the way through the far turn. Then, when they went into the stretch, the horse wanted to take off. They passed the grandstand and poor Shoe was practically standing straight up in the stirrups trying to hold him back. It was another six furlongs until they turned into the stretch again. I had never seen a jockey ride like that for so long. Shoe dropped down finally and Deux-Moulins won. Shoe looked exhausted after the race but he wasn't mad. A winner was a winner.

Some jockeys, when they get to become stars, don't look for other rides when they fly in for one big stakes. But Shoe always was willing to ride one of my platers whenever I asked him.

I really pressed my luck one day at Hawthorne. Shoe was coming in from California to ride in the Gold Cup. Thinking that he wouldn't turn me down, I named him to ride a filly I was running in the second race.

The time for the first race was approaching and I still hadn't seen Shoe. The stewards were bugging me to name another jockey, but I kept telling them not to worry. Shoe would be here. I went outside to wait. Pretty soon Shoe pulled up in a cab. I went up to him and asked whether he'd ride my filly.

"Does she have a shot?"

"Yeah."

"I'll ride her."

He won.

BOBBY USSERY

Great rider and very strong. He could over-power a horse, like Arcaro, Brooks and Fires.

Ussery rode a horse for me that refused to win. The first time, the horse hung nearing the wire. Ussery jumped off the horse and called him a bastard. The second time, after the horse got beat in a photo, Ussery spat at the horse and cursed him again. When I ran the horse back, I named another jockey, Johnny Sellers.

I passed Ussery in front of the jockey's room an hour before the race and he started yelling at me.

"How come you didn't ride me?" he said.

"You spit on the horse and cursed him. You hate him, and you're asking me to ride you? Are you nuts?"

Sellers won.

ISMAEL "MILO" VALENZUELA

He was Kelso's regular rider. A great hairy-ass jockey—like Arcaro, Cordero, Eddie Belmonte—Valenzuela never gave anybody an edge. I saw him ride a terrific race one day at Hialeah. There was a horse on the inside of him and another on the outside. Milo would push the inside horse and then massage the outside one. All the while he was riding the hair off his mount. And he won the race. The two jockeys claimed foul, but they didn't get it. I told Valenzuela that if he ever rode a horse for me like that I'd pay him three jock mounts.

JACINTO VASQUEZ

A good jockey and probably the best exercise rider in the country. He's out every morning working horses in New York, Florida or wherever. He really gets along with horses and will make a good trainer some day.

Maybe even a stand-up comic. He was riding for me in Florida one day and the horse ran out.

"What happened?" I asked.

"Run this horse a little farther," he said.

"A mile and an eighth, you mean?"

"No. From here to New York."

JORGE VELASQUEZ

I rode him on a horse at Gulfstream early in 1981. The horse fell and Velasquez went sprawling, breaking his collar bone. He lost his Kentucky Derby mount because the horse was scheduled to run a week later in one of the big preps and Jorge wasn't expected to be ready to ride for more than a month. I felt terrible. I called his home a couple of times, wanting to say how sorry I was, but every time somebody answered the phone all I heard was Spanish.

Things turned out well for Velasquez, though. He wound up on Pleasant Colony, who won the Derby and the Preakness and finished third in the Belmont.

The next time I saw Velasquez was in 1985 just after his horse, Proud Truth, was disqualified in the Flamingo. The race was given to Chief's Crown and I went over to tell Velasquez that it was too bad the decision went against him. He pushed me away, saying, "You're no friend of mine. You didn't even come to see me when I got hurt on your horse."

Slap, slap, slap. What could I say?

•
_____

Six

An Excuse
for Every
Occasion

"Well, what's the excuse this time?"
"Too horny."

In 1968, I was running Frigid Aire II in the
Man o' War Stakes at Belmont. The time for the
post parade was nearing, so the other trainers
and I started toward the paddock to saddle our
horses. Frigid Aire was a "studdish" horse;
sometimes he'd act up out in the open where he
could see and smell other horses. I feared the
worst, so I asked the paddock judge whether I
could saddle Frigid Aire away from the other
horses.

151

"If he acts up, you can move him," the judge said.

"It may be too late then," I said.

"No, we'll watch. I want him saddled with the rest of the horses."

That was that. I couldn't call the judge a jerk. So I turned away and told my groom to take the horse to his paddock stall.

As soon as Frigid Aire got near the other horses, he went bananas, like some guy who walked into a room with naked women lounging all over the place. There weren't any fillies or mares in the race, but my horse didn't know that. He knew he didn't want to fool with the horses stalled next to him; they smelled like stallions. But he figured those horses down the line were fillies and mares just waiting to get it on with him. So he started whinnying and shrieking, rearing up and fighting the groom who had a hold of him. Frigid Aire's pecker came out about a foot and a half and he was swinging it back and forth like a batter taking practice cuts.

"What did I tell you?" I said to the paddock judge.

He didn't waste time arguing. He called out and told somebody to start bringing in buckets of ice water. When they were delivered, we formed a bucket brigade, with the last guy in the line throwing the ice water at my horse's pecker.

After God knows how many dousings, Frigid Aire quieted down. The shock treatment killed all the romance in him. He was exhausted and soaking wet, not just from the cold shower but also from sweaty exertion. It was as if he'd already run a mile. Or laid five mares.

In the Man o' War, Frigid Aire finished fifth, beaten by about five lengths. He woulda, coulda, shoulda been in the money if he hadn't run his race in the paddock.

One guy I knew had a similar problem with a hog he trained. For weeks he couldn't figure it out. The horse was sound, but his races were below par and so were his workouts. He's perk up some in the afternoon, but the next morning he seemed all worn out again. A vet was called in to examine the horse and blood samples were taken. The tests came back and showed nothing. Meanwhile, the trainer was getting heat from the owner. "Get him running or I find myself a new trainer."

Then one night, on a hunch, the trainer went to the barn. The next day he called up the owner.

"I figured out what's wrong with your horse," he said. "He's been playing with himself."

"What!"

"Horses are like people. They get horny."

"How the hell does a horse play with himself?"

"Well, he gets a hard-on and starts rubbing it against his belly. Pretty soon he pops. You go pop, pop, pop three, four times a night and the last thing you want to do at six in the morning is exercise."

The trainer fixed the horse up with a ring that went around his cold pecker. Now the horse couldn't get hard. He probably thought it fell off because he had been playing with it too much.

The ring worked like a charm but not like magic. Before, the horse had been a horny hog. Now he was just a hog. The trainer had to come up with different alibis to explain to the owner why this son of No Account out of Can't Give It Away wasn't winning.

Horse racing wouldn't be horse racing without excuses. The funny thing is, many of the excuses are legitimate. Even if the horse is fit and well-placed, something can, and usually does, come up before or during a race to screw things up. It's the groom who mucks out the stall, but a trainer has to be handy with the shovel too.

"What happened?" the owner asks.

"Bad break," the trainer says. "You must have seen it."

"I didn't see anything and the horse didn't show me anything."

"Well," the trainer says, getting a good grip on his shovel, "your horse broke slow and just as he came out of the gate that horse outside of him crossed over right in front of him and your jockey had to snatch up and drop back."

The trainer waits for an oh-I-see nod, but he gets nothing. So he starts shoveling.

"You know, I'm thinking we need another jockey."

"What's wrong with the one we rode today? Everybody else rides him."

"He's good, don't get me wrong. But I've been thinking we need a real gateboy, someone who can get your horse to break like *that*—boom!— just as the gate opens. Yeah, another rider might be the answer. What do you think?"

"I think maybe I need a new trainer."

The trainer nods his oh-I-see-you-want-to-be-a-rat-bastard nod.

"What have I got to show for my investment? Out of the money seven times, including today."

"Do you want to drop him down?"

"What, even more? I'll lose him then."

The trainer nods slowly. The only way the owner is going to lose this horse is if the water wagon runs him down.

"Well, it's your horse, although my wife," the trainer says, giving his embarrassed laugh, "my wife thinks that sometimes I think it's *my* horse. The amount of time I spend with him, I mean. A couple weeks back, for instance, he had this cough and I was pretty worried. I must have told you about that. I didn't? Well, I meant to. Anyway, I got this special straw that doesn't cost much extra and it's real clean, no dust, you know, almost sanitary. You get regular straw and it's got a lot of dust. Horses aren't too fussy, so they just eat it. I figure that's why he's coughing. Well, I get this special straw and the next day— boom!—your horse stops coughing. Most trainers probably would have called in the vet and the vet would have given him some shots or taken some blood tests. That all costs money, and I don't want to throw away money when I think there's an easy answer. You've got a good horse here, sir, and I think it's just a matter of time before we get him running the way I know he can run. But, like I say, he's your horse."

The owner doesn't know what to say. Finally, he mutters, "Yeah, that's right, it's *my* horse," and walks out of the barn without looking back. He's smiling to himself. He's thinking the trainer is probably crapping in his pants now with worry. One last chance. He'll give that jerk trainer one last chance, and if the horse doesn't finish in the money, then—boom!—so long, loser. The trainer, he means.

No sweat, the trainer says to himself. Sure, the guy's mad now, but he's also confused. Keep him confused and he'll grab at any straw. Next time the horse runs, and loses, he'll give the owner another excuse. Blinkers, maybe.

The best excuse is: "The horse didn't like the strip." This is the all-purpose alibi. Hard, soft, sloppy, muddy, cuppy. Whatever the strip was, the horse didn't like it.

When a trainer like Allen Jerkens or Charlie Whittingham or Woody Stephens says his horse lost because he didn't like the strip, the owner is going to believe him because neither Jerkens nor Whittingham nor Stephens has to lie to an owner or play stupid games. When the trainer who's handling cheap horses uses the strip excuse, the owner may believe him the first time, and maybe the second time. But the trainer takes a big jump in brass when he tries it a third time. That's alibi abuse, and when you get caught, you pay.

Why risk it when there are always jockeys to blame?

—"Did you see the hold the jockey had on him in the backstretch? He was choking him. Your horse wanted to go to the lead and the jockey was goddam nearly choking him. That's why your horse hung in the stretch. The jockey's good, don't get me wrong. He wins races on other horses, but we'll just keep him off this horse."

—"I told that jock to wake the horse up on the way to the post—hit him on the ass, put him on his toes. He didn't do it. The horse came out of the gate like an elephant, a slow elephant. He would have *flown* out of there if the jock had followed orders. I'm through with him."

—"I asked that jockey if he was going to make the weight. Can't afford to give away an ounce in this race, I said. No sweat, he said. Make it easy, he said. Do you know what happened? He was in four pounds over. I can't guarantee a jock's weight, sir. I'll know better than to use him next time. He cost us a race and a bet."

The truth is that at any meeting, the top 15 jockeys in the standings are pretty much the same as far as ability goes. Sure, some horses do require a certain type of jockey (a strong, muscular rider, say, instead of a 100-pounder whose technique means diddley-squat on a runaway), but having Laffit Pincay or Bill Shoemaker in the saddle isn't going to make any difference if the horse can't run.

Like the strip excuse, the jockey alibi also can get old fast. After five jockey changes, even the dumbest owner will get suspicious, so the trainer has to go into his feed bag for another treat to keep his employer wagging his tail.

Bad luck is handy because it gets everybody off the hook. A trainer who doesn't blame others can't be all bad.

—"The jockey broke (lost) his whip."

—"Did you see it? Your horse was making a good move, but he got carried out at the head of the stretch."

—"It wasn't the jockey's fault. He got trapped on the rail. Your horse didn't have racing room."

—"Luck of the draw. He hates the No. 1 post. Look, five starts back he had the pole and wasn't even close. I guarantee you that with an outside post, he can beat this same bunch."

Next to bad luck, conspiracy always is good for three or four losing efforts.

—"Nobody can kid me. A few trainers here are in with the track superintendent. They've got the track like cement. You know our horse loves a cushioned strip. Those guys have horses that like a firm strip. I may tell the track owner what's going on around here. Somebody has to look out for our interests."

—"He got a lot of sand in his eyes. He didn't break too good, and before you knew it he was way behind and getting all that loose sand kicked in his face. I think we should complain. The track isn't sprinkling down the strip enough."

—"Hell, we should have won at least five races at this meet. We haven't won one. These jockeys might be in cahoots. Don't you get that feeling, sir? The jockeys, they're all Mexican, or Puerto Rican, or Spanish something. Everybody's a goddam Carlos, or a Jose. I don't know what in the hell is going on, but I'll find out for damn sure. I think it might have started when we canned Ramon."

—"Did you see the odds drop on the winner? Somebody knew something about that winner. Nobody is going to tell me that something isn't going on."

—"That goddam assistant starter had a hold of our horse at the break. He didn't turn him loose at the bell. He must have bet another horse. The next time I see an assistant starter grab our horse's bridle, I'm going to report him to the stewards. I don't care if our horse is acting up. I don't want anybody holding him back."

—"Everything happens to us. They have 10

good valets to saddle the horses and we get a third-stringer. He couldn't even make it as a jockey in the bushes, so he decides to be a valet. He wasn't strong enough to tighten the girth and the saddle slipped on our horse right after the break. The jockey almost fell off."

—"The next time we have a horse entered, I'm going to get a steward to watch the guys drawing the post positions in the morning. You know as well as I do we haven't drawn a single post in our favor the whole meeting. That's why we haven't had any luck. I'm through getting pushed around like a dog. I hope you feel the same way, sir."

The backstretch help at any track is always badmouthed. Not without good reason too. The best grooms I ever had were Tom Lloyd and Wendell Griffin. Griffin worked for me in the late 1960s. Since then I haven't had a groom who was worth a dozen horse buns.

—"I think the bandages on this horse were too high. Heck, the groom put them up almost to his knees. That prevented him from taking his best stride. I saw the groom do it and I was going to mention it but something else came up. Trouble with grooms is they think they're trainers. The next time we're going to run him with short bandages and he'll probably win."

—"I'm going to fire that pony boy. I told him to warm our horse up a lot and get the stiffness out of him. Did you see what he did? He just walked with him to the gate. He gets $12 to warm up the horse, to get him jogging for three or four minutes, and all he does is walk him around. I'm through with him."

Equipment and horse ailments are always good excuses because they confuse the hell out of owners.

—"The horse got his tongue over the bit. I think we'll have to run him with a tongue strap the next time out. As you know, the strap will keep his tongue in place so he doesn't roll it back in his throat and half-choke himself when he's running. That's probably why he was running so poorly. We'll use a strap the next time out, and I'm sure he'll do much better."

—"The blinkers I had on him are full-cup blinkers. He couldn't see too much with them. He used to run pretty good with them, but horses are like people. They change. He might need blinkers with the little holes so he can see the other horses better."

—"Maybe he needs French blinkers. They're wide open so he can see a lot in front of him and not too much behind him. I tried him with those blinkers once before and he ran pretty good. But I thought he could run much better, so I put the full-cup blinkers on him. Now I think I'll go back to the open blinks."

—"I think this horse needs a shadow roll so he won't be jumping at shadows. The jockey said that on the first turn the horse got spooked by something and wanted to bolt. I worked the horse with a shadow roll a couple of times, and he worked pretty good. Once he didn't, though, so I left it off today. I'll put it back on the next time, and he'll run much better."

—"I told the goddam blacksmith the horse wears a size 6 shoe and he said the horse took a 5. I could tell our horse wasn't putting out right after the start. What size shoe do you wear, sir? An 11? How would you like to run in shoes that are a size 10? It would cripple you, right?"

—"God darn, he lost a shoe in the race. I told the goddam blacksmith to watch out because I noticed sometimes that the horse has loose shoes. He must hit the ground a certain way. I'll get on the blacksmith this time, and your horse will run much better, sir, much better."

—"Maybe we ought to steam his head out. When he got back to the paddock, I saw some mucous. Maybe our horse needs his head cleared. I thought he needed it before, but I didn't want to fool with him because he was showing signs of coming around. But we'll steam his head out two, three times, and we'll run him in 10 days."

—"You know that ankle he had that was a little inflamed? Well, when he came out of the race, it blew up a little bit more. But he'll be OK because we're going to put him on ice and give him some butazolidin. We'll get that down tight and walk him a few days. The next time out he'll probably win."

—"The horse ran down behind on his heels. See where he scraped them? He didn't bleed, but you can see the marks there. He's hitting hard. I put a little patch on there, but he's going to need bandages."

—"I think I'll leave the bandages off in front. He wasn't striding just right. He's not sore, he's not lame. Don't worry. You don't have to sell him. I'll put these bandages on his hind legs and they'll get a little support. He'll run much better, don't worry. Those bandages in front threw him off."

—"I think we'll run him with a girth piece. The regular jockey's girth sometimes rubs the horse's belly the wrong way. When we use the girth piece—what's a girth piece? Oh, it's a strip of rubber or padding that fits inside the regular girth. A lot of big stables use it, sir. The regular girth can pinch the horse's skin. Using a piece makes it much easier on the horse's belly. Your horse will be more comfortable, and he'll run much better. It has to move him up a few lengths."

—"He needs a nose band. I think he was running with his mouth open. That's no good for him. The nose band, I probably don't have to tell you, sir, wraps under his chin and keeps his mouth closed a little bit. And it keeps him from swallowing all the dirt that hits him in the face. We'll put a nose band on, and it should help plenty."

—"This horse might have bled in the throat. We're going to scope him. The jockey said he wasn't breathing just right. It could be that he'll even hemorrhage, so we'll keep a close watch on him. But even if he doesn't bleed, we're going to have him scoped tomorrow, because I always had a suspicion that this horse was a bleeder."

—"This horse acts a little stiff in his shoulders. No, he's not sore, he's not broke down. Don't worry. We'll run him in a couple of weeks. But I think I'll put a little Bigol oil on his shoulders and massage him the next time he runs. I think that's why he lost, sir. He was a little tight in his shoulders."

—"We may have to blow him up. No, no, no. Not blow up boom! I mean blow up with air. His shoulders. We'll get the vet to take his needle and bulb and put air into the shoulders so they're not so tight. The air will loosen him up and give him the freedom to stride out. I've seen it move up a horse a million times. He'll even work better the next time."

—"The jockey said the horse wasn't taking hold of the bit. That could be our problem, sir. His teeth. He's a 4-year-old, so he's probably got caps. No, sir, not the porcelain kind. These caps are natural. They grow on the back teeth, and sometimes a horse with caps can't get a hold of the bit. I know this horse hasn't had his teeth done in about six months. It's hard to find a vet who'll do teeth, but they tell me there's a guy around here who'll knock off those caps. He charges about $30, but it's worth it. Trust me."

—"Maybe we shouldn't have run him. Before the race he missed a meal one day. Maybe I said something to you about it. No? Well, maybe I didn't. Anyway, I think something's bugging him. Maybe he's got worms. We'll give him a worm ball, and you watch, he'll work much better. We worm a horse about every three or four months. This horse hasn't been wormed in six months. I was thinking about doing it before the race, but thought, 'Well, we'll run him once.' Maybe I said something to you, 'Run him once and see how he goes.' Well, maybe I didn't mention it."

—"You know this horse is rheumatic. The jockey said he didn't extend himself at the start, but he did through the stretch. What I think I'm going to do the next time is put some Bigol oil on hot towels and keep them on his back before he leaves the stall. It'll loosen him up. I'm pretty sure the stiffness cost him the race. This is a nice horse. We'll keep him and run him back."

—"I'll run the horse with a burr so he won't bear out. You put that burr on the outside part of the bit and the bristles will poke him in the jaw when he tries to go out. Didn't you see him try to get out on the turn? You can't win doing that. We'll put the burr on him the next time, and I'm sure he'll run much better. He can't run any worse, right?"

Another excuse that's worth mentioning is one that is used only in extreme circumstances. It's called the truth. Trainers with hogs seldom can afford to tell an owner why his horse hasn't won a race and probably never will. It's when the trainer has another owner lined up that he can be honest.

"Who is this?"

"It's me, sir."

"What time is it?"

"It's a little before five."

"What the hell are you doing calling me at five in the morning?"

"Oh, I'm always up at this time, sir. I'm here at the barn getting ready to work the horses."

"Something wrong with my horse?"

"No."

"Then why are you calling me?"

"I just wanted to tell you that your horse is OK."

"You told me that last night."

"That's right. You called at 11, didn't you? You always call around that time, three, four times a week, to ask about your horse. And what do I always say?"

"What are you talking about?"

"I always tell you that your horse is fine, don't I? And I always ask you not to call me that late at night because I get up at 3:30 every morning."

"You're my goddam trainer. I pay you. I have a right to call you anytime I want to."

"That's what you always say."

"Get to the goddam point. Why did you call me?"

"Your horse, sir."

"What about him? You said he was OK."

"Oh, he's OK. He's as fit now as when you got him. You paid $20,000 for him, didn't you? You bought a 4-year-old who ran only once when he was 2, didn't run at all when he was 3, and finished last, last and next to last in his three starts before you showed up. Tell me, why did you buy him?"

"I liked his breeding."

"His breeding? What do you know about breeding? You may know a lot about bimbos, sir, and you may know a lot of selling dresses—isn't that what you do?—but I haven't met an owner of cheap claimers yet who knew anything about breeding."

"You're fired!"

"And your horse can't win at $20,000, he can't win at $15,000 and he won't win at 12-5, 10, 7-5 or 5. He's got bad hocks, bad ankles and absolutely no heart. You paid $20,000 for a bum, sir. Have a good day."

Seven

Read Your Bible . . . and Pray

My father used to spend a lot of time reading the Bible. I guess he liked the stories. Look cross-eyed at God and you pay. Toe the line and you could wind up as a gold medalist in the sling-shot competition. I'm a lot like my father. I have my bible, too. It's called the *Daily Racing Form* and I never go to my place of worship, the race-track, without it. Like the real Bible, it has terrific stories in the chapters and verses of the past performances. You want a miracle? How about 12^{15}, 12^{20}, 9^{11}, 6^8, 1^1. You want a rout of the Philistines? There's Secretariat's 31-length victory in the 1973 Belmont Stakes. Or how about a plague of locusts? It's all in these numbers: 1987 23 0 0 0 $0.

The *Form* is like the real Bible in another way: It's open to interpretation. The best interpreters are the best handicappers and as a handicapper I think of myself as a biblical scholar.

—In 1969 the horse racing magazine *Turf and Sport Digest*, in a one-shot deal, kept a record of newspaper handicappers all over the country. I finished first.

—The best meeting I ever had was at Hialeah in 1972. That year the track had the middle dates in the Florida racing season, and any handicapper will tell you that races run during that six-week stretch are the toughest to pick. For one thing, the fields usually are full. For another, there's always a constant stream of new horses coming in from all over the country, making it difficult to compare the abilities of the runners. Despite those obstacles, I scored 33 percent winners. When you consider that a handicapper is doing well if his winning percentage is 27 or 28, the 33 percent I recorded was out of this world.

—And in 1987, during the Hawthorne meeting, I had one of my better hot streaks. In one nine-day stretch of racing—81 races—I picked 46 winners. That's a winning percentage of 57 percent.

If I'm so sharp, why aren't I rich? You sound like my mother.

"So tell me."

"I'm just a lousy bettor, ma."

"You pick five winners and you lose money?"

"They were short-priced. Not worth it."

"What is this 'short-priced'?"

"Favorites, ma. A waste of time. Bet 10 bucks and get back 13."

"That's so bad? Three dollars out of nothing. God, He can make something out of nothing. But you, you're too good for that? Hyman. Mr. Big Shot here says he's better than God."

It's a curse, this betting. I've been around race-tracks for 60 years and I know that betting is a losing proposition for 99.9999 percent of the horseplayers. Don't press me for statistics. What point is there in gathering facts to support what I know is true? Will I gag if I drink water straight from the Chicago River? Will my heart stop if some luscious babe presses up close to me? Trust me. Don't bet.

But that's like telling a fat man, "Don't eat too much." He's going to eat. And you're going to bet. The only advice I have is: If you're going to stuff yourself, do it once or twice a day, when you're really hungry. The same thing goes for betting. Don't snack constantly. Stick to a diet of playable races.

In this chapter and the next, I'll teach you something about handicapping, which is how a horseplayer figures out whether a race is playable. I'm not going to load you up with charts and graphs and statistical stuff from computers. That's what other handicappers do when they write books claiming that *Yes, you can beat the races*. But their "winning systems" are so complicated that you feel like a dummy; you need an IQ that's larger than a trifecta pool to understand what the hell they're talking about. I guess if you dazzle people with enough "facts," you can say anything. Me? I take a more basic approach to handicapping, with the idea that *No, you can't beat the races, but you can have a little fun and you don't have to go home feeling like a jerk because you lost the rent money*.

The only material you'll need is a *Form*. I've got mine in front of me somewhere. I'm waiting for the Gentile kid to come up and turn on the lights.

THE SPORT OF KINGS?

First, a few thousand discouraging words. You can't talk to a horse, so already you're behind the eight ball. You can't ask him how he feels, or how he likes the weather and the strip, or how he likes the jockey who'll be riding him, or the groom who rubbed him down and walked him around the shed row. You can't ask him about his knees, or his hocks, or his ankles, or his tight shoulders. You can't ask him whether he got enough Lasix so he won't hemorrhage. You can't ask him the one question that you're dying to know the answer to, which is: Are you, for God's sake, going to run your race today? You can ask all these questions of the trainer, but he'll be wrong more times than he'll be right because he can't get it from the horse's mouth, either.

The blood and guts of horse racing isn't the Kentucky Derby or the Arlington Million. It's the hog races and claiming events. It's not Secretariat going for the Triple Crown or Alysheba breaking John Henry's record for winnings. It's 6-, 7-, and 8-year-old horses that have been passed around more times than blame itself. Horse racing is not the sport of kings. It's the sport of veterinarians. If thoroughbreds were people, 80 percent of them would call in sick on the day of the race.

"Boss, I can't walk today, much less run. My feet hurt, my knees, my hocks, my shoulders, my back hurts, even my teeth hurt. I think I'll stay in my stall today. I'll be up and about next week."

So what does the trainer do? The only thing he can. Freeze the poor sunuvabitch, then send him to the races. The trainer may have an owner who's driving him crazy, complaining about the money he's paying the trainer, anywhere from $40 to $75 a day, and not getting a cent of purse money because the horse hasn't run in weeks. The racing secretary may be having trouble filling races, so he's leaning on the trainer to enter his horse even if he's not quite fit. (If the trainer refuses, he won't win points with the secretary and may not get as many stalls as he needs next year.) So, the trainer says what the hell, he'll race the horse into shape. Who knows? Maybe the horse will win because he'll be competing against other outpatients.

That, my fellow broken down horseplayers, is horse racing.

THE BASICS

There are four major types of races: stakes and handicap, allowance, claiming and maiden. Within each category, there are different levels— usually determined by purse. In Chicago, the purses for stakes and handicaps can range from $30,000 to the Arlington Million. Allowance purses are from $10,000 to $30,000. Claiming races are run for as little as two tickets to a Bears game to as much as $15,000. Purses for maidens are usually for no less than $7,500.

The stakes and handicap races attract the Secretariats and Alyshebas. (They also can attract mediocre horses, such as those that manage to get into the Kentucky Derby, run out, and are never heard from again. When that happens, you know that the owner was calling the shots. He just wanted tickets to the Derby and a little horse-world attention.) The difference between stakes and handicaps is one of weight or weight assignment. In some stakes such as the Triple Crown events, all the colts carry the same weight and fillies get a five-pound allowance. In other stakes, horses weight themselves. Each may start out at 122 pounds and pick up or lose pounds depending on his past performances. Alysheba, for example, might pick up six more pounds, 128, based on money winnings or number of victories. The least impressive horse in the field might come in at 110. In a handicap race, the weight is assigned by the racing secretary. He might give Alysheba 130 pounds, and put 108 on the longshot.

The next category is the allowance race. There are two kinds: open and conditioned. In an open allowance, which are rare in Chicago, the only condition is age, as in "for 3-year-olds and up." Weight is assigned on the basis of age. Three-year-olds will carry five fewer pounds, and fillies will get an additional five-pound allowance before September 1, and three pounds after that date. Next to stakes and handicaps, open allowances are the toughest races and they attract quality horses.

A conditioned allowance restricts a field to horses that meet certain conditions, such as money earned, and/or races won, and/or the type of races won, and/or sex. They are assigned weights based on their recent record.

Here are the condition lines for two allowance races:

1 MILE. PURSE $19,000. 3-year-olds and
upward. Weight, 3-year-olds, 117 lbs.;
older, 122 lbs. Non-winners since August
25 allowed 3 lbs.; July 25, 5 lbs.; a race in
1988, 8 lbs.

1 MILE. PURSE $18,000. 3-year-olds and
upward, non-winners of two races since
August 25 other than maiden or claiming.
Weight, 3-year-old, 117 lbs.; older, 122 lbs.
Non-winners since August 25 allowed 3
lbs.; two races since June 25, 5 lbs.; a
race, 8 lbs.; two races in 1988, 10 lbs.

The first allowance race is open to any horse
that is at least 3 years old. It'll be tougher than
the second allowance, which is a conditioned
event. It's restricted to horses 3 years old and up
that have not won two races during the period
specified.

Like allowance races, claiming events can be
open or restricted, but they differ in one important aspect: A trainer can lose his horse if another trainer puts in a claim before the race. A
runner that has been doing well against $10,000
horses won't suddenly be entered against $5,000
dogs. The trainer probably would pick up an
easy purse, but he would most likely lose his
horse through a claim. When there is a dramatic
drop in class, from $10,000 to $7,500 or $5,000,
that usually means the horse isn't worth $10,000
and the trainer is seeking the right level of com-

petition. It also means the horse has more than the measles and the trainer wants to get rid of him.

Without claiming events there would be no racing. Sore horses have to be entered someplace because they still represent sizable investments. An owner may have $20,000 tied up in a thoroughbred that he can't sell for $2,000. He feels he's got to get some return on his money, so he tells the trainer to race the horse or the trainer can kiss his $40 a day goodbye.

Claiming horses might be as young as 2 or as old as 12. The oldest horse I ever had was Gala Serenade, who was 10 years old on January 1, 1989. I claimed him for $12,500 in 1986, and won about five or six races with him. Then, in May of 1988, I ran him in a $5,000 claiming race. I figured that no trainer in his right mind would want a 9-year-old horse. He went off as the 8 to 5 favorite and finished second, beaten by two and one-half lengths. If that wasn't bad enough, some hungry trainer claimed him. The next time Gala Serenade ran, three weeks later, I claimed him back. For $6,500. That probably set some sort of record—a 9-year-old horse getting claimed twice in one year. Maybe it wasn't the smartest move I'd ever made, but I knew he still had some racing left in him. Probably more important, I knew what was wrong with him. His hocks weren't too good, he couldn't race in the heat, and he bled. Other than that he was in great shape. I don't mean that to be funny. Claiming horses are a lot like used cars. At least with your clunker you know its problems and peculiarities. When you get a new used car, it'll take you a while to figure out how to get it running smoothly.

The worst race is for maiden claimers. Imagine a horse that has run 10, 15, 20 times and has yet to win. If a horse is worth next to nothing, this is the race for him. The crappy tracks use maiden claiming events as one-half of the daily double, or as a trifecta race. The betting is good because the fields are big and payoffs can be in the thousands.

There are bad maidens and there are good maidens. The good maidens run in non-claiming maiden races. These events are called maiden special weight, which means only that all of the horses carry the same weight. Maiden races carry larger purses than the average claiming race because unlike claimers, young maidens haven't proven themselves to be bums. Horses that break their maiden early, jump right up to the allowance class. Those that haven't won after five races, say, usually are dropped to the maiden claiming level. The only type of horse that gets umpteen chances to prove himself is the one that cost $50,000 or more. A 1,000-pound, $50,000 lemon? Nah. Not my horse.

There are two types of maiden races: for 2-year-olds and for 3- and 4-year-olds. The better of the two is the race for juveniles, the young colts and fillies just starting out on their racing careers. The race for older maidens is for horses that either didn't win a race in their first year of competition, or did not race at all. Horses in the latter group either had physical problems, or were slow to develop because they weren't broken in properly as yearlings.

Finally, there is a strange bird of a race called a starter handicap. Most of our starter handicaps are $7,500. That means a horse must have started in a race for $7,500 claimers since a specified date. The "handicap" means that the racing secretary assigns the weights.

In starter handicaps, it's not surprising to find the top-weighted horse carrying 10 or 15 pounds more than the next horse. The weight disparities approach those that you see in rich races, where one horse clearly is tons the best.

WINNING FAVORITES

Over all, betting favorites win about 31 or 32 percent of the time. It doesn't matter where you're betting at—Santa Anita, or Hialeah, or Aqueduct, or Fairmount Park—the favorites win, on the average, almost a third of the races. But one thing any aspiring handicapper should know is that the percentage of winning favorites slips as the quality of the horses goes down. I know there are some who say that the 31 or 32 percent figure applies to all races, from cheap claiming to stakes. But I don't buy that. You can't tell me that betting favorites in $3,500 claiming races win as many times as they do in $100,000 stakes. That just doesn't make any sense.

I checked the charts of the races that were run during Hawthorne's meeting in 1988. In 841 races, the favorites won 270 times for a 32.1 winning percentage, which is about right. But when I broke down the races into seven categories, I came up with these winning percentages:

TYPE OF RACE	NUMBER OF RACES	WINNING FAVORITES	% OF WINNING FAVORITES
$10,000 and under claiming	268	82	30.6
$20,000 and under claiming	49	8	16.3
Over $20,000 claiming	34	11	32.3
Maiden claiming	95	31	32.6
Maiden special weights	121	40	33.1
Starter handicaps	15	6	40.0
Allowances, stakes, handicaps	259	92	35.5

It doesn't take a wizard in statistics to know that in some categories—such as starter handicaps and claiming races above $10,000 and $20,000—I have too few races to draw firm conclusions. But the two categories that I'm interested in—claiming for $10,000 and under, and allowances/stakes/handicaps—each group has more than 250 races, a pretty fair sampling. The betting favorites in the richer races won 35.5 percent of the time; the winning percentage of the cheapie favorites was 30.6. The difference is almost 5 percent! That's a lot of mutuel tickets that don't have to be eaten.

In richer races, the horses are more likely to run truer to form because they are in better condition and the fields are smaller, creating fewer traffic problems. You bet to win in a $30,000 allowance race; you bet gimmicks in a $5,000 claiming event.

READING THE *DAILY RACING FORM*

Each race supposedly matches horses of more or less equal ability. But we all know that isn't true. Some animals look like horses and eat like horses, but they don't run like horses. The *Form* will help you spot these phonies. But first, you have to know how to read the past performances.

Here's one for a horse called Joy Underthe Falls, who was entered in a six and one-half furlong race for $5,000 claimers on October 5, 1988, at Hawthorne. The conditions: 3-year-olds and upward, and non-winners of two races since August 25.

Joy Underthe Falls previously raced on September 19, 1988, in the seventh race at Hawthorne. The distance was 1 mile 70 yards. The leader during the race (not Joy Underthe Falls, mind you) went the first four furlongs in 47

1st Hawthorne

6 ½ FURLONGS. (1.14⅘) CLAIMING. Purse $5,300. 3-year-olds and upward. Weight, 3-year-olds, 117 lbs.; older, 122 lbs. Non-winners of two races since August 25 allowed 3 lbs.; a race, 6 lbs.; a race in 1988, 8 lbs. Claiming price $5,000. (Claiming races for $4,000 or less not considered.)

Joy Underthe Falls — **B. g. 7, by Taylor's Falls—Robb's Joy, by Daryl's Joy**
Br.—Van Berg Jack C (Ill) — **1988 8 0 0 1 $2,185**
Own.—Schiffner F J et al **114** **Tr.—Schiffner Frank J** **$5,000** — **1987 11 0 4 4 $31,892**
Lifetime 60 14 11 9 $283,392 — **Turf 27 10 4 5 $196,632**

19Sep88-7Haw	170 :47 1:14 1:462sy	7½	114	32½	21½	811	820¼	Fires E4	8000	50-27	Mudskippr,Mthw'sMrk,HyLookAtM	8
30Aug88-9Haw	6½f :223 :454 1:172ft	12	114	66	65¼	88	813½	Torres F C8	12500	72-19	DshTheMusic,MxB.,Dwn'sBehving	10
23Jly88-10Haw	1 1/16 Ⓣ:461 1:104 1:414fm	5	114	11	2hd	910	1018¾	Fires E2	25000	— —	Tht$fysrinbow,MsteroftheGm,Trvr	10
11Jly88-8Haw	1 1/16 Ⓣ:483 1:13 1:433fm	14	115	62¾	52½	41¼	74¼	Razo E Jr7	Aw19000	— —	ShrpSwingr,Jck'sKingdom,BgBobct	9
22Jun88-6Haw	1 Ⓣ:473 1:122 1:364fm	4¾	114	66½	43½	44½	35½	Razo E Jr6	25000	— —	ActonEvdr,Progstrn,JyUndrthFlls	10
9Apr88-4Spt	6½f :232 :47 1:181ft	4½e	114	62¾	64	67½	59¼	Frazier R L7	25000	77-18	Shelter, That's A Blunder,Saverton	8
17Mar88-9Spt	1 :492 1:14 1:402ft	5½	114	65¼	53¼	42½	53¾	Razo E Jr3	25000	74-28	JustZck,TryOncMor,Tht'sABlundr	10
29Feb88-8Spt	6f :24 :473 1:123ft	5½	114	815	86¼	65	914	Razo E Jr2	Aw22000	73-27	Proud Dhabi, Rad, Romeo's Bullet	10
2Oct87-8Haw	7f Ⓣ:231 :463 1:234fm	*6-5	114	2hd	21	32½	35¾	Meier R2	Aw17000	89-12	Lekey,StgeExecutiv,JoyUndrthFlls	8
23Sep87-7Haw	1 Ⓣ:494 1:143 1:401gd	*8-5	114	3nk	1hd	21½	34¼	Meier R4	Aw19550	74-27	Rongk,Zupprdo'sLov,JoyUndrthFlls	7

Sep 13 Haw 4f ft :493 b **Aug 23 Haw 3f ft :382 b**

seconds, six furlongs in 1:14, and the full distance in 1:46 2/5. The track was sloppy. Joy Underthe Falls went off at 7½ to 1 odds, and carried 114 pounds.

The next four columns are "calls," which are provided by the *Form's* chartcaller. He gives you the position of the horse at various stages of the race. At the first call Joy Underthe Falls, showing some speed, was in third place, 2½ lengths behind the *leader*, not the second-place horse. He was second, 1½ lengths back, at the second call. Then his problems took over. He dropped to last, 11 lengths back, and kept on falling behind until he crossed the wire 20¼ lengths behind the winner.

The rest of the line tells you that Earlie Fires was the jockey; Joy Underthe Falls had the No. 4 post position; the event was an $8,000 claiming race; the horse's speed rating and variant was 50-27; the first three finishers in the race were Mudskipper, Matthew's Mark and Hey Look At Me, and there were eight horses in the race.

To figure Joy Underthe Falls' time for the 1 mile 70 yards, add one-fifth of a second for every losing length (a half-length or more counts as a fifth of a second) and tack that onto the time of the winning horse. Twenty lengths divided by five (the number of fifths in a second) equals four full seconds. So, Joy Underthe Falls crawled home in 1:50 ²/₅.

Using the horse's final time, the *Form* comes up with his speed rating for the race. The rating compares his time with the track record in force prior to the opening of the current meeting. The record is assigned an automatic 100. Joy Underthe Falls' time was 10 seconds slower than the track record of 1:40 ²/₅. The number of fifths in 10 is 50. Subtract that from 100, and you get Joy Underthe Falls' speed rating: 50.

The *Form* also provides a second set of numbers called the track variant. The variant of 27 means that on that particular day the average final times of the winning horses over the sloppy track was 5²/₅ seconds (5 times 5 plus 2 equals 27) off the track record, at whatever distance. (I'll have more to say on speed figures later.)

Joy Underthe Falls' past performance reads like the medical chart of a patient in intensive care. For today's race on October 5, the 7-year-old gelding is carrying 114 pounds, the fewest allowable, because he hasn't won a race in a year. His record shows that the closest he has gotten to winning in eight starts in 1988 was a third-place finish. He also was winless in 1987, although he finished in the money 8 times in 11 starts. The 1988 season has been a disaster. A horse that likes to race near the lead, he couldn't get off better than sixth in his first five races of 1988. On July 23, in a $25,000 claiming event, he took the lead after the break, but then the roof caved in. Joy Underthe Falls was rested for more than a month. Then he was entered in a race for $12,500. By doing that, the trainer, Frank Schiffner, was admitting that his horse had problems. Against $12,500 claimers, horses he could have beaten two years ago with one leg tied behind him, Joy Underthe Falls finished eighth, beaten by 13½ lengths. He ran even worse the next time out. He was beaten by 20¼ lengths going against $8,000 claimers!

In his prime, Joy Underthe Falls was a fine turf horse. (His grass races are indicated by the symbol ⑦.) He won 10 times in 27 starts on the grass and finished in the money 19 times. Over all he has won almost $300,000. The old gelding with the crutches didn't appear as though he'd ever win on the turf again. But lo and behold with a tub of ice and a few butazolidin pills, he found himself in June and won a $9,000 starter handicap race at Hawthorne. In his day he could have beaten horses worth $50,000. Class does show up.

WORKOUTS

A horse's workouts, if any, are listed below the past performances. They state in bold type the date of the workout, track, distance and time. My advice on workouts is: Don't get too worked up over them. I know horseplayers who'll throw out a horse because he doesn't have at least one current workout listed in the *Form*. And there are even those who choose horses mainly on the basis of workout times. Oh my back! What they don't know! Some horseplayers must think the *Form* really *is* the Bible.

The only time I pay attention to a listed workout is when a horse has a fast time for five furlongs or farther. (I don't know whether he actually worked that fast, but I can't afford to ignore it.) By "fast," I mean one minute or less for five furlongs, 1:14 for three-quarters, 1:28 for seven furlongs, and 1:42 for a mile. Workouts run at three or four furlongs don't tell you much, because most horses can show speed for short distances. Workouts beyond four furlongs tell you more about a horse's ability.

Fast times tell me something, but so can the absence of listed workouts—for good horses. (Cheap horses will have few, if any, workouts listed. Sore horses are often galloped into racing shape.) Early in the racing season, a good horse that races every two weeks is worked at least twice before his next start. Later, in the fall, he may need only one workout between races. When a good horse doesn't show *any* current workout, something's wrong. Either the clocker blew it or the trainer was successful in hiding the workout.

If workouts sound screwed up and unreliable, that's because they really are. The system has more holes than I have dead mutuel tickets. I'll just list the biggest ones.

1. The past performances may show that three days before the race, four of the horses in the eight-horse field breezed five furlongs in a minute, two others went 1:02 and one went 1:04. What does this tell you? Nothing, really. Why? Because you don't know what weight any of the horses carried. The horse that went 1:04 might have been carrying an exercise rider who weighed 130 pounds, while the others might have been ridden by jockeys who each weighed no more than 110. That's why a mediocre workout signifies nothing. A fast workout, on the other hand, almost rules out an exercise rider because no one but a jockey could get the horse to run that fast.

2. Although there is a racing rule that says all workouts must be recorded and published, train-

(Courtesy author)

This is yours truly with one of my stakes horses, Sport
King, around 1970; for once, I got to be better
dressed than the horse.

Anyone can use the graded form—this hot dog seems to be getting his information from the horse's mouth.

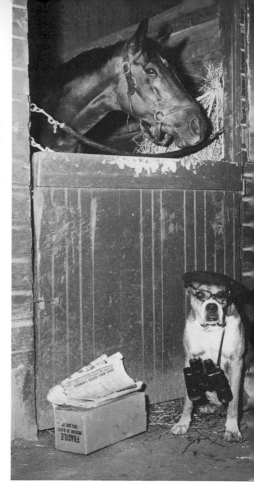

These thoroughbreds at Arlington Park seem to be saying "Bring on the feed and we'll put on the speed."

(Courtesy author)

(Courtesy author)

Above. Sport King is a thing of beauty crossing the finish line first in a 1970 allowance race at Laurel Race Track in Maryland. *Below.* Trying to get a few words from the winner.

(Courtesy author)

(Courtesy Jim Raftery, Turfotos)

Here we are, grinning like proud parents, with my great sprinter Glass House. Steve Brooks rode him to victory for me in 1963.

I told you I get some of my best tips from a little bird.

(Courtesy author)

Off to the races, dressed
to the nines, when I was
in my prime.

(Courtesy author)

Having good
relationships with
jockeys like Carlos
Marquez is an
important part of
my handicapping.

Arlington Park just before it opened in 1939.
Below. And again...horses parade in the paddock
of Arlington International Racecourse on opening
day, June 28, 1989, in Arlington Heights, Ill. The
dramatic new plant is really something with a
six-story grandstand and clubhouse. On the first
day I had four winners on top plus the perfecta.

One of a patient breed of horse players, Herb Forneck is a ticket picker—he checks to see if discarded tickets are "live," bending the rejects and flipping them behind him so he knows not to check them again. Yes, he made a living that way for years.

Below. Taking a break from column writing while waiting for inspiration to strike.

(Courtesy author)

Above. One of the perks of being the president of the Horsemen's Benevolent and Protective Association is hobnobbing with bigwigs like Illinois governor James Thompson and his wife Jane. *Below.* The horses come and go, but Fern and I have stayed together.

(Courtesy author)

All photos courtesy Chicago Sun-Times *unless otherwise noted.*

ers can hide workouts at certain tracks by sneak-
ing onto the strip and "daylighting" their horses
—that is, work them in the dark before the
clocker shows up at first light.

3. The rules also say that before a trainer can
get onto the strip with his horse, he must check
in with a "spotter." The trainer must tell the
spotter that Bag O Beans, for example, "is going
to work three-quarters from the five-eighths
pole." Trouble is, a racetrack may have three
gaps along the fence where horses can come onto
the strip, but it will have only one or two gaps
covered by spotters. When horses slip through,
the job of identifying them falls on the clocker. If
he's good, no problem. If he isn't, big problems
(if workouts mean anything to you). The clocker
may time horse A when actually he's horse B.

4. Even if trainers do check in with spotters,
they have been known to lie if they think they
can get away with it. "Bag O Beans" may, in fact,
be another horse—a better horse—in the trainer's
stable. If the trainer is successful in disguising
his good horse as Bag O Beans, he can hide a
workout.

I can't blame the trainer too much for trying to
be sneaky. He figures he stands to lose if too
many people know too much about his horse.
Does Carson's tell Field's? Say his $20,000
claimer works five furlongs in :59. If the workout
appears in the *Form*, he's telling other trainers

that his horse is sound and is going good. Some of them may start asking questions here and there to check whether his horse really did work :59. If they're satisfied, they may come snooping around the barn to look at the horse. That leaves the trainer of the horse in a pickle, right? What is he supposed to do? Run his horse for $20,000 and have somebody claim him? Or scratch him and lose out on a chance to pick up a good purse?

Another thing to ignore: At some tracks a horse isn't allowed to run unless he has had a workout listed in the last 30 days. That's to protect the public, the tracks say. That's crap, I say.

Some track official will go up to the trainer and say, "Hey, you've got to give me a workout for your horse, otherwise he can't run."

"OK," the trainer says. "He went five-eighths in 1:05."

"Thanks," the official says and walks away.

Then the track announcer gets on the public-address system and says, "We have a recent workout for so-and-so. He went five-eighths in 1:05 on August 22."

There's a problem with asking a trainer to provide a workout for his horse. The tracks, though, haven't figured that out yet.

SPEED FIGURES

Another thing that makes me laugh are the *Form's* speed figures, the combination of the

speed rating and track variant. According to fol-
lowers of these speed figures, one set of numbers
is meaningless without the other. A horseplayer
who goes for speed figures likes a horse that consistently gets 100 "points."

Me? I like fast horses, all right, but I don't have
much use for the *Form's* speed figures. Don't get
me wrong. I look at them. A horse that received
a 110 in his last race is hard to ignore, especially
if no other horse in the field has a rating above
95. But that only happens when some horse like
Lost Code comes to Chicago and meets some of
our local "stars." You don't need a speed figure to
tell you which horse has the edge. That's pretty
clear when you check the horse's record and his
earnings.

Look at these two races, both run at six and a
half furlongs over a fast track at Hawthorne in
September 1988:

:23^1	:46^3	1:18^1	1$^{1\frac{1}{2}}$	1$^{\frac{1}{2}}$	1^2	1$^{1\frac{1}{2}}$	**82-21**
:22^2	:45^3	1:18	1^3	1$^{3\frac{1}{2}}$	1^5	1$^{5\frac{1}{2}}$	**83-20**

The first race was won by a $5,000 claimer
named Speedy. The second was won by Squeaky
Sneakers, a $16,000 claimer. What if these two
met in their next race? How would you grade
them? Based on their speed figures, each receiving 103 points, the two horses are equal. But the
final times tell you that Squeaky Sneakers is a
length better than Speedy. And the pace of the

race, the fractions set by the leader (or leaders), puts even more distance between the two.

Speedy ran the first two furlongs in :23^1 in rushing to a fairly easy lead. Squeaky Sneakers was three lengths ahead at the first call after going the first two furlongs in :22^2. Speedy covered the next two furlongs in :23^2, compared with Squeaky Sneakers' :23^1. Speedy's time was slower even though he was beating back a challenge; Squeaky Sneakers, on the other hand, was widening his lead. Speedy went the final two and one-half furlongs in a quick :31^3 as he held on to win. Squeaky Sneakers ran the last leg in :32^2, adding another half-length to his lead even though he was probably hand-ridden through most of the stretch. My guess is that if these two horses met, Squeaky Sneakers would easily win the speed duel, leaving Speedy with a blown engine and a speed figure around 90.

Another problem with speed figures is the track variant. It usually says more about the quality of horses that ran that day than it does about the condition of the strip. Speedy ran his 1:18^1 on September 8, a Thursday. The strip was "fast" and the variant was 21. Two days later, on September 10, a Saturday, when the good horses were entered, the variant over the "fast" strip was 16. What if Bag O Beans, another $5,000 claimer like Speedy, ran 1:18^1 to win the only dog race on the card? Bag O Beans's speed figure would be 82-16. Now, what if Speedy and Bag O

Beans faced each other in their next race? Is Speedy, whose speed figure was 82-21 the last time out, five lengths better than Bag O Beans? That's what the numbers say.

Speed figures are of even less value when you're trying to compare horses that have raced at different levels and at different tracks. About the only instances where speed figures have any validity are when you're comparing horses that have raced at a same price, at the same track, and on the same days. But, then, what could speed figures tell you that times and the finishes could not?

THE MANY FACES OF "FAST"

While I'm on the subject of junky bits of information, I'll mention the strip, or what passes as the description of the racing surface. What does it mean when the strip is called "fast"? Does it mean that a cheap horse will run six furlongs in 1:13, and an allowance horse will cover the distance in 1:11? Or does it mean that the strip is packed tighter than plywood? Or does it mean that the track superintendent scraped the strip overnight, so the depth of the cushion is three and a half inches all the way across, from rail to outside post?

A racing strip can change from day to day, from hour to hour. In one race it can favor speed;

three hours later, the strip can be "tiring," giving horses that come from behind the edge. Some days horses that get caught on the rail will run as if on a treadmill; other days, the rail means a sure victory. And sometimes a strip, after a rain, will lose some of its cushion and develop a "path." If a horse gets to the path first, he can cruise home.

Yet the term "fast" applies to all those racing conditions. So what does "fast" mean? I guess it's a weather report: "It didn't rain yesterday, and it's not raining now, so let's call the track 'fast.' "

Well then, how about "good" and "sloppy"? "Good" can mean it rained last night or early this morning. "Sloppy" can mean it was raining an hour before post time or it's raining now. Helpful? Hah!

The condition of the strip is affected by the elements—the sun, wind, and rain—and the track superintendent's crew. When the weather is hot, sunny, and windy, the strip will become loose, or tiring, unless the proper amount of water is sprayed on the sand between races. Water packs and tightens the strip; horses will go faster because their hooves don't dig in as much. Think of a beach. You can run faster if you're near the water's edge because the sand is moist and firm. Farther away from the water, the sand is dry and loose and running is more of a strain.

Strips need water, but too much of it leads to screwy racing. A strip is banked on the turns and crowned ever-so-slightly on the backstretch as well as the homestretch. When it rains, water carries away some of the cushion as it runs off the track and most of that sand settles along the rail. It can cost a horse a few lengths if he runs in the deeper part of the strip.

If slop favors any runner, it is a speed horse with a post off the rail. If he can get out front, he won't have horses kicking mud in his face. He also may be helped by the fact that some of the cushion has been washed away. The times over a sloppy track can be as good as when the strip is fast.

But sloppy strips are like cheap horses: unpredictable. Which horses are going to slip and slide? Which ones aren't? Which horses are going to be bothered by flying slop? Which ones aren't? That's not horse racing. It's bingo. You want to take a chance? Not me. I'll spend the day eating chocolate ice cream.

A strip that's drying out is just as bad as slop. When rain washes away some of the sand, parts of the strip will have less cushion and will dry faster. Some horses have a hard time striding out when the strip is constantly changing under them—from dry to wet and back to dry again. They become tentative when they can't grab hold.

And after the strip has thoroughly dried out, unless it is scraped and the sand redistributed, the rail will become like a sand dune and the parts of the strip that have lost some cushion likely will develop a path. It'll usually be on or near the crown. The path may have only two inches of cushion and it's worth a length or two to the horse that can reach it first. Again, am I supposed to pick the horse that I think will hit the wire ahead of the others or the one that will be first to the path?

Good racetracks measure the depth of the cushion every day; they try to stay within a quarter-inch of the desired depth, whether it's three and a half inches or whatever. Most tracks, though, wait until the horsemen complain hot and heavy before doing anything because taking care of a strip costs money. Picking winners is hard enough when the horses are cheap. I don't need track owners who have all the qualities of maiden claimers.

Eight

Class Will Tell

This is where we stand even before we begin to handicap a race:

1. The condition of the horses is a guessing game. You figure that only fit horses are running, but that is rarely the case.
2. The condition of the strip is a guessing game, too. You can only hope that, barring rain, today's strip will be similar to yesterday's in terms of speed and, if any, bias.

That's two strikes already. In baseball, you'd be guarding the plate. In horse racing, you're just stepping into the batter's box with the idea of smacking a home run. That's not too smart, but that's horse racing.

When I handicap I'll choose a horse on the basis of at least three and as many as 10 factors:

1. Class
2. Most recent races
3. Trainer
4. Condition of the strip
5. Post position
6. Distance
7. Breeding (only for a horse that hasn't started many times)

If, after weighing all those factors, I still can't split two or three horses, I'll look at:

8. Jockey
9. Weight
10. Workouts

CLASS

Speed, stamina, and heart. Those are the ingredients of what I call "class." Every horse has class, but he possesses it in degrees relative to other horses. Alysheba has more class than Gala Serenade, and my horse has more class than the dogs that run in $3,500 claiming races at Balmoral. Those $3,500 claimers, in turn, are better than the $2,500 horses that run at Fairmount Park or Charles Town, West Virginia. But as the level of racing goes down, so does the importance of class. In cheap claiming races, the condition of the horse comes into play to a much greater degree.

When I handicap, I want to look for the likely winner, not the likely survivor. But sometimes I feel like a general asking for one volunteer to charge up the hill against enemy fire. I've got the Dirty Dozen in front of me (or at Sportsman's, where the field is smaller, the Tentative Ten). Nobody steps forward. Instead, 11 of them take a step back, leaving one "volunteer."

When you're looking for a volunteer in, say, a $15,000 claiming race, consider these points:

1. It's usually best to select a horse that is running for the same price, or is being raised a bit.

2. If a horse ran for $25,000 last time and is running for $15,000 today, he's taking a big drop. That usually means he's hurting. The best medicine a trainer can give him (other than complete rest) is cheaper company. Check his previous races. Against better company was he beaten by 25 lengths? Or was he beaten by only 10 lengths? If the latter, class may give him the edge.

3. If a horse ran for $20,000 last time and is running for $15,000 today, he may be worth a second look. Go back three or five races. Was he running for $15,000 then? A horse that is drop-

ping but returning to his class level is more dangerous than one that is just dropping. One horse showed enough potential to merit stepping up in class; the other is on the decline.

4. If all the horses appear evenly matched, look around for speed. If one horse has a lot of speed and the others don't have any, the speed horse will have a tremendous advantage. He won't be challenged and will have more in reserve for the stretch.

5. Stakes races are the easiest to handicap because the best horses usually have won the most money. If three or four horses have earned similar amounts, check the number of starts. A horse that has won $200,000 in 10 starts is classier than one that has earned that much in 20 tries. If money doesn't help in determining class, compare the horses on the basis of where they raced. A horse that has won his races at tracks like Suffolk Downs, Rockingham or Detroit probably may not be good enough to beat a horse that has been winning at Belmont, Aqueduct, Gulfstream Park, Santa Anita, Hollywood Park and even Churchill Downs.

MOST RECENT RACES

1. Unless a horse won his previous start by 10 lengths, one race doesn't say much about form. Go back three, four races. If he finished third, second, third, and first, he may win again today

Drummer's Prince
Own.—Gray R H Sr
112^5
Gr. g. 5, by Sharp Drummer—Gobaidge, by Iron Warrior
Br.—Whited D E (Ark) — 1988 12 1 0 0 $3,780
Tr.—Gray Richard H Jr — $7,500 — 1987 11 1 1 1 $3,400
Lifetime 38 2 1 6 $11,950

22Aug88-3Haw	6f	:22^2	:46^2	1:12 ft	56	119	$9^{8\frac{3}{4}}$	9^{8}	9^{12}	$9^{20\frac{3}{4}}$	Lindsay R^2	7500	60-25	HvyPockts,QtclmDd,HghCommnd	10
8Aug88-3Haw	6f	:22	:45^4	1:12^{2}ft	73	114^5	10^{12}	10^{14}	11^{15}	$11^{17\frac{1}{2}}$	Aguilar R^{12}	7500	61-23	HighAchievmnt,YrdBoss,CrfrPrinc	12
1Aug88-5Haw	$6\frac{1}{2}$f	:22^3	:45^3	1:18^{1}ft	14	117^5	$5^{5\frac{1}{2}}$	$7^{8\frac{1}{2}}$	$7^{7\frac{3}{4}}$	$8^{14\frac{3}{4}}$	Aguilar R^8	7500	67-20	Acoxadoodle, Yard Boss, A Big Cat	8
22Jly88-3Haw	6f	:22^1	:46^2	1:12^{3}ft	80	111^5	6^{6}	$5^{4\frac{1}{2}}$	3^{1}	$1^{\frac{3}{4}}$	Aguilar R^7	7500	78-17	Drummer'sPrince,FastndRel,J.Gunn	8
13Jly88-5Haw	$6\frac{1}{2}$f	:22^2	:45^4	1:20^{1}ft	82	114^5	8^{12}	8^{14}	$9^{8\frac{1}{2}}$	$9^{7\frac{3}{4}}$	Aguilar R^3	7000	64-16	CoffeyvilleKid,TallBid,SavgeSimon	9
29Jun88-3Haw	6f	:22^4	:47^3	1:14 sy	65	111^5	$8^{8\frac{1}{2}}$	$8^{8\frac{3}{4}}$	7^{7}	$7^{8\frac{1}{4}}$	Aguilar R^{12}	7000	63-28	Exponent,Jay'sTotor,MarquisOfDe	12
15Jun88-3Spt	6f	:24^2	:48^4	1:15^{3}ft	70	110^5	5^{4}	$5^{4\frac{1}{4}}$	$5^{6\frac{1}{2}}$	$7^{4\frac{3}{4}}$	Aguilar R^5	4000	67-31	Nolips, Cynosura, Little BidBetter	10
10Jun88-5Spt	$6\frac{1}{2}$f	:22^3	:47^2	1:20^{4}ft	60	110^5	$2^{\frac{1}{2}}$	1^{1}	6^{9}	$9^{17\frac{1}{2}}$	Aguilar R^9	4000	55-25	FirstCsting,Sndy'sCltic,BhvingNtiv	9
3Jun88-3Spt	6f	:23^4	:48^2	1:14^{2}ft	132	110^5	$9^{6\frac{1}{4}}$	$8^{7\frac{1}{4}}$	$8^{6\frac{1}{4}}$	$6^{6\frac{3}{4}}$	Aguilar R^4	4000	71-25	VgorosDncr,Dwn'sDrmmr,DscoTco	10
18May88-1Spt	6f	:24	:49	1:14^{3}ft	52	117	$8^{6\frac{1}{2}}$	$8^{7\frac{3}{4}}$	8^{11}	$7^{14\frac{1}{2}}$	Suman S^3	4000	62-29	Long Gyland, ‡Trevian,LandShark	10

at the same price. If he finished seventh, seventh, seventh, and first, chances are his victory was a fluke. Everything fell into place for that dog to win: The better horses got into trouble and the pace was just right.

2. There are times, though, when there is a good reason for a dramatic turnaround. Trainers don't perform miracles, but sometimes drugs do. Lasix is a medication that is given to a horse that hemorrhages. Blood will collect in his trachea and he won't be able to breathe properly. A horse that can't breathe can't run. In most cases, a dose of Lasix will prevent bleeding and that can lead to dramatic improvement in a horse that is getting the medication for the first time. I've seen first-time Lasix users run their eyeballs out. The next time out, a Lasix horse may not run quite as well, but he usually will run better than he did before he was diagnosed as a bleeder.

Here's Goose's Gold's past performances going into a $7,500 claiming race on September 5, 1988, at Hawthorne:

```
Goose's Gold                        B. g. 3, by Red Wing Bold—Goose's Joy, by Jesterson
                                    Br.—Gosselin John W (Fla)              1988 10  1  0  0      $5,205
Own.—Gosselin Jack          106⁵   Tr.—Berns Linda Gibson      $7,500     1987  6  1  0  0      $6,990
                                    Lifetime   16  2  0  0   $12,195
8Aug88-3Haw  6f :22  :45⁴ 1:12²ft  16 113   2½  2½  2½  79¼  Ward W A 11    7500 69-23 HighAchievmnt,YrdBoss,CrfrPrinc 12
  8Aug88—Bled
15Jly88-3Haw  6½f:22³ :45⁴ 1:18¹ft  35 111   1¹  1hd 8⁹ 9¹4¼ Marquez C H Jr 9 8000 67-22 BoldTry,I'mABadBoy,SomedyMybe 9
3Jly88-1Haw  6½f:23  :46³ 1:18 ft   9½ 108   2¹  7¹² 8²5 8³1¼ Fuentes E R 8  10000 52-25 Someday Maybe, Detail, Billy Brad 8
28May88-4RD  5½f:23  :46 1:05²ft    9½ 1065  2ʰᵈ 2² 5⁹ 5¹⁰  Dolton C J 2  15000 78-21 Rhubick, TallMeadows,RunninDevii 7
13May88-5CD  6f :21¹ :45¹ 1:12 ft  16 1117  2² 2¹ 3²½ 75¼  Buckley P R 4  10000 77-15 Dross, Highland Bay, U Time Jig 12
13Apr88-7Kee  6f :22¹ :45 1:10³ft   92 1087  3½ 44½11¹6¹12²¾ Murray J H 5 Aw19800 66-15 UnitedTims,HtchrHill,BlurdMmory 12
29Mar88-4Crc  6f :22² :46⁴ 1:14³ft   7½ 1097  1¹ 1¹¼ 1hd 75¼ Vives J C 2   12500 72-27 SprkIngAppl,SqurOn,Ppp'sFzzbstr 12
1Mar88-2GP  6f :22²  :46 1:23⁴ft   42 1067  12½ 15 14 1⅜   Munoz O R 4   10500 76-23 Goos'sGold,LoThLon,GrshwkStngr 12
23Jan88-2GP  6f :22²  :46⁴ 1:22⁴ft  13 114  32½ 46 11²3¹¹22½ Penna D7    10500 54-24 King'sBnnr,RginthThron,KppDncr 11
12Jan88-5GP  6f :22²  :46¹ 1:24⁴ft  112 114  3² 32 9¹3¹0¹0⅔ Penna D 12   20000 64-25 Phute,HomerJons,Lou'sProudStvn 11
 ●Sep 1 Haw 5f ft :59¹ h      Aug 26 Haw 4f ft :49² b      ●Aug 18 Haw 6f ft 1:16³ h      Aug 5 Haw 4f ft :49 b
```

The *Form* tells you that in his last race Goose's Gold "bled." When you see that it's 1 to 10 that the horse will receive Lasix next time out. Some horses that are regularly treated with Lasix will bleed through the medication. "Bled," however, applies only to bleeding horses that have not been Lasix users. The *Form* also provides a Medication List (on the same page where you find their "Experts' Selections") that tells you which horses are running with Lasix, and which horses are receiving the medication for the first time. It's good to check the Medication List for first-time users, because the past performances won't always show that such-and-such a horse bled for the first time in his most recent race.

The Medication List for September 5 says that Goose's Gold is a first-time Lasix user. So, what effect did the Lasix have? He finished second, beaten by only two and a quarter lengths.

Don't get the idea that all first-time Lasix horses go up several notches in class. If a horse hasn't shown *anything* in his previous races,

FIRST RACE
Hawthorne
SEPTEMBER 5, 1988

6 FURLONGS. (1.08⅕) CLAIMING. Purse $6,800. 3–year–olds and upward, non–winners of three races. Weight, 3–year–olds, 116 lbs.; older, 122 lbs. Non–winners of two races since August 1 allowed 3 lbs.; a race, 5 lbs.; a race in 1988, 8 lbs. Claiming price $7,500. (Claiming races for $6,250 or less not considered in estimating allowances.) 67th DAY. WEATHER CLEAR. TEMPERATURE 62 DEGREES.

Value of race $6,800; value to winner $4,080; second $1,360; third $748; fourth $408; fifth $204. Mutuel pool $119,740.

Last Raced	Horse	Eqt	A.Wt	PP	St	¼	½	Str	Fin	Jockey	Cl'g Pr	Odds $1
24Aug88 ^{9}Haw^{4}	Foxy Model	b	3 113	6	2	$2^{2\frac{1}{2}}$	2^{5}	1^{hd}	$1^{2\frac{1}{4}}$	Baird E T	7500	2.30
8Aug88 ^{3}Haw^{7}	Goose's Gold	b	3 109	9	1	$1^{2\frac{1}{2}}$	1^{hd}	2^{6}	2^{4}	Schaeffer G A^{5}	7500	3.10
29Aug88 ^{3}Haw^{7}	First Long Pants		3 113	7	9	8^{1}	5^{1}	3^{3}	$3^{1\frac{3}{4}}$	Clark K D	7500	a-2.40
12May88 ^{7}Spt^{7}	Cement Son	b	4 117	1	6	5^{hd}	6^{hd}	$5^{2\frac{1}{2}}$	$4^{3\frac{3}{4}}$	Frazier R L	7500	5.40
23Jun88 ^{5}Haw^{6}	Double Will	b	6 114	5	4	6^{hd}	$7^{\frac{1}{2}}$	6^{2}	$5^{1\frac{1}{4}}$	Sellers S J	7500	20.60
29Aug88 ^{3}Haw^{10}	Jan's Buck		4 114	8	3	7^{1}	8^{3}	7^{3}	6^{5}	Meza N	7500	12.70
22Aug88 ^{3}Haw^{10}	J. Gunn	b	3 113	2	5	3^{2}	3^{hd}	4^{hd}	$7^{\frac{1}{2}}$	Torres F C	7500	13.50
22Aug88 ^{3}Haw^{9}	Drummer's Prince		5 112	4	8	9	9	$8^{1\frac{1}{2}}$	$8^{1\frac{1}{4}}$	Aguilar R^{5}	7500	31.50
22Aug88 ^{3}Haw^{5}	A Big Cat	b	4 114	3	7	4^{2}	4^{hd}	9	9	Fires E	7500	a-2.40

a–Coupled: First Long Pants and A Big Cat.

OFF AT 1:31. Start good. Won driving. Time, :22⅘, :46⅗, :59⅕, 1:12⅗ Track fast.

Official Program Numbers

$2 Mutuel Prices:			
6–FOXY MODEL	6.60	3.60	2.40
8–GOOSE'S GOLD		4.20	2.60
1–FIRST LONG PANTS (a–entry)			2.20

B. g, by Reality and Reason—Nearctic Fox, by Nearctic Traveller. Trainer Boyce Neil. Bred by Shelley M C (Ore).

FOXY MODEL moved up to engage GOOSE'S GOLD on the turn, brushed several times with that rival upper stretch, then drew clear late under strong handling. The stewards failed to allow a claim of foul against the winner lodged by the rider of GOOSE'S GOLD. GOOSE'S GOLD broke alertly to rush up and take a clear early lead, responded when engaged by the winner, brushed several times with that one upper stretch, then faltered late. FIRST LONG PANTS rallied willingly. CEMENT SON made a mild late gain inside. DOUBLE WILL raced evenly. JAN'S BUCK improved position without threatening. J. GUNN forwardly placed inside, gave way in drive. DRUMMER'S PRINCE showed little. A BIG CAT gave way between rivals straightening for home.

Owners— 1, Shelley Melvin C; 2, Gosselin Jack; 3, Cowan C C Jr; 4, Jer-Ed Farm; 5, Schuh William A; 6, Reifer James; 7, Bowline Ray; 8, Gray R H Sr; 9, O'Keefe Peggy.

Trainers— 1, Boyce Neil; 2, Berns Linda Gibson; 3, Hazelton Richard P; 4, Harris Rickey B; 5, Salvino Owen C; 6, Reid David R; 7, Bohn Bernard F; 8, Gray Richard H Jr; 9, Hazelton Richard P.

Overweight: Goose's Gold 3 pounds.

nothing is going to help him—nothing legal, anyway.

3. At the $15,000 claiming level a horse usually runs once every 10 days or two weeks depending on his basic soundness. If he hasn't raced in a month, he's hurting. Maybe the month's rest has helped him. Maybe not. This isn't to say that horses don't win after a long layoff. Many do, but most don't. Stakes horses are worked hard to prepare them for racing. Cheaper horses get into shape by being raced.

4. There may be legitimate excuses for a long layoff. If *none* of the $15,000 claimers in today's race has run in the past month, that means there

wasn't any race for them. If the past performances show that some of them ran in a $15,000
claiming race two weeks back, you will have to
investigate further by checking that day's *Form*
and that race's chart.

The *Form* will tell you whether the horse you
like—let's call him Bag O Beans—was entered. If
he was entered and didn't run, it was because he
either was on the also-eligible list and didn't
draw in, or he was scratched. If he was
scratched, the race chart will have that information, but it won't explain why the trainer made
that decision. It may have been because the strip
was sloppy, or it may have been because the
trainer didn't feel Bag O Beans was ready.

But if you're a sometime horseplayer, you don't
have old *Forms* stacked up neatly in your house.
The only information you have on Bag O Beans
is what is in today's *Form* and that just isn't
enough. It's better to play it safe, and throw out
Bag O Beans with your dead mutuel tickets.

5. Good horses get good treatment. A horse
worth $25,000 will be rested and given a chance
to recuperate and should be in good shape when
he returns to action. When he gets back to racing, keep an eye on him. You don't pick him, of
course, in his first race back. But you see in the
Form that he laid up there second, third, or
fourth for a quarter. At the half he was third,
fourth, or fifth, before finally losing by 10, 12, or
15 lengths. He was "dead short," a trainer would

say. He wasn't fit enough to go the distance fast. But the next time out he's second, second, third, fifth, and gets beat by seven lengths. Watch out. That horse is ready to win. He needed those two starts.

6. Along with the Medication List, the *Form* will note the equipment changes made by trainers for horses running today. If you notice that a young horse (2 or 3 years old) running in fair form is wearing blinkers for the first time, give him an extra point in your ratings. The blinkers may be just the thing he needs to keep his mind on racing. Remember Dixieland Brass? He was beaten by 20 lengths in his debut. Then he started running with blinkers. He quickly became one of the top 3-year-olds in the country and figured to be the second choice in the 1989 Kentucky Derby until he broke down in the Florida Derby. But like Lasix, blinkers won't do much for a horse that's beyond help.

7. When thoroughbreds hear the bell, they all want to break out of the gate like gangbusters. Those that break slowly are sore. In distance races, these horses sometimes can work out of their soreness. They'll pick up enough ground in the stretch to make you think that, with a good start, they'll get up next time. In most cases they won't.

8. In better races, a horse that is coming off a grass race will pick up a little speed when he's returned to the dirt. That's an old trick. Horatio

Luro, who won two Kentucky Derbys, would get his horse ready for the dirt by shooting a grass race into him. The grip that a horse gets running on the turf sharpens his stride, and it carries over to the next race. Of course, this tactic won't help a horse that can't run on the dirt.

9. If a horse has run two putrid races on the grass, forget him on the turf. Horses spend most of their first two years of life running around on the grass, but some can't race on it. I don't know why. I had a horse called Futuresque who won a series of races on the dirt, one after another. Then I entered him in a grass race at Washington Park. As soon as he broke from the gate, he went to the outside fence and stayed there throughout the race. He must have got beaten by 30 lengths. I couldn't believe it. I ran him again on the grass. The same thing happened. I never ran him on the grass again.

TRAINER

The horse deserves 90 percent of the credit for winning (and 90 percent of the blame for losing). The next biggest hand should go to the trainer. I'd give him between 5 percent and 8 percent on the applause meter.

A good trainer is like a mother. He knows what's good for a horse. He calls in the vet when the horse is sick, gives him his vitamins and has his teeth checked, gets angry when he does something bad and rewards him when he's a good boy. A good trainer makes sure his horse gets the right amount of exercise, not too little, not too much. And, most important, he doesn't send him out to play with horses that are faster than he is.

A good trainer develops horses. More of his horses will move up in class than will drop down and he's less likely to run hogs. He may not lead in the trainer standings with the most victories but he will win at least 15 percent of his races. The local trainers that rate high with me include Jere Smith, Neil Boyce, Harvey Vanier, Carl Bowman, Jerry Calvin, Frank Schiffner, Paul Darjean, James Levitch, Noel Hickey, Tom Dorris and Dan Switzer.

Dead-serious handicappers keep meticulous records on trainers and try to find training patterns. That's fine for them, but you've got a job, a wife, some kids and a mother who wonders why you don't come over more often. You can't waste your time studying old *Forms*. If you can't split two horses on the basis of form, go with the horse whose trainer has shown he can win a good percentage of his races.

CONDITION OF THE STRIP

A handicapper must know whether a track favors speed or gives the edge to horses that come off the pace. And he must know whether it has any bias. The best way to get a line on strip conditions is to go to the track every day for a week and analyze the races. A very general pattern will emerge and it will hold true until nature or the track superintendent steps in and changes the rules of the game. Then it's back to square one.

But the casual horseplayer can't go to the track every day. About the best he can do when he does go to the track is to lay off the first race and try to pick up clues.

How did the winner win? Did he lead wire to wire? Did he come from the middle of the pack? From far back? Did he win on the rail? Did he stay off the rail throughout the race? What was his winning time? How does it compare with his last time out?

Here are some general observations you can make from watching one race:

1. Jockeys know where the strip is fastest. If they stay on the rail, that means the rail is fast or at least not deep. If there is only one speed horse in the race, he will have an advantage.

2. If an unchallenged speed horse stops in the stretch, the track probably is loose and tiring and will favor strong closers.

3. Winning time is important, but only if it's really fast or really slow compared with the time registered by the same horse in his previous race. Comparing times is tricky because time depends

on pace. Say, in his last race, Bag O Beans went six furlongs in 1:14 winning wire to wire. Today, he ran 1:13 against the same company but finished third. Is the track faster today? Hard to say. When he won wire to wire, Bag O Beans might have been the only speed in the race. Today, he went head and head with another speed horse. They set a fast pace as they battled for the lead and both eventually died in the stretch.

4. If an odds-on favorite ran out, study the replay of the race and try to figure out what happened. If he had traffic problems or got carried out wide or had some kind of bad racing luck, his performance probably won't tell you much about strip conditions. But if he looked to have a shot coming into the stretch, ask these questions: Was he a speed horse that died? Was he a closer that failed to get up? Was he on the rail? Off the rail? Answer those questions and take it from there.

DISTANCE

Most horses can win only within a narrow distance range: six furlongs to seven furlongs; seven furlongs to 1¹/₁₆ miles, and 1 mile to 1¹/₈ miles. Some horses, though, can give a game enough effort running long or short. Here's what you should consider when you come across a router running in a sprint, or a sprinter going long.

1. A horse coming off a route is likely to be fit and that's often the difference in a race. But he also tends to have problems doing those early quick fractions. If he's meeting quality sprinters, he probably won't finish in the money.

2. A horse coming off a sprint may have an edge in a route race. In the sprint, he was pushed all the way, going one-quarter in, say, :23, a half in :46 and change, and three-quarters in 1:12. Going a route, he doesn't need those fast fractions and still may be able to take an easy lead. He can go :24, :49, 1:14, and still have a lot left for the finish.

BREEDING

Forget the breeding on an older horse. When talking about a 5-year-old, somebody might say, "Look, this horse is by Old Frankfort. He must be pretty good." He was a 2-year-old by Old Frankfort and it didn't help him. I don't care if he was by Alydar or Bold Ruler. If he was a hog then, he's a hog now. Unless a horse is winning, forget the breeding once he's past 3 years old.

And forget his breeding for the grass. They say it's hereditary but that's bunk. Practically all horses like the grass. They're born on it. They spend the first year and a half of their lives on it, running around, filling out, growing up. Most horses run better on grass because they don't have dirt and sand flying in their face. Very, very seldom will you hear a trainer say, "My horse can't run on the grass." I said it with my horse, Futuresque, but he was a strange one.

The only time that you've got to know something about breeding is when you're handicapping a race for 2- or 3-year-olds making their first start. The *Form* publishes the *American Racing Manual*, which gives you all the information on the big studs in the breeding shed, and how much was paid for each yearling sold the previous year. You can check the book to compare the price tags of the horses running today. A $50,000 horse may run faster than one bought for $25,000. At least that's what the owner of the $50,000 horse hopes. The only trouble with bringing the *Racing Manual* to the track is that it's very heavy. You could get a hernia.

JOCKEY

If you're looking for handicapping help, you can get it from the jockey. The better jockeys will get the better horses. In Chicago, Pat Day always will be on one of the favorites. What Day and other good riders do is allow the horse to run his race by keeping him out of trouble. If the horse doesn't have it in him to win, no rider can help him. Even jockeys will tell you that.

"You've got to be on your stock," Day told me.

"That's the number one thing. It doesn't matter who you are, if you're not on a contender, you can't get the job done. The difference between the best riders and the rest of the riding colony is that the best riders make the fewest number of mistakes. I have not yet seen a rider put a horse over his back, carry him down the stretch, and win. I have seen riders make a number of mistakes and cost the horse the race, when in fact the horse should have won. I've also seen horses that probably weren't the best horses that day stay out of trouble and get the job done.

"They figure a fifth of a second is equal to one horse length. It doesn't take very long for a fifth of a second to pass. You figure that in the whole field, from the first horse to the last, there's maybe two seconds difference, maybe 10-12 lengths separating the whole field. It doesn't take but one tiny mistake during the course of the race to cost you."

Walter Blum, a two-time national champion and now a steward, breaks it down this way: The horse is 80 percent, the trainer is 10 percent, and the remaining 10 percent is split evenly between the groom that rubs the horse ("the rapport he has with the horse means a helluva lot to the horse") and the jockey.

"The jockey means a great deal," Blum said, "but by the same token I think 90 percent of the jockeys are decent jockeys. You take the top 15 jockeys at a meeting. Anyone is satisfactory to me. As long as they can keep the horse out of trouble and use good judgment, any jockey can ride a horse as good as the next jockey."

POST POSITION

Post position is a factor when the rail is lightning fast or quicksand deep. If it's fast, the jockey wants to get to the rail as quickly as possible and an inside post helps. If the rail is deep, the jockey with an inside post may lose precious lengths trying to get outside.

Also, horses with outside posts are at a big disadvantage in certain races because the first turn comes up too soon. Horses on the outside have to be rushed in order to get into position. By doing that, jockeys are taking something out of their mounts early in the race. Horses with inside posts have an edge in:

— 1$\frac{1}{8}$-mile races over Arlington Park's 1$\frac{1}{8}$-mile track.

— 1$\frac{1}{16}$-mile races over Hawthorne's one-mile strip.

— Mile or 1$\frac{1}{16}$-mile races, or six-furlong events, over Sportsman's five-eighths-mile track.

WEIGHT

Don't worry too much about weight unless there is a dramatic shift. If A beat B by three lengths last time, and B is carrying seven fewer pounds today than A is toting, B is going to close the gap and maybe outrun A. But most weight gains or losses aren't that great; they're usually one to four pounds. About the only thing I check when I notice a shift in weights is the distance. If the race is a sprint, I'll usually disregard a shift in weight. If it's a route, I'll consider making a switch because the longer you carry the extra weight, the tougher it is.

WORKOUTS

Fast workouts can't be ignored because they may be true.

PICKING THE WINNER

Here are two of the more than 580 races I handicapped during the Hawthorne meeting in 1988. I picked the winner of each race. No, they weren't my only winners.

6 FURLONGS. (1:08 1/5) ALLOWANCE. Purse $18,000. Fillies and mares, 3-year-olds and upward, non-winners of two

races other than maiden or claiming.
Weight, 3-year-olds, 116 lbs.; older, 122 lbs.
Non-winners of two races since July 25 allowed 3 lbs.; a race, 5 lbs.; a race in 1988,
8 lbs. (claiming races not considered.)

SILVER CAPER

She has run against four of the horses in today's field, and hasn't finished ahead of any of
them. Last time out, on August 18, she was
fourth, 11½ lengths behind Avie Jane, and 6
lengths in back of Just Sweetness. On July 29,
she lost by a nose to Just Sweetness. On July 8,
she ran out, beaten by 8 lengths by Moonshine
Mishap. On June 24, she ran second to High
School Band, losing by 4 lengths. Silver Caper
showed that she has decent speed, going six furlongs in 1:11 in winning a $17,000 allowance
race on August 5. She runs a better race if she's
rated off the lead. The competition today is too
tough.

JUST SWEETNESS

A good, consistent filly. She hasn't raced much
in 1988. She was "dead short" in her first race
on July 8, then hung on to win the next time out.
She was beaten by 5½ lengths by Avie Jane in
the August 18 race. She's a 3-year-old running
against 4-year-olds, but it shouldn't hurt her too

213

14 DAILY RACING FORM, THURSDAY, SEPTEMBER 15, 1988

7th Hawthorne

6 FURLONGS. (1.08⅕) ALLOWANCE. Purse $18,000. Fillies and mares. 3-year-olds and upward, non-winners of two races other than maiden or claiming. Weight, 3-year-olds, 116 lbs.; older, 122 lbs. Non-winners of two races since July 25 allowed 3 lbs.; a race, 5 lbs.; a race in 1988, 8 lbs. (Claiming races not considered.)

Silver Caper

Gr. f. 3, by Silver Nitrate—Caper Road, by Kennedy Road

Br.—Zimmerman Mary M (Ky) 1988 6 1 2 0 $18,220

Own.—Zimmerman Mary **113** **Tr.—Levitch James M** 1987 1 1 0 0 $4,200

Lifetime 7 2 2 0 $22,420

18Aug88-8Haw 6f :222 :463 1:114ft 2½ 115 2½ 2hd 44 411½ Ward W A4 ⒻAw19000 70-24 Jin'sCommnd,AvieJne,JustSwetnss 6

5Aug88-1Haw 6f :22 :454 1:11 ft 2¼ 114 22½ 21½ 2hd 11 Ward W A4 ⒻAw17000 86-17 SilverCper,GrçefulNncy,ChoicDncr 6

29Jly88-7Haw 6½f :223 :454 1:183ft 8¾ 115 21 11 1hd 2no VlenzulPA4 ⒻAw16000 80-21 JustSwtnss,SilvrCpr,ButifulMountn 8

8Jly88-7Haw 6f :22 :461 1:122ft *3-2 114 34½ 54 52 58 VlenzulPA2 ⒻAw16000 71-23 MoonshnMshp,RdGrdn,FoxFtGnny 10

24Jun88-7Haw 6f :221 :462 1:123ft 14 112 42½ 35 43½ 24 Lindsay R1 ⒻAw16000 74-26 HighSchoolBnd,SilvrCpr,MissLkvll 12

9Jan88-9Tam 6f :223 :464 1:134sy 21f 113 94 912 913 711¼ GonzlezIJr6 ⒻHibiscus 65-19 BillofSale,LeveItBe,KissYourStutz 13

9Jun87-2Rkm 5f :222 :472 1:011ft 23 118 1112 910 55½ 11 Gonzalez I Jr9 ⒻMdn 78-20 SilverCper,RoylRxson,RdWingQun 12

9Jun87—Fractious gate,dr

Sep 2 Haw 4f ft :49 b Aug 27 Haw 4f ft :49 b Aug 13 Haw 4f ft :49 b Jly 24 Haw 4f ft :50 b

Just Sweetness

Dk. b. or br. f. 3, by Mr Leader—Inner Command, by Delta Judge

Br.—Johnson & Madden (Ky) 1988 3 1 0 1 $12,650

Own.—Canonie Marialyce **113** **Tr.—Hoffman Kenneth E** 1987 8 1 4 2 $16,500

Lifetime 11 2 4 3 $29,150

18Aug88-8Haw 6f :222 :463 1:114ft 4¾ 115 53¼ 3½ 32½ 35½ Fires E2 ⒻAw19000 76-24 Jin'sCommnd,AvieJne,JustSwetnss 6

29Jly88-7Haw 6½f :223 :454 1:183ft 5 112 32 51¾ 2hd 1no Fires E2 ⒻAw16000 80-21 JustSwtnss,SilvrCpr,ButifulMountn 8

8Jly88-7Haw 6f :22 :461 1:122ft 7¼ 112 11½ 11 21 47 Fires E9 ⒻAw16000 72-23 MoonshnMshp,RdGrdn,FoxFtGnny 10

30Oct87-9Crc 170 :481 1:141 1:47 ft 16 112 11½ 1½ 3½ 87¾ ValienteD 1 ⒻGardenia 67-17 BrLind,ProperEvidenc,MyLdyG.P. 10

20Sep87-3Crc 1 :50 1:151 1:421ft 6¼ 112 11½ 12½ 13 2hd Valiente D 2 ⒻAw16900 77-16 SmlngTun,JustSwtnss,Chrstn'sMgc 6

12Sep87-1Crc 6f :23 :472 1:14 ft *1 117 1½ 1hd 2hd 1hd Valiente D 6 ⒻMdn 81-17 JustSweetnss,JtTrd,Christin'sMgic 8

29Aug87-4Crc 6f :223 :46 1:13 ft *3¼ 116 64 66 34½ 31¾ Suckie M C 11 ⒻMdn 84-13 MirnaM.,OkayBabe,JustSweetness 11

19Aug87-6Crc 5½f :23 :473 1:074ft 3¼ 116 52¼ 41¾ 21½ 21½ Suckie M C 6 ⒻMdn 84-15 PlesurbleQust,JustSwtnss,DrstRos 12

19Jly87-5Crc 5½f :232 :474 1:073sy *2¾ 115 2½ 2hd 2½ 23½ Suckie M C 8 ⒻMdn 83-21 DmondSnjt,JstSwtnss,Popgosthlsl 11

4Jly87-1Crc 5½f :23 :483 1:083ft 5½ 115 74¼ 43½ 2hd 22 Suckie M C11 ⒻMdn 80-16 FirlyChrming,JustSwtnss,MssJmm 11

4Jly87—Bore in

Fond Wishes

B. f. 4, by Topsider—Remember Me Too, by Reviewer

Br.—Nuckols Bros (Ky) 1988 18 2 3 3 $39,471

Own.—R L Reineman Stable Inc **117** **Tr.—Springer Frank R** 1987 10 1 0 3 $10,500

Lifetime 28 3 3 6 $49,971 **Turf 2 0 0 0**

1Sep88-9Haw 6f :22 :453 1:111ft 11 117 88¼ 79½ 64¼ 21½ Miller S E 6 Ⓕ 16000 83-18 DorothyRidge,FondWishes,Escltion 9

14Aug88-5Cby 6f :23 :46 1:121ft 3½ 119 54 66 79 78¼ Evans R D 3 Ⓕ 16000 77-15 CoolBobb,MnDocN'M,Infltn'sWndy 7

29Jly88-8Cby 1 Ⓣ:4621:1011:362fm 53 119 36 917 931 941 Evans R D 8 ⒻAw13000 47-15 Janjac, Special Victory, Dissembler 9

17Jly88-6Cby 6f :23 :462 1:113ft 5¼ 121 64¾ 63¾ 57 611½ Evans R D 1 ⒻAw13520 76-13 Stilted, Early Answer, Stats Missy 7

28Jun88-5CD 6f :213 :454 1:114ft *2 116 34 21½ 12½ 13 BrumfildD 1 ⒻAw24870 84-22 FondWishs,LgisltvDnc,MssChfHmp 6

3Jun88-7CD 6f :221 :462 1:111ft 4¾ 112 69 67 67 48¾ Fires E 5 ⒻAw22125 78-21 SnshnAlwys,MssChfHmp,RsontoBb 7

25May88-5CD 6f :221 :463 1:113ft *3-2 112 67½ 52¼ 52 32¼ Fires E 5 ⒻAw20325 82-19 BlueTango,ResontoBb,FondWishes 6

14May88-6CD 6f :214 :46 1:113ft *2¼ 117 67 42¾ 31½ 12¼ Brumfield D 6 Ⓕ 25000 85-20 FondWshs,IOwIOwGogg,OnLckyGrl 8

5May88-4CD 6f :222 :473 1:133ft 6 117 116¾ 84¾ 22 21¼ Allen K K 8 Ⓕ 25000 73-23 ChristineCrne,FondWishes,Jessem 12

13Apr88-3Kee 6f :222 :451 1:113ft 8½ 112 68½ 57 43½ 44¾ Allen K K 4 ⒻAw19800 79-15 MysticlSunris,Giggltr,SoftlyDncing 6

Aug 9 Cby 4f ft :493 h ●Aug 4 Cby 4f gd :523 h Jly 24 Cby 4f ft :503 h

Avie Jane

Ch. f. 4, by Lord Avie—Omaha Jane, by Our Michael

Br.—Gibson C E (Ky) 1988 8 0 3 1 $11,064

Own.—Sugar Hill Farm **114** **Tr.—Switzer Daniel G** 1987 5 2 0 2 $10,800

Lifetime 13 2 3 3 $21,864

18Aug88-8Haw 6f :222 :463 1:114ft 9 114 3½ 1hd 1hd 2no Silva C H5 ⒻAw19000 82-24 Jin'sCommnd,AvieJne,JustSwetnss 6

4Aug88-1Haw 6f :22 :454 1:113ft *2½ 114 1hd 1hd 11 22¾ Silva C H5 Ⓕ 16000 80-13 Rich'nCremy,AvieJne,BrillintBullet 7

13Jly88-1Haw 6½f :224 :463 1:183ft 8-5e 114 11½ 11 1hd 1nk † Lindsay R8 Ⓕ 16000 80-16 ‡AvieJne,NvjoBlossom,Pick'sChick 8

†13Jly88—Disqualified and placed second; Bled

30Jun88-8Haw 6f :223 :47 1:133ft 13 121 65¼ 56½ 55½ 64 Torres F C9 ⒻAw17000 69-28 ShrpType,LdyLibby,UncertinVoyge 9

17Jun88-8Spt 6f :234 :484 1:152ft 2½ 115 511 58 67½ 513 Baird E T2 ⒻAw23100 60-33 Lou'sLogic,ShrpTyp,PrincssofWigs 6

2Jun88-7Spt 6½f :23 :472 1:191ft 7½ 115 1½ 2hd 2hd 3½ Torres F C2 ⒻAw21300 80-26 That's A Doll, Afloat, Avie Jane 7

20May88-8Spt 6f :233 :474 1:134ft 15 115 65¾ 89 87¼ 64 Torres F C4 ⒻAw20400 77-29 Lurn'sDncr,PrincssofWigs,TTntrum 9

12May88-8Spt 6f :232 :464 1:123ft 19 116 59½ 511 59½ 512 Torres F C5 Ⓕ 25000 75-21 RunWild,HoldYourTan,QuakerType 9

12May88—Bore out early.

1Aug87-5Bir 6f :223 :462 1:131ft *1 115 1hd 31 44 75½ Smith L S5 ⒻAw10000 75-22 HghMnmums,MryJcqln,MgnfcntSz 7

23Jly87-9Bir 6f :223 :454 1:114ft 7¼ 114 1hd 11 13 16½ Babij S5 ⒻAw9000 88-18 Avie Jane, Panhellenic, Cox's Note 7

Aug 10 Haw 3f gd :39 b Jly 27 Haw 5f ft 1:06 b

High School Band — Own.—King Farms — **111**
Dk. b. or br. f. 3, by Vencedor—Riffin' the Blues, by Stevward
Br.—Summerplace Farm (Ky) — 1988 8 2 1 2 $24,360
Tr.—Hoffman Kenneth E — Turf 1 0 0 0 $1,320
Lifetime 8 2 1 2 $24,360
11Aug88-8Haw 1 1/16 :463 1:121 1:453ft 4 112 26 1hd 43½ 410½ Baird E T5 ⒻAw19000 59-20 Tht'sADoll,PreciousTiffini,NoblDm 8
21Jly88-8Haw 170 :472 1:124 1:423ft 4½ 114 2½ 1½ 22 36 Baird E T4 ⒻAw17000 83-15 MissLkvill,JustRoyl,HighSchoolBnd 6
8Jly88-8Haw 1 Ⓣ:4711:1131:37 fm 6 113 32 22 35 45 King ELJr6 ⒻAw25300 — — Outofthebluebell,LilStrkr,TriflinGl 10
24Jun88-7Haw 6f :221 :462 1:123ft 13 113 64½ 45 31½ 14 KingELJr11 ⒻAw16000 78-26 HighSchoolBnd,SilvrCpr,MissLkvll 12
14May88-9Spt 1 :482 1:141 1:393ft 13 112 2½ 79½ 714 729¼ KELJr4 ⒻMata Hari H 53-20 ValidVixen,MartiniNTwist,DerDusty 7
27Apr88-5Spt 6½f :224 :471 1:192sy 4½ 113 22 2hd 15 113 King E L Jr3 ⒻMdn 80-28 HghSchoolBnd,Lovslot,TrffcBuldr 10
11Apr88-6Spt 6½f :233 :482 1:212ft *8-5 113 2½ 2½ 22½ 32¾ King E L Jr2 ⒻMdn 67-29 PlfcrMrn,TrffcBldr,HghSchoolBnd 10
18Mar88-6Spt 6f :241 :48 1:143ft 9¾ 121 88½ 55 53 21 King E L Jr10 ⒻMdn 76-26 StntoSlk,HghScholBnd,Sctt'sTttr 10

Dear Dusty — Own.—Dykema C C — **108**
Ch. f. 3, by It's Freezing—Dusty Lace, by Dust Commander
Br.—Dykema Carl C (Ky) — 1988 8 0 1 3 $24,213
Tr.—Yanez Moses R — 1987 9 2 1 2 $24,532
Lifetime 17 2 2 5 $48,745 — Turf 2 0 1 0 $6,140
5Sep88-5Haw 7½f Ⓣ:241 :4711:301fm 9½ 112 85½ 811 43½ 21¼ DouglasRR5 ⒻAw25000 — — GoingYourWay,DearDusty,TriflinGl 9
25Aug88-8Haw a1 Ⓣ:4811:1421:393fm 5¼ 110 31½ 1hd 33½ 46¾ DouglasRR6 ⒻAw19000 — — Avie'sDouble,NobleDm,MyGrtFolly 7
14May88-9Spt 1 :482 1:141 1:393ft 5½ 114 32 11 32 36¼ RzEJr6 ⒻMata Hari H 76-20 ValidVixen,MartiniNTwist,DerDusty 7
27Apr88-6Kee 6f :222 :45 1:114ft 37 112 86¾ 910 710 610¼ Allen K K 2 ⒻAw22000 73-22 Volterr,ClssicCrown,MotherofEight 9
15Apr88-7Aqu 7f :222 :45 1:223ft 23 112 67 613 414 514 RomeroRP 1ⒻAw32000 74-23 Avie'sGal,OurGallmr,GoldenT.Dncer 9
31Mar88-7Aqu 1 :452 1:10 1:363ft 37 113 24 32 31½ 34 RomeroRP 3ⒻAw33000 79 30 Topicount, Our Gallamar,DearDusty 7
20Mar88-8Aqu 1⅛ :47 1:114 1:502ft 64 112 55 612 624 627¾ LovatoFJr 7ⒻRuthless 55-27 Aptostar, Sham Say, Joe's Tammie 7
27Feb88-8Aqu 6f ⊡:222 :4611:11 ft 33 114 53½ 52 44 36¾ Kaenel J L 2 ⒻCicada 82-19 FeelTheBet,BoldLdyAnne,DerDusty 6
16Dec87-8Haw 170 :46 1:122 1:433gd *4-5 114 2hd 1hd 35 211 Razo E Jr 2 ⒻDurazna 73-19 RollMeTwice,DrDusty,Outofthblubll 7
3Dec87-7Haw 170 :47 1:143 1:454sy *8-5 119 2½ 12½ 110 114 Razo E Jr 3 ⒻAw14700 73-29 Dear Dusty,RollMeTwice,It'sSoNice 9
Sep 4 Haw 3f ft :372 b — Aug 20 Haw 1 ft 1:44 b — ●Aug 13 Haw 7f ft 1:302 b — Aug 6 Haw 4f ft :513 b

Moonshine Mishap — Own.—Frank Jerome — **117**
Dk. b. or br. f. 4, by Pumpkin Moonshine—Dewan's Mishap, by Dewan
Br.—Foyt Anthony Joseph Jr (Ky) — 1988 9 2 2 3 $31,367
Tr.—Twardy James E — 1987 19 3 0 4 $27,330
Lifetime 33 6 2 8 $65,206 — Turf 5 0 0 0 $3,120
25Aug88-3Haw a1 Ⓣ:4621:1311:39 fm 4¾ 119 35½ 33 35 47¾ Torres F C 1ⒻAw19000 — — DremLeder,RusticCedr,Sndi'sDlight 7
4Aug88-8Haw 6f :222 :45 1:102ft *8-5 122 21½ 22½ 21½ 31¼ Torres F C 1ⒻAw18000 88-13 LdyLbby,Jn'sCommnd,MnshnMshp 6
28Jly88-7Haw 6½f :223 :451 1:17 ft 3½ 122 52¼ 5¾ 21 2nk Torres F C 1ⒻAw17000 88-12 Aflot,MoonshinMishp,PrciousTiffin 7
20Jly88-7Haw 6f :222 :46 1:102ft 5½ 119 75¼ 66¾ 43½ 22¼ Ahrens L 5 ⒻAw18000 86-15 Ails,MoonshineMishp,YoursAnytim 8
8Jly88-7Haw 6f :22 :461 1:122ft 5½ 117 66 65 11 14½ Torres F C 6ⒻAw16000 79-23 MoonshnMshp,RdGrdn,FoxFtGnny 10
30Jun88-5Haw 6½f :224 :464 1:20 ft 6¼ 112 69¾ 78¾ 42½ 31½ Torres F C 7 Ⓕ 22500 71-28 BrodwyKthy,GntlVxn,MonshnMshp 8
11Jun88-4Spt 6f :24 :481 1:14 ft 3 115 611 58 46½ 46½ MrqzCHJr2 ⒻAw20100 73-25 Jin'sCommnd,MissLkeville,UnBelDi 7
27May88-8Spt 6f :24 :474 1:141ft 7 115 511 58½ 55½ 31½ MrqzCHJr3 ⒻAw20100 77-28 UncrtnVoyg,Lo'sLogc,MnshnMshp 6
16May88-9Spt 6f :233 :472 1:134ft 9 115 87¼ 53 3½ 1nk Torres F C8 Ⓕ 16000 81-24 MoonshnMshp,UncrtnVyg,NstyNkk 9
2Dec87-9Haw 6½f 1:183ft 5¾ 116 96¾ 88½ 74½ 55¼ Ahrens L10 Ⓕ 16000 75-24 Big Sparkle, Gender Gap,AFullJet 10
Sep 10 Haw 4f ft :503 b — Aug 16 Haw 4f ft :50 b

Riton — Own.—Franks John — **108**
Ch. f. 3, by Shecky Greene—Ritura, by Ridan
Br.—Axmar Stables (Ky) — 1988 4 0 0 0
Tr.—Catalano Wayne — 1987 3 2 1 0 $14,120
Lifetime 7 2 1 0 $14,120
18Aug88-8Haw 6f :222 :463 1:114ft 24 112 1½ 41 610 615½ RydwskSR3 ⒻAw19000 66-24 Jin'sCommnd,AvieJne,JustSwetnss 6
4Mar88-8OP 6f :214 :453 1:102ft 11 115 2hd 53½ 89¼ 815¼ Day P1 ⒻAw15000 73-22 Fr'sTem,WhitesburgExpress,IceTch 8
31Jan88-10FG 6f :214 :453 1:114ft 7½ 112 74¼ 89¼ 814 821¼ Romero SP 3ⒻThelma 65-20 BreezingTer,Vnit'sSpecil,Srh'sRose 8
8Jan88-8FG 6f :223 :472 1:132gd 7 119 1hd 53 610 614½ Leblanc KP1 ⒻAw9000 63-32 PocketBaby,Srh'sRose,Vnit'sSpecil 8
8Jan88—Tight quarters.
10Dec87-10FG 6f :22 :464 1:134ft *6-5 119 1½ 11 11½ 12 Murray K C4 ⒻAw8200 76-21 Riton, Poleeced, False Glitter 9
4Oct87-4Haw 6f :22 :453 1:133ft *1-2 119 21½ 21 21½ 21 MurrayKC6 ⒻAw13000 72-29 Ailsa, Riton, Navajo Blossom 7
23Sep87-6Haw 6f :221 :454 1:124ft 4½ 119 3½ 12½ 15 18 Murray K C5 ⒻMdn 77-18 Riton, Cinderella Bay, Ackrobast 12
Sep 9 Haw 4f ft :50 b — Sep 2 Haw 4f ft :471 h — Aug 12 Haw 5f ft 1:033 b — Aug 3 Haw 4f ft :473 h

much because she's in good form. She won an allowance race later than the other horses, so she doesn't get a six-pound weight break a 3-year-old gets in September. She should threaten, but that's about all.

FOND WISHES

She finished a good second in her only race in Chicago, a $16,000 claiming event, which means that today she's going up several notches in class. She ran with better while at Churchill Downs, but went off form after being shipped to Canterbury Downs in Minnesota. Maybe she didn't like the strip. There's no way of knowing what class she was meeting at Canterbury because purses are higher at Churchill. Her last race doesn't convince me that she'll get the job done here. She'll threaten, but that's about all. Fond Wishes, incidently, looks like another Futuresque. Check her race on the grass on July 29.

AVIE JANE

Look out. She should go off as one of the betting favorites. She's coming off three solid second-place finishes. She's a runner, and she has heart. She wants to race in the lead and will fight to keep it. Three races back she bled, but hung on. Also, Dan Switzer is better than an average trainer and the teacher helps. None of the horses that beat Avie Jane is in today's race. The turning point for her came on when she bled. The next time out, on August 4, she ran with Lasix. Since then she hasn't had a bad race. Things add up for her to win. She makes this a playable race.

HIGH SCHOOL BAND

She's a horse. Just a horse. Nothing special. She has some speed but tires. She got beat by 10 lengths in her last start, a distance race. A lot of guys don't mind horses coming off a route to a sprint. I do. They lose their speed.

DEAR DUSTY

She came out of New York and California, where she ran against better horses. She's got three things going for her. One, she's the class of the race; she ran in stakes at Hawthorne and Aqueduct. Two, she's a 3-year-old and will be getting a break in the weights. And three, she's coming off grass races, which tends to give a horse a bit more speed. The only problem I see, and it's a big one, is that she's not a sprinter.

MOONSHINE MISHAP

She's a nice filly, consistent, and has won $65,000, which is tops among the horses here. She has good speed and has won six races in her life. She'll probably be the favorite. The only bad thing I see is that she's coming off a mile race. Even though her last race was on the grass, she might not be able to run the quick fractions she'll need. She's a better bet for her next race, whether a route or a sprint.

SEVENTH RACE
Hawthorne
SEPTEMBER 15, 1988

6 FURLONGS. (1.08$\frac{3}{5}$) ALLOWANCE. Purse \$18,000. Fillies and mares. 3-year-olds and upward, non-winners of two races other than maiden or claiming. Weight, 3-year-olds, 116 lbs.; older, 122 lbs. Non-winners of two races since July 25 allowed 3 lbs.; a race, 5 lbs.; a race in 1988, 8 lbs. (Claiming races not considered.)

Value of race \$18,000; value to winner \$10,800; second \$3,600; third \$1,980; fourth \$1,080; fifth \$540. Mutuel pool \$91,436. Perfecta pool \$72,204.

Last Raced	Horse	Eqt.	A.	Wt	PP	St	1/4	1/2	Str	Fin	Jockey	Odds \$1
18Aug88 ^{8}Haw^{2}	Avie Jane		4	114	4	3	2^{hd}	5^{hd}	2^{hd}	1^{nk}	Silva C H	6.00
25Aug88 ^{3}Haw^{4}	Moonshine Mishap	b	4	117	7	5	5^{1}	3^{hd}	1^{1}	2^{4}	Torres F C	1.50
11Aug88 ^{8}Haw^{4}	High School Band		3	112	5	6	8	8	5^{1}	$3^{1\frac{1}{2}}$	Baird E T	9.20
1Sep88 ^{9}Haw^{2}	Fond Wishes	b	4	117	3	8	7^{3}	4^{hd}	$3^{1\frac{1}{2}}$	$4^{1\frac{1}{4}}$	Clark K D	6.10
18Aug88 ^{8}Haw^{4}	Silver Caper		3	113	1	7	4^{hd}	$6^{1\frac{1}{2}}$	6^{2}	$5^{\frac{1}{2}}$	Frazier R L	12.60
18Aug88 ^{8}Haw^{3}	Just Sweetness	b	3	113	2	4	$3^{1\frac{1}{2}}$	1^{hd}	$4^{\frac{1}{2}}$	$6^{2\frac{3}{4}}$	Fires E	13.10
5Sep88 ^{5}Haw^{2}	Dear Dusty		3	112	6	1	$6^{1\frac{1}{2}}$	7^{4}	8	$7^{1\frac{1}{2}}$	Diaz J L	2.80
18Aug88 ^{8}Haw^{6}	Riton		3	111	8	2	1^{1}	2^{1}	7^{1}	8	Marquez C H Jr	27.10

OFF AT 4:10. Start good. Won driving. Time, :22$\frac{3}{5}$, :46$\frac{4}{5}$, :59, 1:11$\frac{3}{5}$ Track fast.

\$2 Mutuel Prices:

4-AVIE JANE	14.00	5.20	3.40
7-MOONSHINE MISHAP		3.60	2.60
5-HIGH SCHOOL BAND			4.40

\$2 PERFECTA (4-7) PAID \$38.40.

Ch. f, by Lord Avie—Omaha Jane, by Our Michael. Trainer Switzer Daniel G. Bred by Gibson C E (Ky).

AVIE JANE broke alertly, was allowed to drop back on the turn, rallied outside in the drive with a rush, gained the lead late and prevailed. MOONSHINE MISHAP moved up on the outside on the turn, closed well to gain the lead in early stretch then could not contain the winner. HIGH SCHOOL BAND outsprinted for a half, improved her position but was no threat to the top two. FOND WISHES rallied five wide entering the stretch then could not sustain her effort. DEAR DUSTY did not menace. RITON was used fighting for the lead.

Owners— 1, Sugar Hill Farm; 2, Frank Jerome; 3, King Farms; 4, R L Reineman Stable Inc; 5, Zimmerman Mary; 6, Canonie Marialyce; 7, Dykema C C; 8, Franks John.

Trainers— 1, Switzer Daniel G; 2, Twardy James E; 3, Hoffman Kenneth E; 4, Springer Frank R; 5, Levitch James M; 6, Hoffman Kenneth E; 7, Yanez Moses R; 8, Catalano Wayne.

Overweight: High School Band 1 pound; Dear Dusty 4; Riton 3.

RITON

She's from a good stable and that's all. Her record is so poor it seems as if trainer Wayne Catalano stuck her in the race just to fill it for the racing secretary.

I've got the race between Avie Jane and Moonshine Mishap. It's tough to split them but I give the edge to Avie Jane because I think she has tremendous courage. In her last race, she went head

2nd Hawthorne

6 FURLONGS (HAWTHORNE; START, FINISH)

6 FURLONGS. (1.08⅕) MAIDEN. CLAIMING. Purse $5,000. 3 and 4-year-olds. Weight, 3-year-olds, 115 lbs.; 4-year-olds, 121 lbs. Claiming price $7,500.

Native Basket

Own.—Watson Jim **115**

Dk. b. or br. g. 3, by Bask—Miz Sassy Brown, by Bold Native
Br.—Watson Jim (Mo) 1988 4 M 0 1 $892
Tr.—Schiffner Frank J **$7,500** 1987 0 M 0 0
Lifetime 4 0 0 1 $892

13Sep88-4Haw	6f	:22^4 :47^3 1:14^{1}ft	62	116	4^3	44½	31½	31¼	Holland M A 6	M7500	69-21	GrssFlyingGren,Rvin'Dvin,NtivBskt	8
22Aug88-2Haw	6½f	:23^1 :47 1:20^{4}ft	11	114	5^6	5^9	71^2	720¼	Fires E 3	M7500	49-25	Misty Castle, Learam,TwoNoTrump	8
11Aug88-2Haw	6½f	:23 :46^2 1:19^{3}gd	7	115	84¾	6^6	61^2	516¾	Fires E 6	M7500	58-20	Bet YourFull,Learam,FabulousCall	12
1Aug88-4Haw	6½f	:22^3 :46 1:18^{2}ft	6¼	114	2½	3^3	51^2	52^1	Valenzuela PA 3	M7500	60-20	Forli Joy, Misty Castle, It's Bill	11

Jly 27 Haw 4f ft :50^4 b

New Paragon

Own. Bulicek Helen **115**

B. g. 3, by Ole Foreman—Bank Audit, by Go to the Bank
Br.—Bulicek Dick W (Ill) 1988 2 M 0 0
Tr.—Lamar Ann M **$7,500** 1987 0 M 0 0
Lifetime 2 0 0 0

14Sep88-3Haw	6f	:22^2 :46^1 1:12^{3}ft	149	116	33½	78¼	92^3	72^8	Meza N 1	[S]M10000	50-19	Blinding, Amazing Zip, Play the J.	12
24Aug88-6Haw	6f	:22^3 :47^4 1:14^{1}ft	17	115	101^2	91^4	92^3	928½	Meza N 6	[S]M10000	41-27	StoneHrborBert,GoodAngle,Bidmr	12

Aug 12 Haw 6f ft 1:20 b

Saginaw Slew

Own.—Sommer L & Houghton R **110^5**

Dk. b. or br. g. 3, by Slewacide—Handy Kandy, by Hurricane Tim
Br.—Dixon Ernest E (Okla) 1988 8 M 0 1 $770
Tr.—Houghton Roy **$7,500** 1987 2 M 0 0
Lifetime 10 0 0 1 $770

7Jun88-4Spt	6½f	:23^2 :47^3 1:21^{1}ft	18	113	55¼	4^6	6^9	61^9	Meier R 4	M7500	52-27	TexsWhistl,FlowingSwift,TuttyM.	10
27May88-4Spt	6f	:24^1 :49 1:16^{1}ft	44	115	75¾	54¾	5^4	34½	Sayler B 3	M7500	64-28	HezaFreezen,SafriLife,SginwSlew	10
16May88-2Spt	6½f	:22^4 :47^3 1:21^{2}ft	27	115	63¼	64¾	78¾	610½	Sayler B 10	M10000	59-24	CrfrPrnc,UnonofNtons,Sgt.TomNx	10
26Apr88-2Spt	6½f	:22^2 :47^2 1:21^{4}ft	57	113	101^5	91^0	69¾	58¾	Sayler B 1	M7500	59-23	BrynL.,TwoNoTrump,WineAndChs	10
26Apr88—Rough trip.													
5Apr88-1Spt	1	:49^4 1:16^1 1:43^{4}ft	60	113	—	—	—	—	Sayler B^9	M7500	— —	SunnyZr,SpringtothTop,WnforTgr	10
5Apr88—Bolted													
25Mar88-4Spt	6½f	:24 :48^1 1:21^{4}ft	94	113	66¼	78¼	71^5	813¾	Melancon KC^3	M10000	54-29	AbNchols,FunnySdUp,TorunTorun	10
14Mar88-4Spt	6f	:24^3 :48^2 1:16 ft	60	116	91^3	89½	91^3	815¼	Sayler B^6	M7500	54-28	‡JohnHermn,TrueRuler,LstBreker	10
3Mar88-5Spt	6f	:24 :49 1:15^{2}ft	19	113	2^{hd}	43¼	101^7	1025¼	Meier R 3	M10000	48-26	Hrry'sDrem,JohnHrmn,GoGorgiGo	10
14Oct87-4Haw	6f	:22^2 :46^4 1:13^{4}ft	33	119	5^2	66¾	101^5	1118¼	Rashall R D 8	M15000	54-25	FrstLongPnts,FdorFbl,FlshCnnctn	12
30Sep87-4Haw	6f	:22^1 :47^1 1:14^{4}ft	29	119	11½	2½	61^2	923¼	Meier R 4	M15000	44-30	FstBrn,FrstLongPnts,HotRockTnt	11
30Sep87—Bore out.													

The Schroeder Boys

Own.—Quarto James&MoebusFrank **115**

B. g. 3, by Giboulee—Princess Abla, by Nodouble
Br.—Manganaro Stable (Ky) 1988 8 M 0 2 $2,183
Tr.—Prochazka James G **$7,500** 1987 6 M 1 0 $3,080
Lifetime 14 0 1 2 $5,263

14Sep88-5Haw	1^{70}	:48^2 1:14^2 1:45^{3}ft	2½	115	3^2	31½	3^6	49½	Pena R R 8	M7500	64-19	Switch Flights, Galaximo, It's Bill	8
14Sep88—Raced outside													
2Sep88-4Haw	1^{70}	:47^1 1:13^1 1:45^{1}ft	14	115	2½	2^{hd}	21½	36¼	Pena R R 3	M7500	70-18	CmmrclT.V.,TndrOffr,ThSchrdrBys	8
22Aug88-4Haw	6½f	:23 :46^4 1:20^{4}ft	25	114	7^8	71^2	51^0	310½‡	Pena R R 9	M7500	58-25	BusyBsk,Wnnr'sStr,ThSchrodrBoys	9
‡22Aug88—Dead heat													
6Jly88-2Haw	1^{70}	:48^1 1:14^2 1:45^{3}ft	15	114	91^0	82^1	82^6	832½	Frazier R L^7	M7500	41-25	OnDisply,CommercilT.V.,DinnrAtS	11
27Jun88-2Haw	6f	:22^3 :47 1:14 ft	47	113	111^5	112^0	91^1	92^0	Frazier R L^{10}	M16000	51-31	BleederBiley,MuchTooCool,RidUp	11
29Mar88-1Spt	1	:48^4 1:14^2 1:40^{3}sy	18	113	81^2	71^5	71^9	521¾	Melancon K C^6	Mdn	55-27	Mrin'sLuck,DustyAppl,Dvil'sNitOut	8
12Mar88-6Spt	1	:50^2 1:15^1 1:43^{4}ft	12	113	4^6	5^7	58¼	58¾	Melancon KC^1	M20000	52-27	TImelessGeorg,EstOnElm,Qudmtic	8
12Mar88—Awarded fourth purse money													
26Feb88-4Spt	6f	:24^3 :48^4 1:15 ft	16	122	91^5	91^2	102^1	1025¼	Meier R^2	Mdn	50-28	Homebuyer,I.B.Confused,SuddnM.	10
9Dec87-2Aqu	1 1/16 [T]	:48^4 1:14^2 1:48^{2}ft	10	114	76½	85¼	86½	77	Venezia M 8	M30000	60-17	Askherout,RiseTheHet,ReviwRdrs	12
18Nov87-4Aqu	1	:46^2 1:12^1 1:38^{3}ft	7½	114	7^6	85¼	84½	75¼	Venezia M^2	M30000	67-16	Tootzew,DimondAnchor,RviwRdrs	13

Aug 13 Haw 5f ft 1:02^3 b **Aug 5 Haw 5f ft 1:03 b**

Winner's Star
Own.—Schuyler Jack & Mckay Dale **110^5**
B. g. 3, by Planetarium—Miss Cactus, by Sun David
Br.—Schuyler Stables (S.D.) **1988 9 M 1 3 $3,593**
Tr.—McKay Dale **$7,500** **1987 0 M 0 0**
Lifetime 9 0 1 3 $3,593

30Aug88-4Haw	6f	:22^4	:47	1:13^{2}ft	6	115	3^2	4^2	4^5	5^{6½}	Douglas R R 3	M7500	67-19	Brilliant Princ, SunGreeter,Learam	9
22Aug88-4Haw	6½f	:23	:46^4	1:20^{4}ft	5¼	114	4^{5½}	3^6	3^6	2^7	Douglas R R 7	M7500	62-25	BusyBsk,Wnnr'sStr,ThSchrodrBoys	9
8Aug88-4Haw	6½f	:22^4	:46^1	1:20^{4}ft	18	115	7^{1¾}	3^2	2^{½}	3^{3¼}	Douglas R R 2	M7500	66-23	BronzSbtg,CmmrclT.V.,Wnnr'sStr	11
2Aug88-2Haw	6½f	:22^2	:45^2	1:18^{4}ft	44	115	6^4	4^7	3^9	4^{8¾}	Douglas R R 5	M7500	70-20	Foxy Model, Ride Up, Learam	12
19Jly88-4Haw	6½f	:22^4	:46^1	1:18^{2}ft	16	114	3^3	3^{5½}	3^{13}	3^{26½}	Douglas R R 3	M7500	54-23	FiveStar'sPece,RideUp,Winner'sStr	9
11Jly88-4Haw	6f	:22^3	:47	1:13^{3}ft	12	114	4^{1¾}	6^{8½}	4^{8½}	3^{10¼}	Razo E Jr 1	M7500	63-23	Rep'sLst,BetYourFull,Winner'sStr	12
15Jun88-2Spt	6½f	:23^2	:47^3	1:22^{1}ft	10	114	5^6	5^{11}	7^{11}	5^{14¼}	Razo E Jr 9	M10000	52-31	IcyDmond,MuchTooCool,BtYourFll	9
15Jun88—Bled															
7Jun88-2Spt	6½f	:23^3	:48^2	1:22^{2}ft	8	115	1^1	1^1	1^{hd}	6^{4¾}	Sayler B 6	M7500	60-27	OurRoylNtv,Dnsrd'Or,UnonofNtons	9
19May88-2Spt	6½f	:23^2	:48^4	1:22^{3}ft	3¼	115	5^7	5^3	3^{4½}	5^{10½}	Sayler B 5	M7500	53-31	Sllvntobsly,DsgndEnrgy,WlcmGst	10

Sep 22 Haw 5f ft 1:03^2 b **Sep 16 Haw 3f ft :38 b** **Sep 11 Haw 3f ft :37 b** **Aug 20 Haw 3f ft :39^3 b**

Roses Best Knight
Own.—Crandall Cynthia **121**
Ch. c. 4, by Best of It—Rose Empress, by Bravest Roman
Br.—Laurell Sally S (Fla) **1988 1 M 1 0 $780**
Tr.—Wade Deanna **$7,500** **1986 3 M 0 1 $1,634**
Lifetime 4 0 1 1 $2,414

27Aug88-4EIP	5½f	:22^3	:46^2	1:05^{3}ft	4	122	2^{hd}	1^{hd}	2^1	2^{2½}	Wade J T 3	M7500	89-08	VigorofGin,RosesBstKnight,BitbyB	9
11Aug86-1Haw	5½f	:22^3	:46^4	1:05^{2}ft	*6-5	116	4^3	5^4	5^8	7^{14}	Richard D^6	M22000	71-21	Two Bagger, GimmeLuck,Palcinto	10
30Jly86-4Haw	5f	:22^4	:47^1	:59^{3}ft	8¾	119	2^{hd}	2^{hd}	3^1	3^5	Moran M T^6	Mdn	89-13	ExistngDsr,SomBdt,RossBstKnght	11
16Jly86-1Haw	5f	:21^4	:46^1	:58^{2}ft	16	119	6^{5¾}	6^{5¼}	5^{5½}	4^{8¼}	Bullard B A^6	Mdn	92-12	RisedDncin',ExistingDesir,CbinDncr	9

Sep 15 Haw 3f ft :39 b **Sep 13 Haw 3f ft :39 b**

Put to Sea
Own.—Loeber M **115**
Dk. b. or br. g. 3, by Golden Act—Sea of Pleasure, by What a Pleasure
Br.—North Ridge Farm (Ky) **1988 8 M 3 2 $4,995**
Tr.—Miller Danny **$7,500** **1987 2 M 0 0 $714**
Lifetime 10 0 3 2 $5,709

2Sep88-4Haw	1^{70}	:47^1	1:13^1	1:45^{1}ft	4½	115	5^{4½}	6^{7½}	6^8	6^{9¾}	Silva C H 8	M7500	66-18	CmmrclT.V.,TndrOffr,ThSchrdrBys	8
17Aug88-4Haw	1^{70}	:48^1	1:14	1:45^{3}ft	3¼	114	2^{½}	3^1	3^{11}	3^{17}	Silva C H 4	M7500	57-24	Evaluator,CommercilT.V.,PuttoSe	12
8Aug88-4Haw	6½f	:22^4	:46^1	1:20^{4}ft	3½	115	10^6	9^{9¼}	7^{8½}	4^{5¾}	Silva C H 8	M7500	63-23	BronzSbtg,CmmrclT.V.,Wnnr'sStr	11
19Jly88-2Haw	6½f	:23	:47	1:21 ft	*4-5	114	6^{6½}	6^{7¾}	4^5	2^{hd}	Silva C H 6	M7500	68-23	Hat Tabbid,PuttoSea,TwoNoTrump	9
30Jun88-2Haw	6½f	:22^4	:47^3	1:22^{2}ft	*9-5	112	9^{11}	8^{11}	5^{4¼}	2^{1¾}	Silva C H 1	M7500	59-28	Danseurd'Or,PuttoSea,NativeTutsi	10
10May88-4Spt	6f	:23^4	:47^4	1:14^{1}ft	*2	113	9^{8¼}	6^8	5^{6¼}	3^{1¼}	Meier R 7	M7500	78-21	HotRockTonite,SafariLife,PuttoSe	9
21Apr88-2Spt	6½f	:23	:47^4	1:21^{1}ft	11	113	10^{11}	10^6	4^{1¾}	2^3	Silva C H 10	M10000	68-22	AmilliumWalk,PuttoSea,LstBreker	10
22Mar88-6Spt	6½f	:23^4	:48^2	1:21^{3}ft	4¾	113	6^5	4^3	4^{6¼}	4^{7¼}	Silva C H 6	M7500	62-24	Baracan, MysteryofLife,SafariLife	10
6Dec87-2Haw	6½f	:23^1	:47^1	1:20^{2}gd	4½	116	10^{7½}	9^{6¼}	4^{8¼}	4^{2¾}	Meier R^9	M13500	68-19	J.Gunn,Tom'sStormyHart,SonaCut	11
12Nov87-2Haw	6f	:22	:46^4	1:13^{4}ft	22	117	12^{20}	10^{12}	7^{8¾}	4^{8¼}	Meier R^6	M13500	64-25	Bold Grise, Dr. Propp, Learam	12
12Nov87—Steadied early.															

Sep 21 Haw 4f ft :51^2 b

Two No Trump
Own.—Romanoff N & Weiss A **115**
Ch. g. 3, by Aloma's Ruler—Two Bidders, by Bold Bidder
Br.—Conway J & Scherr N (Ky) **1988 12 M 2 3 $4,373**
Tr.—Tomillo Thomas F **$7,500** **1987 0 M 0 0**
Lifetime 12 0 2 3 $4,373

13Sep88-2Haw	6f	:22^4	:47	1:13 ft	12	116	4^{¾}	4^2	8^{15}	8^{21½}	Rydowski S R 8	M7500	54-21	RoylPumpkin,SunGretr,PurplSilks	10
13Sep88—Fractious.															
30Aug88-2Haw	6f	:22^1	:46	1:12^{4}ft	5½	115	7^{4¼}	7^{12}	8^{15}	8^{18½}	Rydowski S R 7	M7500	58-19	WllerWllBnger,VnNuys,Revin'Dvin	10
22Aug88-2Haw	6½f	:23^1	:47	1:20^{4}ft	4¾	114	3^2	2^{½}	2^{hd}	3^{6½}	Rydowski S R 5	M7500	62-25	Mist; Castle, Learam,TwoNoTrump	8
8Aug88-4Haw	6½f	:22^4	:46^1	1:20^{4}ft	9½	115	8^{3¾}	4^2	5^{3½}	6^{6½}	Rydowski S R 10	M7500	62-23	BronzSbtg,CmmrclT.V.,Wnnr'sStr	11
19Jly88-2Haw	6½f	:23	:47	1:21 ft	2½	114	3^{1½}	2^{½}	1^{1½}	3^{hd}	Rydowski S R 3	M7500	68-23	Hat Tabbid,PuttoSea,TwoNoTrump	9
27Jun88-4Haw	6½f	:23^2	:48^1	1:21^{2}ft	3½	113	1^{hd}	1^1	1^{1½}	2^{1½}	Rydowski S R 9	M7500	64-31	Tuffy M., Two No Trump, Ramzoe	11
16May88-2Spt	6½f	:22^4	:47^3	1:21^{2}ft	4½	113	1^{hd}	1^{hd}	3^{3½}	5^{9½}	Rydowski S R 1	M10000	60-24	CrfrPrnc,UnonofNtons,Sgt.TomNx	10
26Apr88-2Spt	6½f	:22^2	:47^2	1:21^{4}ft	6¾	113	3^3	2^{1½}	2^{hd}	2^{½}	Rydowski S R 10	M7500	67-23	BrynL.,TwoNoTrump,WineAndChs	10
26Apr88—Bore out, lugged.															
5Apr88-1Spt	1	:49^4	1:16^1	1:43^{4}ft	5	113	3^1	1^{hd}	5^6	8^{13¼}	Rydowski S R 4	M7500	48-31	SunnyZr,SpringtothTop,WnforTgr	10
25Mar88-4Spt	6½f	:24	:48^1	1:21^{4}ft	11	113	4^{3½}	4^3	6^{13}	4^{8¼}	Rydowski S R 2	M10000	60-29	AbNchols,FunnySdUp,TorunTorun	10

Barrickman's — Dk. b. or br. g. 4, by Whitesburg—Commie, by T V Commercial
Own.—Tonka Wombli Fm — **121** — Br.—Jonmac Farm (Ky) — Tr.—Kerns Fred — $7,500
1988 8 M 1 1 $1,151
1987 4 M 1 0 $880
Lifetime 12 0 2 1 $2,031

24Aug88-2EIP	1	:46^{1}	1:11^{4}	1:38^{1}ft	4¼	122	8^{11}	6^{7}	4^{4½}	5^{9}	Troilo W D 9	M5000	75-09	Winnin'Willim,BstofGld,Hlly'sPrid	10
9Aug88-10EIP	7f	:23^{4}	:47^{2}	1:24^{3}ft	5¾	122	11^{6½}	9^{5¼}	6^{5¼}	6^{10½}	Troilo W D 1	3500	79-07	AntiqueAttck,CptinHmmer,IslsByI	12
27Jly88-1EIP	1⅛	:47	1:12^{2}	1:51^{3}ft	5	118	5^{6}	5^{3}	6^{4½}	6^{10¼}	Troilo W D 6	3500	72-12	Fipstrt,RitchieExpress,GimmeSpc	10
21Jly88-3EIP	1	:47	1:12^{2}	1:40 m	6¾	119	5^{6}	4^{2½}	3^{3}	3^{¾}	Troilo W D 6	3500	74-24	MSpclPtrck,MrchntBnkr,Brrckmn's	9
13Jly88-1EIP	1	:48	1:13	1:41 m	48	122	5^{3¼}	5^{2½}	3^{2}	2^{1}	Troilo W D 2	3500	69-25	Lindale,Barrickmn's,BodciousSon	12
3Jly88-4EIP	6f	:22^{4}	:46^{2}	1:12^{2}ft	31	122	11^{14}	7^{15}	5^{9½}	5^{6½}	Humphrey M 4	M3500	76-10	JonthnForbs,KntckyCoppr,TmTdr	11
5Jun88-2CD	6½f	:23^{1}	:46^{4}	1:19^{1}ft	110	112	4^{3}	8^{7¾}	12^{13}	12^{13½}	Troilo W D 1	4000	70-17	VorheesFlight,Requ,IrishExubernc	12
11May88-1CD	6½f	:23	:46^{4}	1:19 ft	98	121	9^{5¾}	9^{11}	10^{15}	12^{20¼}	Murray K C 12	M10000	65-20	StrghtnOt,Nvonod'sLst,MyLstDllr	12
24Oct87-6RD	6f	:22^{4}	:46^{2}	1:12^{4}ft	62	116	4^{5}	4^{6}	9^{17}	10^{19¼}	Bomer T C 10	7500	60-23	JckTheSilor,RogerAlfrd,FthrSoup	10
15Oct87-1RD	170	:48^{1}	1:15	1:47 ft	4	118	8^{13}	10^{11}	12^{28}	12^{38¾}	Bomer T C 8	M7500	26-26	ProgrmDrctor,Bob'sI.G.A.,Illmntn	12

Purple Silks — Dk. b. or br. g. 3, by You E X—Pink Purple, by Funny Fellow
Own.—Hondo Ranch — **115** — Br.—Hondo Ranch (Ill) — Tr.—Kirby Frank J — $7,500
1988 4 M 0 1 $743
1987 0 M 0 0
Lifetime 4 0 0 1 $743

13Sep88-2Haw	6f	:22^{4}	:47	1:13 ft	77	116	5^{2¼}	5^{2½}	3^{4½}	3^{7½}	Sayler B 9	M7500	68-21	RoylPumpkin,SunGretr,PurplSilks	10
17Aug88-4Haw	170	:48^{1}	1:14	1:45^{3}ft	78	114	1^{½}	4^{3½}	4^{19}	5^{33}	Ward W A 1	M7500	41-24	Evaluator,CommercilT.V.,PuttoSe	12
11Aug88-2Haw	6½f	:23	:46^{2}	1:19^{3}gd	40	115	10^{7¾}	10^{13}	8^{15}	7^{19¼}	Sayler B 5	M7500	56-20	Bet YourFull,Learam,FabulousCall	12
30Jun88-2Haw	6½f	:22^{4}	:47^{3}	1:22^{2}ft	11e	113	6^{8}	9^{13}	10^{9½}	8^{11¼}	Sellers S J 7	M7500	50-28	Danseurd'Or,PuttoSea,NativeTutsi	10

Aug 10 Haw 3f gd :40 b   Aug 8 Haw 5f ft 1:05^{2} b   Aug 1 Haw 5f ft 1:03^{2} b

and head with Jin's Command before losing out. She's ready to win.

The second example is a dog race, run September 27, for maiden claimers. At this stage of the game, breeding means nothing. These horses haven't shown any promise, so the trainers and owners of these bums are telling the world that they can buy any of them for $7,500.

> 6 FURLONGS. MAIDEN. CLAIMING. Purse $5,000. 3 and 4-year-olds. weight, 3-year-olds, 115 lbs.; 4-year-olds, 121 lbs. Claiming price $7,500.

NATIVE BASKET

He was beaten by 1½ lengths in his last start, his best race yet. His other starts were awful to godawful. I give him a shot, but a small one. His last race might have been a fluke. I like his trainer, Frank Schiffner. He tries hard but he can't carry the horse. Two races ago Native Basket was beaten by 20 lengths. That means he ran six and a half furlongs in 1:24 ⁴/₅, which is just about what I could do it in if I didn't have so many ailments.

NEW PARAGON

Every dog has his day, but it won't be New Paragon's today. I hope trainer Ann Lamar doesn't die of despair. She deserves better horses.

SAGINAW SLEW

He hasn't raced in almost four months. He had a few good races at Sportsman's, but it's doubtful he can threaten after such a long layoff. His form is so poor he reminds me of some of the horses at Balmoral. I hear some guy tossed some dog biscuits on the track at Balmoral and the horses thought it was feeding time.

THE SCHROEDER BOYS

He's by Giboulee out of Princess Abla, who is by Nodouble. Great bloodlines. He cost $21,000 as a yearling, according to the *American Racing Manual*. Now the owner is willing to dump him for $7,500. I don't think he's worth even that much. What's worse, he's running today at six furlongs and he has shown that he can't handle a sprint.

WINNER'S STAR

Maybe he's about ready to win. He'll have to go down to the $5,000 maiden-claiming level to find weaker company. In his most recent races, he has been doing something, threatening and then falling back. He's also carrying five pounds fewer than he did in his last start because an apprentice will be up. He has been off a month after a heavy August schedule. That may hurt him. But I still think he's the best of a rotten group.

ROSES BEST KNIGHT

In his first race after a two-year layoff, he finished second in a five and a half furlong sprint at Ellis Park. He has speed, but I don't think he has any stamina. The horse that beat him last time out, Vigor of Gin, was pulling away. Roses Best Knight had the same problem in the other races. Still, he has got a shot and may go off as the betting favorite.

PUT TO SEA

Here's another blue blood that's on the block for $7,500. He's back at the right distance, but that may not help him. I guess the trainer figured his closer needs a longer race, so he ran him twice at a mile and 70 yards. He showed nothing both times. Put to Sea still may develop into a decent horse, but the fact that he's coming off a route probably will hurt this time.

TWO NO TRUMP

He has some speed but he has developed some problems. Only a horse that's hurting will fall back 13 lengths just like that in a sprint.

BARRICKMAN'S

The only times he was close were when he ran on an off track. This is a 4-year-old who has won only $2,031.

PURPLE SILKS

He turned in a decent performance after bombing in a route. Your guess is as good as mine as to what he'll do today.

This is a classic example of an unplayable race. I'll go with Winner's Star by default. I don't think any of the others will finish second.

SECOND RACE
Hawthorne
SEPTEMBER 27, 1988

6 FURLONGS. (1.08⅘) MAIDEN. CLAIMING. Purse $5,000. 3 and 4-year-olds. Weight, 3-year-olds, 115 lbs.; 4-year-olds, 121 lbs. Claiming price $7,500.

Value of race $5,000; value to winner $3,000; second $1,000; third $550, fourth $300; fifth $150. Mutuel pool $53,988. Perfecta pool $47,145.

Last Raced	Horse	Eqt.	A.	Wt	PP	St	¼	½	Str	Fin	Jockey	Cl'g Pr	Odds $1
30Aug88 ^{4}Haw^5	Winner's Star	b	3	110	5	10	7^1	$5^{1\frac{1}{2}}$	$1^{\frac{1}{2}}$	1^3	Aguilar R^5	7500	7.80
24Aug88 ^{2}EIP^5	Barrickman's	b	4	121	9	8	10	$6^{1\frac{1}{2}}$	2^1	$2^{\frac{3}{4}}$	Clark K D	7500	17.30
13Sep88 ^{2}Haw^3	Purple Silks	b	3	115	10	2	2^3	2^3	$3^{2\frac{1}{2}}$	$3^{\frac{1}{2}}$	Sayler B	7500	14.40
7Jun88 ^{4}Spt^6	Saginaw Slew	b	3	115	3	4	$4^{\frac{1}{2}}$	4^{hd}	5^1	$4^{1\frac{1}{2}}$	King E L Jr†	7500	34.60
14Sep88 ^{5}Haw^4	The Schroeder Boys	b	3	115	4	9	9^{hd}	9^{hd}	$7^{1\frac{1}{2}}$	$5^{1\frac{1}{2}}$	Frazier R L	7500	2.30
27Aug88 ^{4}EIP^2	Roses Best Knight	b	4	121	6	3	1^{hd}	1^{hd}	$4^{1\frac{1}{2}}$	6^{hd}	Wojtas D A	7500	3.20
13Sep88 ^{4}Haw^3	Native Basket	b	3	115	1	5	$5^{2\frac{1}{2}}$	7^3	8^3	$7^{1\frac{1}{2}}$	Holland M A	7500	8.40
13Sep88 ^{2}Haw^8	Two No Trump	b	3	115	8	6	3^{hd}	$3^{1\frac{1}{2}}$	$6^{\frac{1}{2}}$	8^1	Rydowski S R	7500	10.30
2Sep88 ^{4}Haw^6	Put to Sea	b	3	115	7	1	6^{hd}	8^{hd}	9^{10}	$9^{11\frac{1}{2}}$	Silva C H	7500	3.90
14Sep88 ^{3}Haw^7	New Paragon	b	3	115	2	7	$8^{1\frac{1}{2}}$	10	10	10	Meza N	7500	106.10

OFF AT 1:56. Start good. Won driving. Time, :22⅖, :46⅗, :59⅗, 1:12⅗ Track fast.

$2 Mutuel Prices:

5-WINNER'S STAR	17.60	5.20	4.80
9-BARRICKMAN'S		14.40	8.20
10-PURPLE SILKS			8.80

$2 PERFECTA (5-9) PAID $219.00.

B. g, by Planetarium—Miss Cactus, by Sun David. Trainer McKay Dale. Bred by Schuyler Stables (S.D.).

WINNER'S STAR lacked speed in the early going, rallied outside on the turn, gained the lead in midstretch then increased his margin under a drive. BARRICKMAN'S rallied five wide on the turn, came on for the place but could not reach the winner. PURPLE SILKS fought for the early lead with ROSES BEST KNIGHT while outside that one for a half then weakened in the final furlong. SAGINAW SLEW went in an even effort. THE SCHROEDER BOYS did not menace. ROSES BEST KNIGHT gave way in the drive. TWO NO TRUMP flashed brief speed. PUT TO SEA was never prominent.

Owners— 1, Schuyler Jack & Mckay Dale; 2, Lauer Penny & Hemminger Martha; 3, Hondo Ranch; 4, Sommer L & Houghton R; 5, Quarto James & Moebus Frank; 6, Crandall Cynthia; 7, Watson Jim; 8, Romanoff N & Weiss A; 9, Loeber M; 10, Bulicek Helen.

Trainers— 1, McKay Dale; 2, Lauer Michael; 3, Kirby Frank J; 4, Houghton Roy; 5, Prochazka James G; 6, Bass Tomi; 7, Schiffner Frank J; 8, Tomillo Thomas F; 9, Miller Danny; 10, Lamar Ann M.

† **Apprentice allowance waived:** Saginaw Slew 5 pounds.

Now that you know how to handicap a race, don't be like the sucker who gets touted off his horse. Racetrackers tell the story of the guy going up to buy a bag of popcorn but coming back with peanuts instead.

"I thought you wanted popcorn," his friend says.

"I did. But I met somebody on the way and he said the peanuts were better."

Stick with the popcorn.

Nine

You Lose Some, and Then Some More

I'm always selling the *Sun-Times*. At the track, if a guy stops me and says he reads the column, I stand and talk with him so the paper and our readers have good relations. If I see a guy reading the *Tribune*, I ask him why.

"Not for winners," I say. "I pick more than the *Tribune*. Buy both papers and you'll see."

I'm never too busy to say hello or shake a hand. I'd even kiss babies but you don't see many of them at the track. Once a kid around 10 years old

came up to me and said, "Mr. Feldman, I read
your column every time. Look, I've got your selections in my pocket." We talked about racing
and then I pulled out a dollar, autographed it and
gave it to him. I do that a lot. I don't always give
away a buck. It's usually a quarter. Kids have fa-
thers and mothers who read.

If everybody on the newspaper tried to sell papers as I do, we'd pick up a lot on the *Trib*. But,
no. Most of them just like to bitch, saying how
the company's screwing them left and right, up
and down. If they saw an empty *Sun-Times* street
box next to a box stuffed with *Tribs*, do you think
any of them would report it to the circulation office? Hell, no.

I can drive down Ontario any goddam day and
see three guys selling the *Tribune* and no *Sun-
Times* guy. I reported it—three, four times—but
nothing happened. I once picked up a circulation
boss at eight o'clock in the morning and drove
him to this one corner where we were getting the
crap beat out of us. Some gal was selling *Tribs*
one after another. No *Sun-Times* guy.

"I used to sell papers," I told our circulation
guy. "I know a hot corner when I see one."

"I'll take care of it tomorrow," he said.

Next day I passed the same corner and nobody
was hawking the *Sun-Times*. I called in.

"Hey, where's our guy?"

"I told him to go across the street in front of
the vegetable store and sell it from there."

"Across the street? The cars don't stop there, for chrissake."

He was just saying he had a guy at the vegetable store. He really didn't. He was humoring me, blowing me off. Screw him. You know what I did? I just stopped getting subscriptions to the paper. We had this subscription drive and I had sold four at the track. Here I was pressuring people to buy the paper and the circulation guy was laughing off a good corner.

Maybe I was depressed. Maybe that's why I decided to call trainer Mack Miller. He would understand. Besides, I had a column to write and he would make a good subject. By mid-year 1987, Miller had three possible Eclipse Award winners—Java Gold, the 3-year-old colt who had won the Travers, Whitney and Metropolitan; grass-running Dance Of Life, and Crusader Sword, a 2-year-old. When late fall rolled around, Java Gold was in retirement after injuring his foot. Dance Of Life was sold and syndicated after fracturing an ankle. And Crusader Sword's career was on hold after popping a knee. It would cheer me up to talk to somebody whose luck was worse than mine.

I had five stiffs in my barn. No, that was wrong. Two of them weren't good enough to be called stiffs. They were eating machines. Worse, they were *my* eating machines. Windy City Son hadn't won a race in more than a year and Lusciously was a 3-year-old maiden filly who was past her prime. They were costing me $40 a day—apiece. Feed, vet care, shoeing, vanning, etc. I also had a 2-year-old colt, Leading BDH, on a farm in South Carolina. That was another $40 a day.

Windy City Son, Lusciously and Leading BDH all were by Old Frankfort, who was standing (and waiting) in stud on a farm in Barrington. That was another $15 a day. Breeding was bleeding me dry. Five years times $40 for Windy City Son came to $73,000. Three years times $40 for Lusciously was $45,800. Leading BDH: $29,200. And Old Frankfort, now nine years on the farm, $50,000. That came to about $200,000. All of that was my own money. Getting into breeding was the biggest mistake of my life.

I got Mack Miller on the phone and we talked about the Eclipse Awards and the horses he was getting ready for the 1988 season. Then I got around to what I really wanted to talk about: his rotten luck. Woulda, coulda, shoulda. Java Gold woulda been named horse of the year, Dance Of Life coulda won honors as best grass horse, Crusader Sword shoulda been a cinch for top juvenile colt. Here was a guy with three sure champions and they all konk out within a two-month period. If anybody had a right to feel gypped, it was Miller.

"I can't get over it, Mack, can't get over it," I said. "I never heard of a guy losing three top horses just like that. Boom, boom, boom. Never heard of anybody with such bad luck."

"Yeah, me neither," he said. "But, Dave, I really can't complain. Look at all the good luck I had all summer."

———

People are always asking a trainer whether he likes his horse. Some trainers will play the tout and say, "Got a shot. Got a real good shot." People take that as inside information and bet the horse. Actually the horse doesn't have a chance, but the trainer figures anything can happen. If by some miracle the bum wins, the trainer will have his hands out expecting his "commission."

Me? I don't believe in touting my horses. I usually say, "My horse figures, if he fires. But I don't know if he's going to fire."

Catch me on a bad day and I can get pretty nasty. I remember once when a friend of mine asked whether I liked my horse.

I looked at him and said, "What are you going to do? Bet him?"

"Yeah, if you like him," my friend said.

"Where were you this morning at 6:30?"

"In bed. Why?"

"You know where I was? I was at the track, and it was cold and it was raining. I got my feet dirty walking through the mud and shit and everything else and you're asking me if I like my horse. I've got $10,000 invested in him. I've been getting up every morning and going through all hell to get him ready and you've been in bed and you're asking me if I like my horse."

"Forget I asked."

"Yesterday afternoon, were you at the office?"

"Yeah."

"What did you do?"

"I sold 8,000 dresses."

"Well, let me ask you a question. Why didn't you call me and ask if I wanted to get in on it? Like, 'Dave, I got some dresses I bought for $3 and I'm going to sell them for $6. I've got 8,000 of them. I'm going to make $24,000 if the guy buys the dresses. Would you like to get in on it?' You didn't call me, did you? You want to get in on my business but you don't want me to get in on your business. And you're in bed when I'm going through the mud and shit, and you want to know if I like my horse. I've got to figure that out later."

I sprained my left thumb. I've got the pain in my back and it's shooting down my leg. And my chest is killing me, *killing* me. Ever since my quadruple bypass in 1979 I've been hurting like a claiming horse. But I've got to keep running. I'm too old to stand in stud.

"No trainer with a yearling on the farm ever committed suicide," Charlie Whittingham said to me once.

Charlie is in his mid-70s, so is Woody Stephens. Mack Miller is getting up there too. They're all going strong.

Training horses keeps you young.

I'm a great trainer but nobody knows it, just me. My training days are just about over so I know I'll never get a horse like Secretariat. I'll always regret that I never had a real champion. I would have liked to prove to others what I know in my heart—that I'm a helluva trainer.

Not ever being a full-time trainer I never had a stable of 30 or 40 horses. The most I ever trained at one time was 12 and usually I had no more than 6. With a small stable your approach to training is different, more cautious. You can't drill horses as hard as you would like because you can't afford to lose any through injuries. Guys like Ben Jones, Frank Whiteley, Sunny Jim Fitzsimmons, they weren't afraid of really drilling their horses because they had plenty of good runners in the barn or back on the farm.

Allen Jerkens once asked why I didn't run Glass House in a stakes race at Sportsman's.

"A lot of horses get hurt there," I said.

"Yeah, but look at how good the purse is," he said.

"Well, you can say that. You're training for Jack Dreyfus. If your horse breaks down, you might have 20 more. If Glass House breaks down, I have no more."

Arlington Park, summer, 1987—two years after the fire that destroyed the grandstand. The temperature was in the 90s every day. The horses were washing out in the detention barn and horseplayers were washing out in the sweltering tents the track was using as makeshift betting rooms. Handle and attendance were way down but Dick Duchossois never squawked. "Something good always comes out of something bad," he said.

Yeah, that's kind of like me. Always looking on the goddam bright side.

The easiest way to make money is to tout people on horses. It doesn't cost you a dime. Racetrackers tell the joke about the rich guy who meets a tout and asks for some hot horses. The tout gives him a horse in each race. They all lose. The rich guy is out a bundle but he says to the tout, "Let's go out to dinner. We'll get a couple of broads and have a good time." They go out and have a good time. Next day, the tout gives the rich guy nine more horses. They all lose.

"Well, you win some, you lose some," the rich guy says to the tout. "Let's go out again tonight."

"Get away from me," the tout says. "You're bad luck."

The handicapper at the *Trib*, Dave Surico, has better comments. He says, "Come catch me." I say, "One to catch." His comments are livelier.

I hate comments. You can't say anything so I don't try that hard. "Pass." "Forget it." "Slowic." "Never." I don't want to waste my time thinking up a clever comment when a horse isn't worth all that thought. I just condemn him. I'll condemn half the field. Some handicappers play it safe. Say there's 10 horses in the field, 8 of them might get a half-assed boost, like "Belongs with these" or "Takes needed drop," just in case a dog sneaks in to win. When I think a horse is dead meat I say he's dead meat.

Since 1975 I've been president of the Chicago division of the Horsemen's Benevolent and Protective Association. It's the worst nonpaying job in the world. I got them the OK to use Lasix and butazolidin. About four guys said, "Good going." The other 600 didn't say boo. Let something go wrong and they're screaming, "It's that goddam Feldman. He was supposed to take care of it. Let's lynch him!"

———————————

Some years back my wife, Fern, and I went to Europe and we signed up for one of those tours of Rome. Somebody had tipped me to check the itinerary very closely, otherwise we'd be seeing 37 churches a day. What interest would I have in seeing old churches? I don't even like old synagogues. So I picked a tour that had only one church on its list of stops. We saw the church and then spent a lot of time walking around by ourselves. I saw where the pope poped and where the pigeons flocked. Pretty interesting if you were Catholic and liked pigeons. After walking around here and there, I had to go to the washroom something awful. I thought I was going to die. I popped my head into one store after another. "Got a toilet here? Toilet. You know, toilet. TOI-LET.... Aaaaah!" Then I saw this place with a bunch of men inside. It must be a brokerage office, I thought. I ran in there and, what do you know, it was a book joint. "Toilet! Toilet!" I yelled and somebody pointed to the back of the room. Horseplayers, God love them. Their horses have gone down the toilet so often that they know the word in any language. When I returned to the room, it was as if I had walked back in time, back to the 1930s. It was like being in Ruby Raff's again. There were sheets on the wall listing the horses, riders and odds; and they were getting the call of the races from all the tracks. Somebody noticed the big diamond horseshoe ring I was wearing and began shouting. I guess he was saying I was one of them. It was like being home.

I've nominated three horses for the Kentucky Derby. One of them was my own, Ray's Blue Man. He ran on Derby Day at Churchill Downs all right, but it was a year later in a claiming race, the last event of the card. That just goes to show how hard it is to know where your horse belongs.

Ask trainer Harvey Vanier who persuaded him to nominate Fortunate Moment for the 1987 American Derby at Arlington Park.

Ask him who said, "Hey, you can win it. You won't be meeting much."

Ask him who kept hammering and hammering until he finally said OK.

Ask Vanier who was responsible for his getting 10 percent of the $95,000 winner's purse.

When I'm at the barn checking on my horses, I feel like a parent who has put his kids in a day care center that's run by people with tattoos on their arms and whips in their hands. Those are very bad signs. But what can you do? You've got to go to work, so you leave your kids there. Same thing with my horses. There's nobody else to take care of them.

The backstretch has gotten worse over the years. Oh, there are still some wonderful people working who love horses and love racing. But more and more you see a lot of mean people who are working in the barns only because they can't find other jobs. Twenty, 30 years ago, it wasn't like that. I didn't have the trouble then that I do now finding a decent groom. This isn't just me saying this. It's every trainer at every track in every state.

OK, grooming horses isn't the best job in the world. The work isn't white or blue collar; it's no collar. For taking care of three or four horses— including rubbing them down every day and shoveling shit out of stalls—a groom earns about $250 to $300 a week. The salary includes a 12-by-12-foot room above the barn that's comfy enough for one person but pretty cramped if the groom is married and has kids. Stoves aren't allowed in the barn, so a groom and his family, if he has any, eat in the backstretch kitchen. The food isn't that bad, but it's not cheap.

A groom's day starts at five in the morning. He checks on his horses and then brings them water and feed for breakfast. After the horses eat, the groom goes into the stalls and tidies up a bit, picking up and getting rid of any loose manure. Then he puts on bandages, brushes each horse and gets him ready for the trainer. All horses, unless they're really hurting, go to the track every day, either to work or gallop. While the horses are working or galloping, the groom tidies up some more, taking out wet straw and more horse buns and rebedding the stall with fresh straw. When a horse comes back, he removes the bridle, saddle and bandages and takes him outside to give him a bath. He soaps the horse down real good and rinses him off. With a scraper, he removes the excess water before toweling him off. Then the hotwalker walks the horse around for 30 minutes or so. After the horse has been cooled out, the groom rubs in oil or liniment into the muscles and then brushes him, running the bristles through the mane and tail to get out dirt and gunk. Pretty soon the horse looks like patent leather. Around 9:30 or 10:00 the groom fixes lunch, hauling a tub of feed for each horse. When they finish, he washes the tubs and hangs them up. By 10:30 or 11:00 the groom's work for the morning is done. Five hours later, he comes back to prepare dinner and clean out the stall again. Then he kisses the horse goodnight.

When his horse runs, a groom has to do nearly

everything twice: bandaging, saddling, brushing and bathing.

For all that, a groom gets his weekly salary, health insurance (usually from the HBPA), a room and a bonus every time one of his horses wins—or, in the case of stakes horses, every time one of them finishes first, second or third. The amount of the bonus depends on the groom's arrangement with the trainer, but it's usually one percent of the purse money. A groom can make decent money if he's taking care of a stakes horse. If his horse wins $2 million in one year, he gets $20,000, which is more than his salary. But most grooms rub four horses whose combined annual winnings won't come to $20,000. What's one percent of 20 grand? A whopping $200.

It's a rough, dirty life. To be satisfied you have to love being around horses and animals or have an ambition to become a trainer. There aren't too many satisfied people on the backstretch.

Today I could never find anybody like Tom Lloyd and Wendell Griffin, who were the best grooms I ever saw. Lloyd was a Welshman who rubbed horses for kings and queens before coming to America. Griffin worked for Ben and Jimmy Jones and was Iron Liege's groom when the colt, with Bill Hartack riding, won the 1957 Kentucky Derby. That was the Derby in which Bill Shoemaker, aboard Gallant Man, blew the race when he stood up too soon, thinking he had already passed the wire. That allowed Iron Liege to sneak in ahead of Gallant Man.

"My horse would have caught him anyway," Wendell said. He never wanted to admit that Iron Liege got lucky.

Wendell was a genius. He could make anything, from hay racks to protective bandages to a stall webbing. And he could handle any horse. He'd talk to them in his quiet, soothing voice and stroke them in a way that would calm and relax the craziest stallion. Walter Blum, the former jockey, says a groom is just as important as a jockey. To me, Wendell was *more* important that any jock.

Wendell didn't smoke or drink and didn't run around with women. The only vice he had was fighting. But he didn't get into that many brawls because he knew his mother, who was back in Ohio somewhere, would raise hell if she heard about it. He was strong as a horse. A blacksmith told me he once saw Wendell hit a guy so hard that he landed 10 feet away. I was glad Wendell's mother approved of me. Wendell once told me, "My mother said I should never work for anybody but you."

I felt terrible when he quit. It was my fault. We were in our barn at Hawthorne and I said something that ticked him. He dropped the brushes he was using to rub a horse and said, "Do you want me to leave?"

He was stubborn and so was I. "Do whatever you want," I said.

Wendell left. Later, I heard he went back to Ohio. Still later, I learned he finally got married to a woman with three kids.

My back! I miss you, Wendell. So do my horses.

———————

My HBPA board wants to impeach me. They're accusing me of being a dictator, of making decisions without consulting them. Well, they're probably right. We had a meeting scheduled with the horsemen at Balmoral and none of the 10 board members showed up, only me. We had two meetings in court and nobody showed up, only me. I put out a newsletter so everybody knows what's going on but my board would rather stay away and squawk.

———————

Training *good* horses keeps you young.

I can't find any buyers for Windy City Son or Lusciously. I can't even *give* them away.

———————

Once when there was a strike at the *Herald-American*, I took a job as a chart caller for the *Form*. I went to Canfield, Ohio, to work the races at the county fair. I remember seeing this filly win three races in three days. I never saw anything like it. Of course she wasn't beating much, but it takes a horse with a lot of guts and heart to run three days in a row, yet alone win every race. I'll never see that again.

———————

Gulfstream Park is the prettiest racetrack in the country, maybe the world. Hialeah Park also is a garden spot and one of the best places to stable a horse for training and racing. Santa Anita looks terrific only because of the mountains. After a while mountains look like big lumps of dirt.

———————

I saw Johnny Nerud at the Breeders' Cup races in 1987. He was saying how he had just sold some horses for $9 million and how he was worth about $20 million. "I know you got yours too, Dave," he said. "I know you're no dummy."

I got pretzels.

———————

Maybe the best feeling in the world is getting 10 to 1 odds on a horse that you know is a cinch.

It was 1971. I claimed a horse called Beat the Traffic for $6,500. I took him to Florida, where he ran out the first few times I raced him. Then he developed an ankle problem. Then he started coughing. I had his head in an oxygen tent while the vet and I worked on his ankle. The vet said, "Get rid of him." I wasn't about to because I knew the horse could run.

After Beat the Traffic finally perked up, I asked Hialeah's racing secretary, Kenny Noe, whether he could put up a $6,500 claiming race for 3-year-olds on the last day of the meeting.

"I've got a horse that's not quite ready," I said, "but he'll be ready on the last day."

Noe said OK. He knew he'd need a few cheap races to fill the program because trainers who were getting ready to ship, stopped entering horses at the end of the meeting.

Three or four days before my horse was scheduled to run, I told jockey Gerry Gallitano to come over and work him.

"Make it late," I said. "I don't want anybody else on the track."

When Gallitano showed up, I told him to work the horse six furlongs. "Work him fast," I said as I put on the blinkers. "I want to see what he can do with these on."

Beat the Traffic went three-quarters in 1:11²/5! That's a good workout for a stakes horse! But my horse wasn't going to face $100,000 animals! He was going against $6,500 dogs! My mouth started to foam.

Later, in the pressbox, I saw Frenchy Schwartz, the *Form's* head clocker. He was sharp, one of the few really good clockers in the country.

"Man, did that horse work good," Frenchy said. "I got him at 11 and 2."

"Aaaaah, so what," I said. "He works like that all the time but can't run in races. He's about broke down. Look at these races. Ran bad every time."

Next day I picked up the *Form* and checked the list of workouts. Beat the Traffic's 11 and 2 wasn't included. For some reason Frenchy hadn't sent it in. Maybe he forgot. My mouth started to foam again.

Race day came and I saw the odds on the board: 10 to 1. I bet $200 to win on Beat the Traffic and keyed him in some daily doubles. When the gates opened, he broke well and went straight to the front. He was ahead by several lengths going into the first turn and widened the lead down the backstretch. Coming into the homestretch he was in front by 6. No one was going to catch him. Midstretch he was in front by 8, and Gallitano was still whipping him. Before the race I told Gerry that my partner and I had put down $100 to win for him. Now, 10 lengths in front and nearing the wire, Gallitano was beating the blue blazes out of the horse's hinder. They crossed the finish line miles in front but Gallitano didn't let up with the whip until they were 50 yards past the wire.

In the winner's circle, I told Gallitano, "Gerry, you just sold the horse."

"Did you lose him?"

"No, I'll lose him next time. What the hell were you doing? You're way out in front and you're whipping the goddam horse. You couldn't win by a length or two?"

I cashed my win and double tickets and walked away from the window with more than $12,000. I won the battle but lost the war. I ran Beat the Traffic back for $10,500 and he was claimed. The horse went on to win $150,000.

I met Dick Duchossois at the hot dog stand and we got to talking. I told him I was doing a column on a couple of jockeys who weren't doing so well.

"It'll be a change," I said, "because most stories are about the top jockeys."

Duchossois's face got serious. "They're not doing well? Let's give them something."

He pulled out his wallet and it was as fat as my midsection. I had to talk him out of it.

It was November 1978, and Bob Carey and I were sitting in a fire engine watching the Hawthorne grandstand burn down.

"Put it over there," Carey said to the fireman with a big water hose. "There. Right there. And don't move it."

The stream of water arched over the flames and landed in the spot Carey wanted protected.

"What do you have there?" I asked. "A bunch of good mutuel tickets?"

No, he said. There was a cement room that held a safe with $3 million in cash.

Oh.

After firemen found gasoline cans on some of the grandstand floors, investigators put two and two together and came up with the mob. Carey had led the fight against the messenger services, which took bets from horseplayers and ran them to the track. Because the messenger services were taking business away from the track, Carey got the other track owners together and took the modern day bookies to court and got them banned. The mob, which had a picce of the action, didn't like that one bit.

I've had a bad habit all my life. I'm always trying to keep people happy. The horsemen, the horseplayers, anybody and everybody. Take, for example, the annual HBPA party. The association pays for it, but I go through hell trying to run a good party. We have two bands, door gifts, raffle prizes. We have anywhere from 350 to 500 people and these parties, in my opinion, are second to none.

Take, for another example, the food I bring in for the guys in the sports department. Maybe 10 times a year I'll come in loaded down with ribs, or these huge kosher hot dogs, or prime rib dinners, or Chinese food from Jimmy Wong's. Of course, I don't pay for the food. Maybe I do in a way because I get the food from people I've helped out trying to keep *them* happy. And maybe I do in another way because I cater these bashes myself, going here and there to get the food and drinks. That's two hours of my time. Must be worth $25 at least.

Take, for still another example, the horseplayers at the track. They come to me with their problems.

"They won't change my ticket even though they punched it wrong."

I'll talk to management right away, I say.

"Look at this hot dog. Ever see anything so small in your life? Cost me $2.50!"

Terrible, I say. I'll talk to the concessions boss.

"The escalator up to the clubhouse ain't working."

I'll get a screwdriver and work on it this afternoon, I say.

The point is, I don't think other people put themselves out as I do trying to make people happy.

———

I'm a pest. Over the years I've gotten in trouble with the *Sun-Times's* division men, the street bosses, when I complained about deliveries. Twice last year the paper wasn't sent to the track. When I called in, some guy said, "I didn't know there was any racing." What a jerk. When you do that, all you're doing is making *Tribune* readers. I don't know about deliveries to the street boxes in front of churches or drug stores; I'm not around there. But I know when papers aren't at the track.

———

The Illinois Racing Board is good for nothing. You're supposed to have workouts. That's a rule. And there's another rule that says there's supposed to be a clocker at every track where horses are stabled. There were a lot of horses stalled at Arlington Park for several weeks while Hawthorne was operating. Those horses were worked but there was no clocker. That's the job of the IRB to make sure that a clocker is present. The public is getting cheated and the IRB either doesn't care or doesn't know the rules.

Gov. Thompson named some beautiful people to the board. Nice guys, all of them. But I didn't ask for beautiful people. I wanted people who knew something about racing.

———

I remember the time when jockey Bobby Ussery came to Florida after a two-month vacation and he said to me, "Put me on a winner."

"You in shape to ride?" I asked.

"Yeah."

I put Ussery on a favorite and he led about 100

yards from the finish line. Then the horse stopped and got beat by half a length.

After the race I asked Ussery, "Did the horse get tired?"

"I don't know," he said. "I was more tired than the horse."

I blew a race by riding an unfit jockey. Like horses, jockeys need races to get in shape. There aren't many riders who can come off a long layoff and still win. Eddie Arcaro and Steve Brooks could. Bill Shoemaker in his prime was another one.

From time to time I have this feature in the paper called "The Bankroll." I start with $1,000 and make bets every day on certain races. It's not real money so I don't take a beating when I lose, except maybe for the cracks I get at the track.

So, I have this bankroll, see, and I'm down to $100. I write in the paper that I may call my friend Ed DeBartolo, the owner of Balmoral Park and a million other pieces of property, and ask him for a grand to tide me over. It's a joke. Ha, ha.

Next day I get a call from Tom Sweeney, the president of Balmoral.

"You're all set on the bankroll, Dave," he said.

"What do you mean 'all set'?"

"You wrote in the paper that you were going to

call Ed. I called him and he said, 'OK. Give Dave $1,000.' "

———————

I have my arguments with track owners, but that's to be expected because we're on different sides of the fence. Most of them are nice guys, though.

Stormy Bidwell plays it fair and square and runs a first-class operation at Sportsman's Park. Too bad it's a bull ring, but that's not his fault.

Dick Duchossois? Racing in Illinois would be nowhere without him. But besides that, I've seen him spend a half-hour talking with some broken down horseplayer or some broken down trainer. When Arlington Park burned down in 1985, he fed the whole backstretch for a week.

Tom Carey, the boss at Hawthorne, has done a lot of things to improve the track, such as building a new turf club, but he still has a long way to go before he has top-class racing.

DeBartolo sold Balmoral. The less said about the new people there the better.

———————

In February 1989, I told Newt Green, who was handling my horses at Gulfstream, to put in a $12,500 claim for a horse called Windspun. He looked pretty good on paper. And he looked even better in person, winning by 12 lengths! Jesus, now I had a decent horse to take to Chicago. I could run him in allowance races at Sportsman's where the purses are pretty good.

I decided to take a chance and run him again because I wasn't scheduled to return home until later in the month. I put him in a $16,000 claiming event and he won by two lengths. But three claims were put in for the horse and I lost him. I felt sick. It was a dumb gamble. I should have known that he would be claimed, even if I had run him for $20,000.

To top if off, the guy I worked for, Walter Mullady, made $12,500—the $9,000 purse and the $3,500 profit on the claim and sale. And Newt, the trainer of record, picked up $900 for his 10 percent. Me, I got what I deserved—nothing.

One of the reasons some top stables won't send horses to Illinois for a meeting is because of the detention barn. No other tracks in the country— or in the world, for that matter—have detention barns. The politicians in the General Assembly, who know nothing about horses or racing, figured they were protecting the betting public by requiring all horses to be "detained" in a barn two hours before post time. But their ruling has had just the opposite effect. It has made Illinois racing even more chancey for the bettor.

It's criminal. Thoroughbreds are high-strung animals and many become upset when they're kept in unfamiliar surroundings for any length of time. They'll kick the walls, maybe injuring themselves, or become so frightened and nervous that they have nothing left for the race. Is that protecting the betting public? Sure, during those two hours, no horse will be injected with any drug. But what is to prevent someone from hopping a horse *before* he is sent to the detention barn? The IRB doesn't realize how effective their urine testing program is. These tests can detect virtually anything in a sample—from banned substances to chocolate ice cream. If a trainer has ideas about drugging a horse, he has to have not only larceny in his heart, but also feathers in his brain. The sharp trainers don't have to be sneaky. The sneaky ones aren't dumb. And the dumb ones can barely figure out which way a horse runs on the track, clockwise or vice versa.

The HBPA and the horsemen fought the detention barn but it was a hopeless battle. The track owners sent us to the gallows by cutting a deal with the politicians: In exchange for supporting the barns, the tracks got off-track betting. And the horsemen got the shaft.

One of the problems of being president of the HBPA is that the horsemen are pretty chicken-

253

shit when it comes to putting pressure on the tracks. The horsemen will never vote to strike. The detention barn was as good a reason as any to stand up and say, "We're not going to enter our horses until the law is rescinded." There was a lot of bitching and moaning, but no one called for a strike.

Too many horsemen are afraid to buck the system because they think the tracks will retaliate by refusing to give them stalls next year. The tracks, though, probably wouldn't hold it against them. The only trainers who might have something to fear are the ones with broken down horses. But if you have decent horses, no problem. And trainers with quality horses can pretty much call their own shots because Illinois tracks are always in dire need of good stock. Those same trainers, though, had better not try that stuff in California or New York, where good horses are more the rule than the exception.

I broke the story that Arlington Park, with its new plant under construction, was going to hold its 1988 International Festival of Racing at Woodbine in Toronto.

It was a crazy time. Dick Duchossois had scheduled a press conference to announce his selection: Woodbine or Keeneland. It was going to be a big deal and Duchossois was trying to make sure that none of his people leaked information to the press.

I didn't need any inside info. I knew it wouldn't be Keeneland because it was too small. The track could hold only 25,000 people. It had to be Woodbine, which had two terrific grass courses and room for 40,000. Trouble was, I couldn't get anybody to confirm it. Because nobody at Arlington would talk, I zeroed in on Woodbine and called every day. Finally, on a Tuesday morning, I got the information I needed.

"Did you get it yet?" I asked.

"I've got a few more things to straighten out," he said.

That was enough. If Woodbine wasn't going to get it, there wouldn't be anything to straighten out. I'd write it for Wednesday's paper. I went out to Arlington Park to make another stab at getting the story from Duchossois. I hung around the track offices for a while, shooting the breeze with various people, and then saw Duchossois. No dice.

I got back to the office and started to write the story. Then it dawned on me. Even though I quoted a Woodbine source in the story, Duchossois might think the leak came from one of his people because I was at Arlington the day before the news broke. I was in a pickle. Do I run with the story and maybe get somebody in trouble? Or do I sit on it for one day, erasing any link with Arlington, and hope that nobody else beats me? I had a responsibility to the *Sun-Times*, but I also felt an innocent person might get hurt. I decided to sit on the story until Thursday's edition. I did my selections and went home.

I couldn't sleep. *The story's going to pop. I know it. I just know it. The Toronto paper will have it. Or the Trib. Or that goddam Daily Herald. Somebody will have it. And I'll be here with my ass spread all over my scoop.*

Four a.m. and I still couldn't sleep. *I should have gone with the story. If it's the Trib or the Herald, I'm going to commit suicide. It's 4:47. The doorman's suppose to bring up the Trib at 5:00.*

Five a.m. Where the hell was the doorman. *Woulda, coulda, shoulda gone with the story. What a jerk.*

Five twenty-six a.m. *The Trib doesn't have it. So far so good.*

The Toronto paper didn't have it and neither did the *Herald*.

The next day I wrote the story that Woodbine would get Arlington's racing festival. I scooped everybody.

———

They say that if you ever went to a sausage factory and saw what they put into those links, you would never eat another sausage. Maybe you can say the same thing about betting on horses. If you ever went to the backstretch and saw some of the people who are supposed to be taking care of horses, you might not ever again want to put down $2 on the nose.

But I guess it's harder to quit gambling than it is to stop eating sausages.

I told this story at Pimlico where they honored me at a party on the night before the 1986 Preakness Stakes:

It was in the late 1950s and I went to Saratoga, New York, to buy a horse for Ethel and Titus Haffa. The horse was owned by Jane Du Pont Lunger. I dealt with her trainer, Henry Clark. I handed him a check for $50,000 and he told me I could pick up the horse the following evening.

The next day I went out to the track and waited at the spot where I was supposed to meet Clark. I waited and waited. Finally I saw him. He didn't look too happy as he walked toward me. The horse had run that day and won but maybe something had happened after the race.

"You won't believe what happened," Clark said, shaking his head.

"Omigod. The horse break down?"

"No. The horse is OK."

Clark said Mrs. Lunger's daughter was in the barn crying her eyes out. She had just found out her mother was going to sell her pet.

"Mrs. Lunger told me to tell you she's sorry," Clark said, "but she can't sell the horse. She asks that you take back the check."

Well, I could have made a big stink but didn't. I took the check and went back to Chicago.

So, now it's 1982, 25 years later, and I'm at the Preakness. I'm going through the barn area on my way to the clubhouse, when I notice this woman walking alongside of me. I figure she's on her way to the clubhouse too. I look at her. She catches me staring at her and gives me a pleasant funny look.

"What's your name?" I asked.

"What's *my* name? What's *your* name?"

"Dave Feldman. You know me?"

"How would I know you?" she said. She isn't scared. Too many people around and besides I look pretty harmless. "Why are you asking?"

"I don't know. What's your name?"

"Annie Jones," she said. "Tell me. Why are you asking?"

"I don't know. If I tell you what I'm thinking you might have me locked up."

"What are you thinking?" She stops walking and I stop walking.

"Well, about 25 years ago, I bought a horse from trainer Henry Clark but he couldn't give the horse to me because the owner's daughter was crying and begged her mother not to sell him. I'm just wondering—it's a million to one shot—but it wasn't you, was it?"

She smiles. "It was me." Annie Lunger Jones. "Omigod," I said. "You're the girl."

"Am I happy I cried," she said. The horse went on to win some nice races and then jumped in shows. Later, he was bred and produced some good foals.

No way my horse should have been 50 to 1. That was the Florida horseplayers for you. Prejudiced. Even back then, in 1952, they figured horses from Chicago were crap.

I was running Light Moon in a $6,500 starter race at Tropical Park. He was coming off an allowance sprint, beaten by only six lengths. Not bad considering he was a router and considering he had been running with a cut in his mouth that hadn't fully healed. Most of the race he had tried to bear out to get away from the bit. Now he was running a mile and 70 yards and the cut was better—not perfect, but much better.

Light Moon had a shot to win. I figured that when I entered him. But I got even higher on my horse after talking to the other trainers in the receiving barn before the race. I saw Paul Kelly and asked him if he liked his horse.

"No," he said. "He hasn't run for quite a while. He's not quite fit."

I saw trainer Slim Pierce and he condemned his horse. Then I asked him about the favorite in the race, a horse Pierce lost through a claim the last time out. "Horses can make liars out of you," Pierce said, "but I never thought he could run a route."

I went down the line and every trainer I talked to said he didn't think his horse could win. Jesus! These guys were all friends of mine; they weren't playing games. I was the only trainer in the bunch who liked his horse!

I got to the paddock and my groom, Tom Lloyd, said, "Boss, he's 20 to 1."

Tom walked Light Moon around the ring and got another look at the tote board. When he came back, he said, "He's 30 to 1!"

After another time around, he said, "Boss, he's 50 to 1! I'm going to bet him!"

"Don't bet him," I said. "If he wins, I'll take care of you."

I put down $100 to win and $150 to place.

The horses broke and my jockey, Earl Knapp, settled Light Moon into the middle of the pack. On the backstretch my horse was just crying to run but Knapp kept his hold until the turn and then let him go. Before the race I had instructed him not to go too far out when going around horses because Light Moon might want to bear out, more out of habit than anything else. Knapp made a tight swing around the horses in front, gained the lead and won going away. He paid $102.50!

I came away from the window with more than

$10,000 and went looking for my groom. Tom was a 90-day wonder. He worked like a dog for three months, then took off and got drunk. I caught up with Tom at the barn and gave him his share, $1,500.

And I didn't see him for a week.

———

You probably find it hard to believe but I'm a fan of the legitimate theater. Plays, I mean. Some years ago, I saw "Three Men on a Horse" nine times.

———

I'm on my way to bet a trifecta—6-8 all and 8-6 all—and this horse owner calls out, "Hey, Dave, sit down."

"Wait a minute—"

"C'mon, sit down. I haven't seen you in a long time."

"Let me go make this bet first."

"Forget the bet. Save your money."

I sit down and we start talking. The bell rings, the windows close and the gate opens. My two horses finish 1-2 and some longshot comes in third. The trifecta pays $446 and I'm sitting there listening to this guy whose name I can't remember.

Woulda, coulda, shoulda....

•

Ten

Saturday, June 3, 1989

I've got Gala Serenade running today in the seventh race at Hawthorne. He's going against $5,000 dogs but that's no guarantee he figures because he's lost against $5,000 dogs before—by 9 lengths the last time out, by 6 the time before that. If he runs his race, he should win by 10 lengths. But I have no idea how he's going to run. I haven't seen him in three weeks, haven't seen any of my four bums in that time. I got out of the hospital two weeks ago. I had the operation that I should have had last November. Never had the time then but I made the time now because the pain was killing me. Now I feel only half dead.

It's nine o'clock in the morning and I'm at the barn looking for my assistant, Jim. I spot him coming out of the tack room. I don't say hello and he doesn't ask how I feel. We sort of hate each other. He thinks he's Ben Jones and that I'm keeping him down, keeping him from becoming a trainer. I hired him because I needed *somebody* to take care of my horses. I just can't get to the barn at six o'clock anymore. Too cold, too damp for a guy with as many ailments as I have. Sure, if I had a million dollar 3-year-old I'd be spending my nights sleeping in the same stall, but I've got two horses with bad knees, another with sesamoid trouble in both hind legs, and Gala Serenade, a 10-year-old with bad feet and bleeding problems. Gala Serenade is still a flat-ass runner when he's right, but I don't get to the backstretch often enough to know when he's race fit. I wish I could rely on Jim to follow orders, but he has a mind of his own and I never know where it is.

"Worked him five-eighths on Wednesday," he says. "Went 1:05 and 4."

"Five-eighths? I told you to work him a half-mile!"

"You said five-eighths."

Forget it, forget it. "You sure he only worked five-eighths?"

"In 1:05 and 4."

"That's not what I heard."

"What is it? You have people spying on me?"

"Nobody's spying on you. Someone just told me that after the workout my horse went around again because the pony boy couldn't grab him. Were you going to tell me that?"

"If I thought it was important."

"You let him run more than a mile three days before he's supposed to race and you don't think it's important enough to tell me?"

"I was going to tell you."

"Who'd you have pony the horse?"

"The regular guy didn't show up. I had to get somebody else."

Jim names the pony rider.

"My back! This horse has an iron jaw," I say. "There's no way that guy can pick up the horse and hold him."

"What am I supposed to do if the guy doesn't show up?"

"Get somebody who can handle the horse, not some half-starved looking guy with bananas for arms."

Then I find out that Gala Serenade was galloped the next two days.

"What are you telling me? He worked more than a mile Wednesday, galloped Thursday and galloped again Friday, and you expect him to run today?"

"You *told* me to gallop him."

"Yeah, but I didn't figure on him going around again when he worked. Hey, that's not Easy Goer in the barn. I've got a bum and you're going to kill him by drilling him too hard."

Jim's going to hit me. I can see it in his eyes. He might send me back to the hospital but I'll get him run off the track. He can see that in *my* eyes.

"I'm going to scratch the horse. He's run his race already," I say. "Besides, the track hasn't dried up enough. He could break down in the slop."

Jim glares at me, then turns on his heels and walks back to the barn.

I guess I'd better not ask him about my other horses. But what's to know. The horses with bad knees probably won't be able to race for another month. The other one, Leading BDH, who I still own because I can't sell him, last ran more than a year ago, on Derby Day in 1988. Most people keep dogs for pets. I have a racehorse and he can't even chase a stick.

Jim is almost to the barn door before he turns again and heads back my way. He's going to hit me.

"You know, anytime you want to can me," he says, "go right ahead. I'm thinking about going to New York anyway."

"Hey, why are you mad at me. You screw up and now you're mad at me. I've got to figure that out."

It's 9:30 and there's nothing more I can do. I've

worn out my welcome at my own barn. My back! I've got to find somebody else and get rid of Jim. Get rid of him before he quits on me. He's honest and hard-working. I'll give him that. And he's intelligent. I'll give him that too. But he's like a horse I had once. This horse seemed to take to training, but every time in a race, no matter what equipment I'd put on him, he'd bear out and run along the outside fence. Then one day, he never went into the turn, just kept going straight. He tried to jump the fence and his legs got caught. It was a miracle he didn't kill himself. But he was through racing. Horses are a lot like people. Some you never understand.

Jim and I part as we always do—as enemies. I get in my car and head for the HBPA office, which is located in a trailer near the backstretch at Sportsman's Park, about a one-minute drive from my barn. I never walk the distance anymore. It takes too much out of me and besides, the backstretch is a mess, especially when it's been raining.

It's supposed to rain some more today but I'm praying it holds off until after the races. The feature is on the grass and there's a horse in it that just *can't lose*—Dixiella, a French-bred that's run in Grade II and Grade III grass races in Europe. In one of them she was beaten by only two lengths by Mill Native, who won the 1988 Arlington Million. Dixiella has been racing in New Orleans and Kentucky since February, with two victories and two seconds in five starts. And all those races were on the dirt! Now she's back on the grass where she's a standout. I made her the best bet in my morning line. I'm going to bet $200 to win and if I'm lucky she'll go off at 2-1. An overlay at 2-1! God, oh, God, don't let it rain! Take my horse. Take Leading BDH. Strike him dead. No, wait! Take the entire HBPA board. Take them. Only don't let Hawthorne take the race off the grass!

Hell, God wouldn't want my board. They'd probably bug Him to death with their second-guessing. *"You shoulda saved this guy, you shoulda damned that guy. Aaah, you don't know what you're doing. You're a jerk, God, a real jerk."*

I hate being president of the HBPA. It's tougher than being president of the United States. At least the president has a party in back of him. I have nothing—no party, no friends, no flunkies, just a board of whiners and back-stabbers. Then there are the horsemen, another bunch of stakes-grade squawkers. It's been that way since 1975 when I was first elected. So why didn't I quit after the first three-year term? Hell if I know. My whole life has been like this. I'm like a guy who stuffs his pockets with dynamite in the morning and spends the rest of the day running around like a crazy man blowing out people's matches. It never occurs to me that all I have to do is take the goddam dynamite out of my pockets.

I walk into the HBPA office and somebody strikes a match.

"Just the man I want to see," says a horseman.

"OK, what can I do for you?"

"I want 30 more stalls. I asked for 60 and Arlington will only give me 30. Can you at least get me 10 more?"

"Look, you know as well as I do that most everybody is getting only half the stalls they asked for. Arlington's got 1,950 stalls and about 3,800 horses set for the meeting. Some top stables are shipping in and you're competing with them for stalls."

"So guys like me, who race here year-round, get the shaft, right?"

I tell him I understand how he feels and that I'm doing everything I can to get money for the horseman who'll have to pay $7 per day, per horse, to stable at Hawthorne and shell out $80 every time, usually once every three weeks, they van a horse to and from Arlington. I tell him I've asked the Racing Board to let us have some breakage money or to let us dip into the money that's held for uncashed tickets. I'm working on it, I tell him. I'm working on it.

"Right now," I say. "Duchossois's agreed to pay $70 every time you run a horse and the HBPA will come up with $100. That still leaves you out a few dollars and that's what I'm working on."

"You'd better do something soon. Time's running out." He stalks out taking his fire with him. Another satisfied horseman.

"Dave!" Another match flares.

It's my secretary.

"Yeah," I say as I catch a glimpse of myself in the small mirror on the wall. I don't look so good. I've got all the signs of major aggravation.

"One of the board members called," my secretary says, "and asked why you aren't working with the harness horsemen to get rid of the detention barn. He said the harness guys are doing everything while you just sit on your duff."

"Who called?"

She names the guy.

"Call that bum up and tell him I *am* working with the harness guys. Tell him I hired a lobbyist to work for us in Springfield. Tell him he would have known all that if he ever bothered to come to any of the board meetings."

The phone rings. "For you," she says. "Pick it up on 6."

"Yeah, this is Dave."

The caller is a groom. "Can you get me a room with a washroom and shower? I've got a wife and two kids, Dave. Do something for me, will ya?"

There are about 1,200 people, including more than 150 kids, living in those small rooms above the barns. Most of the rooms don't have plumbing; the bathrooms and showers are located at the end of each building.

"Have you talked to your trainer? He's the one who should talk to the backstretch boss."

"He did but they told him all those rooms were filled."

"I don't know what I can do then."

"Don't people with kids come first? I know some single guys got those rooms. What do they need 'em for?"

I'm a nice guy, I think. My heart's in the right place. But I don't have too much pity for people who raise kids on the backstretch. It's no place for families. Some tracks, in fact, don't allow kids to live in their barn rooms. That's smart. Kids need swings, slides and those things that go up and down, whatever you call them. They don't grow up right seeing a lot of broken down people every day, and learning woulda, coulda, shoulda before reading, writing and arithmetic.

"There's nothing that says families get first crack at those rooms," I say, "but I'll talk to the guy running the backstretch. I'm not promising anything, though."

I click the groom off and call the backstretch office. Just as I figured. No rooms, no way, fat chance, forget it.

Complaints and requests, all morning long. What am I doing about this? Can you help me with that? There's no end. I've got a Snickers bar and I'm supposed to feed the entire population of Ethiopia. I look outside, up at the sky. My back! It's going to rain. Even money it's going to rain. Worse, 2 to 5.

It's 12:30 p.m. and I'm sitting in the Gold Cup dining room waiting for my food. Sportsman's serves great meals and Arlington probably will too. I can't say much for Hawthorne's food, though. Today I'll go with a salad, soup and fruit. Not much to ruin there.

I'm at my usual table, not too far from where the maitre d' posts himself. I've got a TV screen close by and the distance to the betting windows won't put a strain on my heart. But I'm going to make just one bet today. Nothing else on the card looks good.

I see a nice-looking old couple head my way.

"Mr. Feldman, how are you feeling?" she says.

I get up and shake hands. "A lot better, thanks."

"Read what you wrote about your operation," he says. "It wasn't serious, was it?"

I explain what it was.

"I know what you went through," he says. "Had the same damn thing myself."

"How long ago?" I ask.

He looks at his wife. "Three years, wasn't it?"

"You were probably in better shape to begin with," I say. "My doc was trying to book bets in the operating room. No action."

She smiles and touches my arm gently, as if I were someone on the verge of tears. "Don't let anything happen to you. What would the horse-players do without you?"

As they start to walk away, he says, "Have a horse for us today, Dave?"

"My best bet. Dixiella in the eighth. But only if they keep the race on the grass."

He checks his program and says thanks.

"Don't you worry about a thing, Mr. Feldman," she says. "Everything will be all right."

"GOOD AFTERNOON, LADIES AND GEN-TLEMEN!"

Jesus, Georgeff! Turn down your goddam speaker! Twenty people just had heart attacks, me included. We've got the loudest and wordiest track announcer in the country. The guy's in love with his own voice. Funny thing, though, people in Chicago love Phil Georgeff. I guess it's a mat-ter of taste. "And here they come *spin-ning* out of the turn..." "There goes so-and-so...like a shot!" "He's pickin' 'em up and layin' 'em down." Just tell me where the horses are, Georgeff. Give me Tom Durkin. He's the best in the country.

Georgeff goes through the program changes—scratches, jockey changes, overweights, added workouts. And he says the third race, a starter in-vitational on the grass, has been switched to the main course. My back! More scratches and jock-eys and weights. Finally, he gets to the feature and, thank God, it's still on the turf! But the soft grass forces two scratches, leaving a field of eight. Doesn't look now that Dixiella will go off at any price.

My food is served but it takes me about an hour to finish because of all the interruptions.

—"I made an early-bird perfecta and when I went to cash the ticket, the clerk said there was a mistake in the program and all he did was give me back my two bucks."

—"Why don't tracks have no smoking areas for people who don't want to breathe the foul air of inconsiderate people?"

—"What's this about the *Form* killing its last edition? That's the one with the latest workouts, for chrissake."

—"Dave, the escalator isn't working."

—"The stews should have set him down. He pulled a horse last week. It was clear as a bell on the replay."

—"Do you think Secretariat could have beaten Citation?"

I don't recognize a face in the bunch but they know me. It's good that they want to talk to me but, Jesus, I want to eat my lunch. I wish I could say, "Come back later." But if I do that the guy will think I'm blowing him off and never buy the *Sun-Times* again. It's my own fault. I write for the two dollar bettors, my Broken Down Horse-players, and I try to look out for them. It's only natural that they think they own my time.

I'm a sitting duck at the table so I decide to head up to the Turf Club. Besides I want to talk to Hawthorne's boss, Tom Carey. I want to know what he's going to do about the feature. Maybe the right word at the right time might sway him. I'm not going out of my way just because of the bet I want to make. I seldom bet anymore. I love class above all but I don't see much of it in the daily cards. I don't think I've played five races a week during the Hawthorne meet. And when Sportsman's was operating this spring, I went four, five days without putting down a bet. With Sportsman's, though, it's not just the racing but also the track itself. A bull ring is brutal. Your horse may get carried out going into the first sharp turn and never recover. Give me a track that's at least a mile around, with wide sweeping turns. Give me horses with some class, not bums with legs frozen like Popsicle sticks so they can run one more race. That's why this grass race means something to me. I think Dixiella has class and I just want to see her run over the kind of course that'll bring out her best.

I punch the button calling for the elevator. The guy standing next to the button gives me a look that says, "I don't need you to show me how this damn thing works." I punch the button three more times, which tells him, "Nothing personal, I'm just in a hurry." He doesn't buy it. He punches the button once, very lightly. No elevator. Disgusted, he leaves. Forget about class racing at Hawthorne. Just give me an elevator that works. Some woman comes up and punches the button. I haven't the guts to look at her. I just punch the button three more times.

What a day! The problem is, it's typical. My assistant Jim wants to strangle me, the horsemen want to shoot me, and my HBPA board wants to

lynch me. My head hurts because of all the aggravation, my chest hurts because of arthritis (so
help me, that's what the doc says now), and my
stomach hurts because I couldn't eat in peace.
And after the races, I've still got work to do at
the paper. I'm half knocked out just thinking
about it. Not much traffic to fight on Saturday, so
I should be able to get into the office in 30 minutes. But the copy deadline for Sunday's final
edition is an hour earlier, 8:30, so I don't get a
break. That gives me about two and a half hours
to do my one-column early line for Monday and
my two-column morning line for Sunday. I have a
column in the early Sunday edition, which is already on the newsstands. I wrote that Friday
night, *after* I did the early line for Sunday, today's
morning line and today's column. It was past
midnight when I left the office. Unless something big happens today, I won't have to change
my Sunday column or write a story, so I've got
that going for me.

Now, if only the elevator would come. The second race has just been run and the horse I picked
in the paper lost. Oh-for-two. No, make that one-
for-three. The elevator door opens.

A short time later, after being told Carey went
downstairs to eat, I'm back in the dining room. I
spot the Careys, Tom and his brother Bob Jr.

I ask Tom, "Are you going to keep the feature
on the grass?"

"As of right now it's still on grass," he says.

It's almost two o'clock.

The phone on the table rings and Carey picks it up. He listens, then says, "OK. Hang on. I want you to talk to Bob." Tom then looks at me and says, "It's off the grass."

Carey says his racing director walked over the turf and said it was too soft. "The horses would dig it up," he says.

"You've got a short meet! So what if they dig up the grass!"

"The strip's too wet, too dangerous," Bob says, hanging up the phone.

"If it's so dangerous, why didn't the other trainers scratch their horses?"

"Our guy says it's raining again," Bob says.

I look out the window. If it's raining, it's only a light mist. "From the looks of the rain, the grass won't get much wetter than it was five minutes ago when you said the race was still on. You've got a $50,000 stakes and it's going to be a nothing race if you make them run in the slop."

No, Tom says, the race is off the grass.

I leave in disgust. Pretty soon I hear the official word over the PA system. Georgeff is telling everybody that the featured eighth race has been switched to the main course. And, he adds, there's another change: Three more scratches.

Now half the starting field is gone, leaving the feature with only five horses. One of the scratches is Josette, a horse with seven victories in 13 starts and $270,000 in winnings. All on the dirt! In fact, Josette was going to make her debut today on the turf. The wet grass didn't worry her trainer, Neil Boyce, but obviously the slop did.

In the clubhouse, I walk around aimlessly, talking to horseplayers here and there. I really have nothing to live for today. Dixiella's still in the race but I have no idea how she'll run in the goo, so I won't bet her. In the dining room, the Careys are probably chewing nails. Maybe I do have something to look forward to: a big laugh.

It comes just before the start of the sixth race. Two horses scratched hours ago. Now another one scratches at the gate leaving a field of five. "THE MUTUEL WINDOWS REMAIN OPEN," Georgeff announces.

The horseplayers scramble to the windows to change their tickets.

Ten minutes later, after the horseplayers have cashed in their dead tickets and bought new ones, Georgeff gets on the PA and says perfecta betting on the sixth race is off. The rules say that a gimmick race must have at least five horses that don't have either the same owner or the same trainer. This race has two horses that could have run as an entry but were listed as separate betting interests in order to fill out the field. My back! It took them 10 minutes to figure that out.

"POST TIME WILL BE IN SEVEN MINUTES. THE MUTUEL WINDOWS REMAIN OPEN."

The horseplayers scramble to the windows again. Tom Carey's probably thinking Duchossois wished this on him.

I stay around for the feature just to see Dixiella. It proves a waste of time. She never makes a move in the slop and winds up far back. What a shame! I don't know whether to cry or scream.

Maybe I'll just cheer. The grand opening of Arlington International Racecourse is only a couple of weeks away and I have high hopes. Groucho Marx's line was: I wouldn't join a club that would have me as a member. My line is a bit different: I wouldn't think much of a track that would have a race for Gala Serenade.

No offense, old boy, but we're talking class.

ABOUT THE AUTHORS

Dave Feldman has been writing his horse racing column for the *Chicago Sun-Times* for more than 40 years. He handicaps nine races a day, six days a week, year round.

Frank Sugano is a copy editor for the *Chicago Sun-Times*.